# Theory of
# Macroeconomic Policy

## M. H.PESTON
*Queen Mary College, University of London*

**Philip Allan**

*First published 1974 by*

PHILIP ALLAN PUBLISHERS LIMITED
RED LION COTTAGE
MARKET PLACE
DEDDINGTON
OXFORD OX5 4SE

0  86003  001  6

Set by E.W.C. Wilkins Ltd., London and printed in Great Britain
by Alden & Mowbray Ltd at the Alden Press, Oxford

# Contents

# Preface

Although the theory of macroeconomic policy has advanced considerably in the past decade, the subject itself is rather short of textbooks. Students are obliged, therefore, to search the journals and select parts of a large number of books in order to gain some understanding of what it is all about, and even then they will find it difficult to arrive at a uniform view of the matter. The textbooks which have been published are admirable in many ways but do not cover at all well the two crucial areas of policy within a dynamic model and policy in conditions of risk and uncertainty.

The reason for the lacuna is twofold. Firstly, some economists whose primary interest is in policy have not been equally interested in theory and have not been acquainted with the technical advances that have recently occurred. Secondly, the relevant problems and methods have been formulated mathematically, and appear at first sight to be extremely hard and abstruse.

The object of this book is to expound the subject at an elementary level. It is intended for economics students in their final year of an honours undergraduate degree course or in the one year masters course. In other words, it assumes a basis of two to three years of economic theory, and one to two years of simple mathematics and statistics. It does not assume that the students are specialists in mathematics, statistics, or econometrics. Equally, students who are antipathetic to any form of analysis, qualitative or quantitative, will not read it with any degree of enjoyment.

To be more specific, the student is assumed to have some acquaintance with the following: (a) the theory of choice (of the household, the firm, etc.); (b) macroeconomic theory including the formulation of macro-models; (c) elementary calculus; (d) elementary algebra; (e) elementary probability and statistics. Some more advanced matters are dealt with in a number of appendices.

My own experience has been that most economics students have got this far by their third year and, indeed, would welcome an opportunity to bring these simple techniques to bear on some interesting problems. What sometimes happens instead is that they are not given a chance to apply them, and they come to the conclusion that their early studies in these subjects were a waste of time. This is a pity, and can easily be avoided by studying a subject such as macroeconomic policy.

In suggesting that one can teach the subject at an elementary level, I am not, of course, arguing either that one can cover all of it or that it is possible to go very far into the fundamental issues. It is possible, however, to offer a serious account of the main topics and to make a good deal of progress using simple examples. Even the theory of optimal stochastic control is intrinsically a great deal easier than much of the economic theory with which undergraduates are expected to cope. Indeed, the difference between an elementary and advanced approach is often little more than that between elementary but laborious methods and advanced but more powerful ones.

While I have called this book the *Theory* of Macroeconomic Policy, my view is that the value of such theory lies in its practical applicability, and that what is set out here is relevant to actual policy making. Examples have been chosen with that aim in mind. Except for certain *obiter dicta* I have not devoted much space to the precise institutional arrangements in the UK, but I do refer in certain places to particular events in UK post-war economic history, and indicate what further reading the student might do to investigate these topics further.

Lastly, the presentation is in many places argumentative. This has been my method of teaching and I have found it to be a successful one. It does mean, however, that students will find some of what I have to say disagreeable and possibly even quite wrong. In addition, bitter experience has shown me that the mathematical parts are also bound to contain errors. Obviously, I would like to hear from those readers who discover them. Apart from that I must express my indebtedness to colleagues at Queen Mary College for critical advice and aid, but utter the usual disclaimer of responsibility on their behalf.

M.H. Peston

# 1
# The need for macroeconomic policy

The need for macroeconomic policy arises because the economic
system does not adjust appropriately to the shocks to which it is
constantly subjected. One view is that over the range of behaviour
in which we are interested the system does not adjust at all and at
best settles down to a new equilibrium some distance from its
desired state until a new shock moves it again. A second view, rather
less extreme, is that there is an equilibrium to which the economy
has a tendency to return, but that this tendency is too slow and
must be accelerated if at all possible. Apart from that, the system
may have a tendency to return to an equilibrium condition, but that
condition or equilibrium path may have certain undesirable properties (for example, excessive unemployment, or too violent fluctuations) which it would be desirable to remove. In other words,
policy may be introduced for two sorts of reasons: to influence
where the system goes, and to influence how it gets there.

It must be said at once that the need for policy does not imply
the feasibility of policy. It could be that, while the uncontrolled
economic system exhibits a great many bad characteristics, we
still do not know enough about its workings to improve its performance. (Indeed, it is important to recognise a substantial body of
opinion amongst economists which says that the economy works
well enough without economic policy, and that most of its short-
comings can be attributed to faulty government policy based on
ignorance.)

A large part of positive macroeconomics is devoted to the
study of the economic system, both in theory and in practice, with

1

a view to throwing some light on how it works and on how it can be made to work better. The theory of macroeconomic policy takes its point of departure from macroeconomics proper, and uses this to determine the likely consequences of particular policies, and to determine better or even optimal policies. (This is meant as a logical proposition. In practice, positive theory may obtain its *raison d'être* from the desire to reach certain ends or to determine the consequences of particular actions. Thus, it is just as true to say that macroeconomics proper takes its point of departure from macroeconomic policy.) It is, therefore, limited by the state of macroeconomics.

The theory of macroeconomic policy is positive economics in the sense that it predicts the consequences of particular policy changes in a way which is subject to empirical test. It may also be a positive discipline in another way, namely in predicting the policy changes themselves as a function of the economic variables. Thus, it may predict the effects of government expenditure on national income, or the effects of national income on government expenditure, or both.

The subject is also normative in the two usual senses of that word. On the one hand, it may be concerned with propositions of the sort, 'If the government wishes to achieve these ends, it should follow policy A', or 'If the government wishes to achieve these ends, it should follow policy A or policy B depending on whether it prefers X to Y'. Now, these are normative propositions in the sense of being concerned with ends and of using the word 'should'. (Related to them are propositions stating what the ends of actual governments happen to be.) They are also positive because they are empirical and testable. On the other hand, the theory of macropolicy is normative in the sense of presenting particular ends, or saying what the ends of governments ought to be. The economist has not hesitated to express himself on such matters and, even where he is more restrained, the very ends he considers in his positive theory may be taken to express a value judgement concerning their significance compared with other ends which are not considered. Related to normative theory in this second sense is a body of economics concerned with the analysis of ends as such. An attempt is made to clarify the meaning of concepts such as full employment, or to ask what lies behind the treatment of them as social ends. This is a logical and philosophical matter and is a form of meta-theory of normative propositions, usually falling under the general heading of welfare economics.

Although we shall cover only a limited amount of the ground in what is intended to be an introductory and elementary book, we shall touch on macroeconomic policy in all of its senses. Our main concern will be with the consequences of particular policies and the analysis of optimal policies. In so far as we shall investigate models in which some or all of public expenditure and taxation are endogenous we shall also be operating on the fringes at least of a positive theory of government behaviour at the macro level. In addition, we have a number of things to say about ends themselves; related to what they are, how they are encompassed in a theory of policy, what meaning can be attached to them, and even what they ought to be.

It is worth saying right away, therefore, that while it is important to recognise that policy can be sub-optimal and that governments are capable of making things worse, the standpoint of the present writer is that macroeconomic policy is both necessary and feasible. Broadly speaking, the system responds to contractionary shocks by reducing real output and employment. Near full capacity working it responds to expansionary shocks by price level increases of a continuing kind. While its responses may be bounded in that output and employment do not tend to zero, or the price level and its rate of change to infinity, it is not self-adjusting in the sense of returning to full employment at constant prices. Thus, arguments based on the Pigou effect or the like are theoretical niceties to do with the ultimate logic of economics; they have little or nothing to do with the operations of an actual economy in practice. It is by no means clear, incidentally, whether the reverse effect is supposed to happen in inflationary situations, and whether a fixed quantity of money is the ultimate deterrent to an inflation. What is obvious is that a great deal of scope remains for improving on the performance of whatever automatic adjustments there are in the system.

In this connection there are two additional points to be made. The sort of economic systems we are talking about (those of the advanced industrial countries) contain significant public sectors. These are not artificial or arbitrary additions to the economy to be discarded at will; they are ignored at his peril by the economist excessively devoted to the theory of individual private sector behaviour. Governments are there. They behave in ways which affect the economy and their behaviour is affected by the economy. Any theory of the automatic adjustment of the economy is, therefore, obliged to explain the role of the government in that adjustment even if the government itself is not engaged in macroeconomic control. The system left to itself, the uncontrolled system, is still one that contains a government and must be studied accordingly.

Secondly, a great deal of writing in the past fifteen or so years has emphasised how difficult economic policy making is, especially when the dynamic stochastic nature of the economy is taken into account. It has been shown how government economic policy can make things worse; indeed, how easy it is for that to happen given the complex situation in which the macroeconomic decision maker finds himself. In the case of the UK it has even been claimed that there have been a number of cases since the war when government intervention has been destabilising. One can refer to the incorrect timing of the devaluation of November 1967 (by about six months), to the insufficient expansionary power of the budget of 1970 (by between £500m and £1,000m), and to the delayed expansion of the budget of 1972 (by six months to a year). It has also been claimed that an improved performance since the war is hardly if at all attributable to public policy. Now, while I shall offer examples of the kind of policy that can make matters worse, it is my view that it is possible to exaggerate the significance of all this, and that the climate of opinion in economics has swung much too far in the cautionary direction. (Of course, it could be argued with some cogency that this is always a desirable thing to do because of the exaggerated claims of politicians.) In practice, public policy has not been as bad as all that, and where it has the reasons do not appear to have been economic. More to the point there is considerable scope on the basis of existing knowledge for improved policy. It is important to distinguish here between two situations in which active policy could be harmful compared with no policy depending on whether or not a better policy was available. Good macroeconomic policies may exist but not be used because the government does not know about them, or has other ends to pursue with which they are incompatible, or even because it is wilfully stupid. While this may discourage the economist, it should not necessarily cause him to doubt the efficacy of the policies as such. It should also be added that it is not helpful to go to the other extreme and, instead of insisting on the mistakes of policy, interpret all public sector activity as optimal by definition. Behaviour may no more reveal government preferences than it does the preferences of the single individual. At either level mistakes may be made; and even if the revealed prefer- ences are taken to be those of the government, it is always possible and sometimes helpful to define social welfare in other ways inde- pendent of the government so as to interpret public policy as sub- optimal relative to it.

This book is largely theoretical and therefore will not devote much space to the description of government and governmental institutions, or to the study of actual policy making. It will also take as given the relevant economic theory and econometric estimates of macroeconomic models. This is chiefly a matter of division of labour, and we refer appropriately to the further reading that a student of policy must pursue. At a more fundamental level, however, it should be realised that our neglect of econometrics is rather unsatisfactory; or more correctly the econometric neglect of policy is unsatisfactory. What I mean by this is that it is crucial to public policy to have some knowledge of the real behaviour, present position, and likely future position of the economy. In large part this is a matter of econometric estimation, and what the engineers call filtering and prediction. What we need to know is a function of what policies we wish to pursue, while our policies will be a function of what we know. It needs to be shown that it is possible to separate knowledge from the policies or the econometrics from the control. In many cases such a division can be shown to be valid; but it would be better still if the general rule in economics was for the two to appear together in the same textbook as indeed does happen in con- trol engineering. The theory of economic policy would be partly a theory of the optimal acquisition and analysis of information on how the economy works, and partly a theory of the use of that information to improve the performance of the economy. At the moment it is not, and in large part we shall take the first task, of data acquisition, as done.

Having said that we shall take the task of formulation and esti- mation of the macroeconomic model as given, this should not be taken to mean that we ignore these and certain closely connected topics entirely. In chapter 8 we discuss the problem of forecasting both in theory and in practice. We also show how the forecasting and control problems are related to each other. In various places in the book we discuss the consequences of the kind of risk and uncertainty due to errors in the specification and estimation of an economic model and more generally how lack of information and imperfect forecasting limit what the policy maker can do. The crucial point to understand is that imperfect information is a constraint on policy and on average involves the decision maker in costs relative to the (notional) situation of perfect information. Optimal policies under imperfect information will differ from those under perfect information and, of course, their consequences will be imperfectly predictable. Moreover, in general, an attempt to remove risk and uncertainty or to behave as if it did not exist will be suboptimal. A serious policy problem in the UK is to convince politicians and officials of these simple points and to accommodate parliamentary government to them. It is optimal to make some mistakes, and members of Parliament should devote some effort to criticising Ministers who use their energies chiefly to avoid error, and not simply concentrate on the errors that occur. At the same time, Ministers should be less cowardly and be prepared to defend policies on the ground that they were still correct in the *ex ante* circumstances in which the decision was made, even if they go wrong in the sense of having undesirable consequences.

A weakness of the economics that we teach at universities and to civil servants is its lack of emphasis on risk and uncertainty. This is partly because these are difficult issues and partly because what we have to say tends to be negative rather than positive. Nevertheless, macroeconomics which is non-stochastic can be seriously misleading. One objective of this book is to show that it is possible to discuss some relevant problems in an elementary (if not too rigorous) way suitable for undergraduate teaching.

The literature on economic policy makes a great deal of fuss about discretionary versus automatic policy making. It is likely that the significance of this distinction is exaggerated relating as it does chiefly to the length of time for which particular decisions are intended to last. We have already remarked that in an economy such as ours the assumption of a government whose macroeconomic impact is zero has little relevance in theory or in practice. The government exists and in general has an impact whether or not it

consciously pursues macroeconomic objectives. Given the existence
of government activity, and given that it takes place in circumstances
and relative to preferences which are constantly changing, it is difficult to see either that it is or should be constant or be a constant
ratio to national income. The notion that public expenditure and
taxation decisions can be fixed for an indefinitely long period of
time (or even that the principles can be fixed according to which
they are decided) is surely rather far fetched either as a matter of
fact or as an objective to aim at. There is nothing in economic
theory or economic research that suggests that this is the case or
should be the case. Even the economists of the new right have a
policy of public sector change (albeit in a downward direction); and
in favoured fields such as military expenditure they certainly favour
the adjustment of government activity to circumstances. Those
other economists who favour long range planning do not mean by
this the taking of once for all decisions, but rather the attempt to
take some account of the possible long term consequences of
decisions. This does not mean, of course, that long term commitments are bad and that frequent changes in policy are good. It does
mean that *sometimes* long term commitments may be bad, and
sometimes it may be valuable to introduce some flexibility into a
policy even at a cost in order to obtain some other benefit or avoid
some larger cost.

If public policy exists and has a macroeconomic impact, the
question must be asked whether and how it can be modified to
improve macroeconomic performance (or at least a remarkable
degree of intellectual restraint is involved in not asking such a
question). Now, it is perfectly possible that the answer is that no
improvement is possible in the present state of economic knowledge or in the foreseeable future. This would not be a matter of
faith, but of theory and fact, and certainly some economists have
come to that conclusion. All that can be added is that others, the
majority, reject such a conclusion as too pessimistic and consider
that consciously directed macroeconomic policy is feasible and
desirable. The point at issue here, however, is not quite that, but
whether macroeconomic decisions can and should be taken effect-
ively once for all and therefore be non-discretionary. Presumably,
what this would mean is that the government would take a view
of the likely course of the economy from now to an indefinite

future in the absence of macroeconomic policy, compare it with
the best feasible alternative state and then take policy decisions
from now to an indefinite future to bring the actual into line with
the best available.

It should be noted immediately that even if this were the correct
thing to do, the once for all decision would not necessarily be a
simple one such as to let public expenditure or the quantity of
money rise at $x$ % per annum, or to let taxes be a constant pro-
portion of all incomes above the lowest quartile. It could involve a
very complicated tax and expenditure package or, more to the
point, it could be in the form of a rule of tax changes (e.g. for
every percentage point that the national income exceeds $y$ % raise
tax rates by $z$ %) which itself would produce a complicated tax
package. Even that, however, does not get us to the heart of the
matter which is that, whatever is decided beforehand, it is a matter
of discretion to follow through with that decision at the moment
it is supposed to take place. As a matter of pure logic the decision
not to do anything or to go ahead with what we had planned is
itself a matter of discretion.

Thus, some economists hold that the chief task of macroeconomic policy is to make occasional far-reaching structural
changes which will assist the automatic working of the system but
not replace it. Others, while not going that far, would limit
policy to correcting only major deviations from the desired state
of affairs. A third group would see policy aiming to correct many
if not all deviations; to engage, that is, in 'fine tuning' of the
economy. There may also be a divergence between those who
emphasise the need to create an environment in which the market
mechanism can work to best advantage, including the strengthening
of that mechanism, and those who argue that macroeconomic
policy must interfere with and limit the market mechanism so that
other methods of resource allocation must be introduced. These are
interesting and important arguments, but they do not turn on
discretion versus rules in any meaningful sense.

The issue is not one of discretion but of the principles of
decision making and the nature of particular decisions, of how
flexible they should be, and of how frequently they should be re-
examined. Even change itself is a matter of definition. If tax rates
are fixed, tax revenues will be variable, but the distinction between

rates and revenues can hardly be one involving the fundamental
philosophy of public policy making. It may be neither rates nor
revenues that are fixed, but the rule or rules that determine them.
But why should fixed rules be regarded as fundamental and, anyway,
what is a fixed rule? Is it the procedure for determining taxes (e.g.
put taxes equal to the difference between desired and actual income
divided by the multiplier), or the procedure for determining this
procedure (e.g. construct a model, posit an objective to be reached,
consider all the available information and determine the correct
policy accordingly)?

As time passes we accumulate knowledge in two senses. Firstly,
we accumulate new observations of the economic phenomena which
we are interested in. Secondly, economic theory and method itself
advances. The latter may be a slow process, but as and when it
happens we should surely take some account of it in our policy
making. The former occurs all the time and must affect the decisions
we take in a particular sense, and sometimes may even affect our
policy rules. In the UK every quarter we obtain new observations of
the many variables that enter into a macro-model (some of them the
results of the very policies we have been pursuing). This enables us to
re-estimate the equations in our model which in turn may modify,
however slightly, our view of the consequences of various policies.
This new information may even cause us to doubt the very models
themselves and lead us to examine new ones. At the same time we
use the latest information to predict the course of the economy over
the next year or way. All of this may lead us to leave policy as it is
to work automatically or as it was previously determined. Alternatively, we may be led to a particular policy change, but of the
sort we have been pursuing heretofore. Yet another possibility is
that we may change the rules of policy making themselves, using
entirely new policies or existing policies quantitatively in a signifi-
cantly different way. All of these changes (or lack of changes) may
be the consequences of rules or principles at a higher level. Thus,
they are simultaneously discretionary and automatic. It seems to
me, therefore, that the debate about a framework for policy has
been slightly misleading. The issue is the use of rules or procedures
versus *ad hoc* and arbitrary behaviour. The former are not identical
with no change, and the latter is not the same as discretionary
behaviour. If by 'discretionary' one means policy that is unjustifiable,

*ad hoc,* or irrational (and plenty of public policy is all of those things), discretionary policy will be rejected by every one. But if one means policy which adjusts to changing circumstances and is decided by policy makers, then all policy must be discretionary.

In sum, this book is about economic policy and its chief purpose is to explain what that is about. Nonetheless, it would be wrong to disguise the attitude of the author, who like all his colleagues is biased, in this case somewhat towards the active and interventionist end of the spectrum rather than towards the passive *laissez-faire* end. Making this explicit enables the reader to adjust accordingly any seeming attempts at brainwashing.

# 2
# The main problems

The simplest problem of economic policy that one can think of derives from the multiplier model of elementary economics. It will be recalled that national income is equal to the level of investment plus the level of government expenditure times the multiplier. In symbols we have

$$Y = M(I + G) \tag{2.1}$$

where $Y$ is national income, $I$ is investment, $G$ is government spending, $M$ is the multiplier.

An increase in government expenditure leads to an increase in national income; a decrease in government expenditure leads to a decrease in national income.

We can treat national income as the *target*, and government expenditure as the *instrument*. The level of the former refers to our ends, so to speak, while the level of the latter refers to our means. Macroeconomic policy, then, will be about the manipulation of means to achieve our ends. If, with government expenditure at a particular level, we expect investment to be such that national income is below its desired level, we can increase $G$ by an appropriate amount. In the reverse case, with expected national income above its desirable level, we can reduce $G$.

We can derive a specific formula for $G$ as follows. Let $Y^*$ be the desired level of national income (e.g. the full employment level). We would like actual national income to equal the desired level.

$$Y = Y^* \tag{2.2}$$

From (2.1), for this to be the case we have

$$M(I + G) = Y^*$$  (2.3)

or

$$G = \frac{Y^*}{M} - I$$  (2.4)

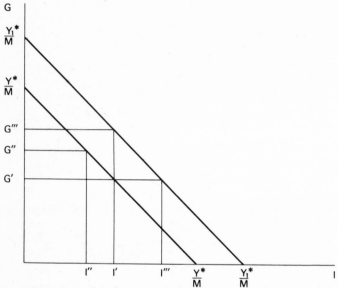

Fig. 2.1

We can plot this equation in figure 2.1. The line $Y^*/M - Y^*/M$ plots $G$ as a function of $I$. It gives us all the combinations of $G$ and $I$ which will generate the desired level of national income. If $I'$ is the expected level of investment then the correct policy is to put government expenditure at $G'$. If instead the expected level of investment were $I''$, the expected level of expenditure would be $G''$.

It is worth noting at this point that, despite our concentration on an extremely simple case, two important conclusions have already emerged. Correct economic policy depends on the desired level of the target to be arrived at, and also on the levels of the other variables that affect the target.

Suppose now that the target level of national income increases.

(This may be, for example, because time has passed and there has been some growth in national productive capacity.) We must now consider the line $Y_1^*/M - Y_1^*/M$ which lies above $Y^*/M - Y^*/M$ in figure 2.1. If it were predicted that investment was going to remain at $I'$, the policy for government expenditure to reach the new target would be to place it at a level equal to $G'''$. It can also be seen that, if investment is predicted to rise as far as $I'''$, the level of the policy variable must remain unchanged at $G'$. (It is even possible that investment is predicted to rise beyond $I'''$ so that government expenditure must be reduced despite the increase in the target level of national income.)

We can illustrate the behaviour of government expenditure through time in two more diagrams. In figure 2.2 we illustrate the behaviour of $G$ and $I$ given the level of desired national income. As $I$ rises $G$ falls by an equal amount, and as $I$ falls $G$ rises.

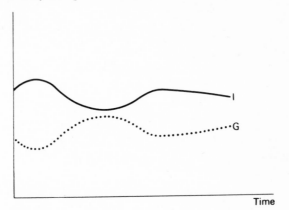

Fig. 2.2

In figure 2.3 we illustrate the behaviour of $Y^*$ and $G$ given the level of expected investment. As $Y^*$ changes, $G$ changes in the same direction but by a smaller amount given by $1/M$. (Do not forget that the multiplier is a number greater than unity.)

In each of these cases we have illustrated a time path for economic policy determined by the target and the expected levels of the other relevant variables. More generally, of course, $G$ will vary as both $Y^*$ and $I$ vary, and will not necessarily bear any simple relation to either of them separately.

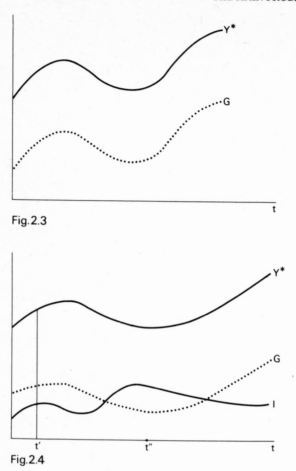

Fig.2.3

Fig.2.4

In figure 2.4 we take the behaviour of $Y^*$ and $I$ as given and
from them derive the correct policy for $G$ over time. Basically, the
behaviour of $G$ is not determined by $Y^*$ and $I$ separately, but by
the gap between them. Thus, at the beginning of the period, although $I$ is rising, $G$ also has to be increased because $Y^*$ is rising
faster. After that for a while $G$ is reduced, although $I$ is also falling,
again because $Y^*$ is falling faster.

In these diagrams we have actually slipped in a major complication – we have made the analysis dynamic. So far this has been

done only in a casual, verbal way and very soon we must introduce
a more serious disciplined analysis. It does, however, enable us even
at this stage to point to some additional important conclusions.

In the first place, our policy programme for government expenditure must now be interpreted as referring to how matters look
at a particular point of time. In terms of figure 2.4, as we are at the
present moment (time zero), $Y^*$ and $I$ look as if they are going to follow
the prescribed paths and, therefore, the instrument $G$ must follow
a particular path. But as far as action is concerned we may only be
committed to the levels of $G$ given by the dotted line up to $t'$. When
we get to that time, things may look different. The target levels
of $Y^*$ or the expected levels of $I$ may not be the same as those
illustrated. We may have changed our minds about the desired level
of national income at time $t''$ or the expected level of investment.
In that case, the policy planned for $t''$ will differ at time zero from
time $t'$.

In other words, policy plans have two time specifications.
They refer to planned policy for a particular date as matters
are seen at a particular date. Macroeconomic policy for 1977 as
seen in 1973 will differ from macroeconomic policy for 1977 as
seen in 1974, which will in turn differ from that as seen in 1975,
which may well differ from macroeconomic policy as carried out
in 1977. (For those interested in such things, we can examine the
conditions for a form of policy equilibrium. An appropriate
definition of this might be that intended policy does not vary with
the date at which we are considering it.) Secondly, having wandered
into dynamics we have now also got ourselves involved with economic forecasting. If we know $I$ for certain, our analysis tells us the
level at which to place $G$. In the real world we do not know $I$ for
certain, but instead have a forecast for $I$. (Actually, the situation
is worse than that; we are unlikely to know present or past values
of $I$ for certain either.) We then have to ask how policy is to be
related to the forecast value of $I$, or to the alternative possible
values of $I$. This leads to considerations of decision making under
risk and uncertainty, to the possibility of matters not turning out
in the way we expected, and to the very deep question of what even
is to be meant by correct policy as opposed to mistaken policy.

Thirdly, it can be seen how difficult the analysis and evaluation
of public policy is bound to be. At the very least figure 2.4 tells us

that in order to discuss public policy satisfactorily we need to have some idea of what the government's objectives were and what they assumed to be the levels of the other forces at work. A simple correlation between government expenditure and one other variable, say private investment, tells us nothing unless we are able to make correct assumptions about a host of other matters. In figure 2.4 there is a degree of negative correlation between $G$ and $I$ which reflects the simple view that variations in the former are used to offset variations in the latter, but the correlation is less than perfect because $Y^*$ itself is also changing.

In sum, our simple model will have to be elaborated in due course to allow both for the explicit consideration of dynamic matters, and also for risk and uncertainty, or what are called stochastic matters. Our equation (2.1) is static and non-stochastic; a quite elementary discussion leads us rapidly to the need for something which is dynamic and stochastic.

We can, indeed, re-examine our elementary problem in the light of our knowledge of macroeconomics and of the requirements of economic management to see a number of other complications that need to be taken into account. Let us start with the multiplier. We know that the value of this is determined partly by the values of such things as the marginal propensity to consume and the marginal propensity to import. In elementary theory we take these things as given and work out the corresponding value of the multiplier. In practice, however, we need to work with the actual values of these parameters that pertain to the UK or US or whatever other economy we are interested in. Since, as a general rule, we cannot predict these values from first principles, we have to investigate the available data to discover their values. We have a problem of statistical estimation or econometrics to solve. What this means, therefore, is that we cannot take $M$ as known for certain; it will be subject to a degree of error dependent on how well we can estimate the consumption function or the propensity to import. More generally, our model may be imperfect because our economic theory is mistaken. It could well be that there is no stable relationship between national income and imports and, therefore, no multiplier to be correctly estimated in the first place. This again takes us into extremely deep waters. It does oblige us to recognise, however, that the uncertainties that limit policy are not simply those derived from the need to forecast the values of so-called exogenous variables; they also come from the imperfections and limitations of economic theory and econometrics.

Having mentioned the difficulties that arise from problems connected with the structure of the economic model, let us look again at the target, in this case the level of national income. In our simple model there appears to be no trouble that can arise here. But we have already noted that we may change our mind over the level to be aimed at. This can obviously arise because of a change of government, or of a shift of power within the governing party, or of the desires and strength of extra governmental forces such as the trades unions. It may be remarked that that is highly unlikely when only the national income is to be taken into account, for surely all will agree that more national income is better than less. Even if this is true, other things being equal, in practice other things are not equal, and account must be taken, therefore, of other targets to be aimed at.

Our simple model pays no attention to the price level, to the balance of payments, to the distribution of income, to regional matters, to growth, or to the environment. This would not be important if they were all positively related to national income so that an improvement in any single variable implied an improvement in all others. It is rarely, however, that one finds oneself in such a happy position. More usually, the problem of macroeconomic policy is about the less than perfect achievement of targets, and the need for trade-off between the degree of fulfilment of individual targets to reach an overall optimum.

A parallel complication arises on the side of the instruments. In our model we have just one instrument, government spending. A more relevant model would include different forms of government spending, e.g. capital expenditure, current expenditure, transfer payments. It would also include taxes of various kinds, the quantity of money, the structure of interest rates, variations in the rate of exchange, controls on the international movement of capital, and direct controls on wages and prices. It may be that in some cases we have room for manoeuvre so that we can consider alternative combinations of instruments to achieve the same set of targets. In other cases, it is precisely the limitations of number and effectiveness of instruments which make us consider trade-offs between targets.

We shall return to the instruments and targets question at greater length below, but it is worth mentioning right away that the distinction between the two sets of variables is not necessarily clear cut. We have referred to government expenditure as a policy instrument, but its level may also be a target in that the government might have views of its desirable level independent of the requirements of macroeconomic policy. Similarly, at times, the rate of exchange or the rate of interest have been target variables and have not been available for use as instruments of macroeconomic policy.

It was clearly true of the Labour government of 1964–70 that they regarded the maintenance of a fixed rate of exchange for the pound as a valuable end in its own right. It has even been suggested that some people were unaware that a variable rate of exchange was available as a policy instrument. It is also true that some of the instruments are constrained; thus, it may be that certain tax rates are only to be changed once a year, or that it is considered undesirable to change government expenditure at any one time by more than a given percentage.

To summarise, the study of macroeconomic policy will involve us in the following:

(a) an economic model made up of several equations and variables,

(b) the dynamic behaviour of that model,

(c) the stochastic behaviour of that model,

(d) policies made up of several targets to be reached and instruments to be used,

(e) policies that are themselves dynamic,

(f) policies which are decisions under risk and uncertainty.

Having said that, it must be added immediately that not everything that follows deals with all these matters simultaneously. Quite the contrary, we shall examine most of them separately, building up to something a little more complete towards the end of the book. Indeed, a great deal of the book is neither explicitly stochastic nor dynamic. This is partly because this is intended to be an elementary treatment of the subject. But it is also because in the present state of economics such static models can still be useful if they are interpreted with care and placed in a dynamic and statistical context. Although our discussion of the dynamics of government expenditure was not mathematically rigorous, we were able to give the flavour of the dynamics in a simple way. This we shall continue to do with various other models that we present.

We have started our treatment of macroeconomic policy from a problem oriented standpoint. Another important step in the analysis of economic policy, whether macro or micro, is to formulate a model of policy making. Many alternative models have been constructed, either implicitly or explicitly, and our purpose will be chiefly to elucidate their possible components.

The simplest approach is to treat the government as a single decision maker with given preferences subject to constraints. The theory of economic policy would then be about which choices maximised the government's utility subject to these constraints. It would involve the study of particular situations and the analysis of actual policy choices together with the derivation of optimal choices. At a more abstract level it might be concerned to emphasise the constraints and hence the cost of one policy in terms of others forgone, together with the need for preferences as a basis for rational choice.

An example of this approach would be the wages and unemployment problem where the now rather empirically discredited Phillips curve is the constraint and the optimum policy would be a point on that curve chosen according to the government's preferences. It could even be said that the best point was one at which the marginal rate of substitution between wage increases and unemployment is equal to their marginal rate of transformation. This is illustrated in figure 2.5. P P is the Phillips curve showing reductions in the rate of increase in money wages as unemployment increases. The broken lines are indifference curves indicating the government's preferences. Utility increases in the direction of the arrow, indicating that the government regards both wage increases and unemployment as bad things rather than good things. The optimum policy is at A where the highest indifference curve reachable, $I_2$, is tangential to P P. Unemployment is set at $U_0$ and the rate of wage increases at $\dot{W}_0$. Should there be some change in the system (for example, a remarkably successful incomes policy) so that a better Phillips curve, P' P' holds, policy shifts to a new tangency at B with unemployment at $U_1$, and wage increases at $\dot{W}_1$.

A great deal of the theory of economic policy is of this form,

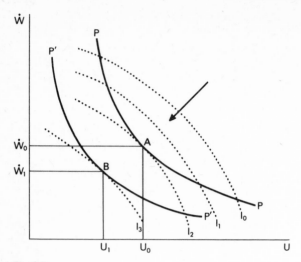

Fig. 2.5

and certainly that is true, either implicitly or explicitly, of much of
the content of this book. Nonetheless it has its drawbacks.

In interpreting this approach we come immediately up against
the normative positive problem, and find ourselves having to answer
the question of whether we are trying to explain what governments
actually do or what they ought to do. Are we saying then that
governments do have preferences and are aware of the constraints
on them, or are we saying that to act properly they ought to formulate their preferences and find out *ex ante* what limits there are to
their actions? Furthermore, is our objective to discover conditions
(notably first-order maximisation conditions) which determine an
optimum, or are we looking for rules which enable our optimum to
be arrived at? And are we also, perhaps, looking for behaviour or
policies as general rules corresponding to changes in external
circumstances?

As far as preferences are concerned, the economist is used to
dealing with multi-decision maker bodies, notably firms, as though
they were single decision makers often with simple preferences, for
example, profit maximisation. The fact that this has been less of
a drawback than might have been imagined, however, is because
a great many of the activities that firms engage in are of little interest
to the economist, and also that little attention is paid by him to

individual firms. It is not obvious that this carries over to government where cooperation and conflict seem to be at the heart of most real problems, and where it is specific government activity that is the subject of discussion. Again, while the economist would not explicitly reject the preferences of shareholders as needing to be related to those of the firm, in practice he tends to take this for granted. The analogous relationship in the public sector cannot be taken for granted and, indeed, the connection, both normative and positive, between individual and group preferences is one of the most complex parts of contemporary economics.

We have referred already to the question of uncertainty and have suggested that, while the world is permeated with risk and uncertainty, theories and models based on an assumption of certainty are still able to yield valuable results. (It may also be agreed, perhaps a little less widely, that a major gap in the subject is the analysis of risk and uncertainty, and it is in this part of the subject, that a breakthrough is most urgently awaited.) We have also said that an analysis of public policy can make some progress while ignoring risk and uncertainty, although pretty well all the major issues that confront us at the present do involve these phenomena. There is, however, one kind of uncertainty that we have not so far mentioned. As far as optimisation is concerned, the government may not know what is an appropriate measure of welfare or be able to devise policies that maximise that level. Its problems may not be internal conflict over preferences, but of not knowing what preferences it ought to have, or what objectives to aim at. If these are to be derived in a satisfactory way from the preferences of individuals, they may even involve insoluble logical problems. Because of the general significance of this subject, we offer a brief discussion of group decision making in the appendix to this chapter.

It follows that a possible model of economic policy might be, and might have to be, constructed on the basis of multiple and conflicting preferences or on no preferences at all. What this does to the concept of optimality is the subject for much more advanced work. At this level, however, we may recognise (a) that the preferences of the government may reflect those of individuals, (b) that the government itself may have preferences, of a paternalistic kind, for example, or simply to be elected, (c) that there may be conflict even between the preferences of members of the government, and (d) that the preferences of civil servants may also be a relevant consideration.

As a practical example consider the history of the devaluation controversy under the Labour government. Much of this must have been a conflict of fact (i.e. about the likely givens of the system), and much a conflict in positive economics about the consequences of devaluation. But some of it was about attitudes to devaluation as such, with Cabinet Ministers, civil servants and economic advisers all seeming to have different preferences about UK prestige, the reliability of the Labour Party, the importance of growth and unemployment, etc. It is hard to interpret all of that in terms of a single factor with given utility function.

Turning to the question of constraints, it may be asked whether here too the analogy of the single decision maker is likely to give rise to a satisfactory model. As far as economic policy is concerned, the way the economy works, in so far as that is known, represents the most obvious restraint or set of restraints on economic policy making. Equally the political system and method of government of a country also are restraints. Governments, whether or not there are written constitutions, are limited in what they can do and in the speed with which they are able to act. In countries like the United Kingdom, and even more so in the United States, the legislative and administrative process acts as a serious restraint on most if not all aspects of the executive business of government. It was suggested that the mini-budget of December 1973, for example, had to be based on public expenditure cuts because it was impossible to raise income taxes quickly enough. While the non-economic environment of the firm may be taken for granted by the economist, to ignore the non-economic environment of government may in practice be a much more dangerous thing to do. The fact, therefore, that that is precisely what happens in this book can be justified only by its elementary and theoretical nature. We must emphasise, however, that the purpose of all this is practical application within the real decision situation of governments.

Referring back to the normative/positive distinction, quite clearly a great deal of the study of economic policy has been about what governments ought to do in the sense of specifying the objectives of government. It has also been concerned with 'ought' in terms of correct policies derived from specified objectives, i.e. if

these are your objectives, this is what you ought to do. In these, as
in other cases of course, the level of abstraction may vary considerably. On the one hand, specific objectives, e.g. the pursuit of full
employment, may be advocated and a specific policy, e.g. a budget
deficit, may be recommended. On the other hand, general objectives, such as responsiveness to household preferences, may be put
forward and general policies, such as the superiority of monetary to
fiscal methods, may be recommended.

It is worth remarking, in addition, that the study of objectives
need not have a normative side to it at all. The student of economic
policy may merely base his work on what he observes governments
to aim at without considering in any way the desirability or otherwise of those aims. He may equally, but more philosophically,
devote himself to such issues as the meaning of economic welfare and
its maximisation, and the nature of objectives which may be pursued
by governments.

We may have, therefore, a spectrum which ranges from such
simple propositions of the sort, 'if the government cuts taxes at full
employment, prices will rise', to the complexities of such propositions as, 'it is meaningless to talk of the objectives of governments
because only individuals can have objectives'. The first kind of
proposition is a part of ordinary macroeconomics and comes into
economic policy because tax rates are one of the policy instruments
at the disposal of the government. The second kind of proposition
takes us right into the fundamentals of methodology, which, like so
many other things, we mention but pursue no further.

We have mentioned the different levels of abstraction at which
the subject has been studied. Parts of it are devoted to examining
and evaluating the consequences of particular policies. Other parts of
it are about general principles of policy. Once again we are really
talking about a spectrum of possibilities rather than a sharp distinction, but it is still worthwhile noting from this viewpoint the different
types of proposition that appear in the subject. The most specific
sort of proposition is of the kind, 'a cut of twenty per cent in the
standard rate of income tax will lead to a one per cent increase in
money national income.' A much more general proposition could
be that optimal macroeconomic control requires 'paying attention
to rates of change of income and prices as well as their level.' More
general still would be such propositions as 'even in pursuing

macroeconomic policies, the government ought to discount the
future in taking decisions which affect investment,' or 'because risks,
when spread over the whole population are immeasurably small, the
government has no need to take account of them in deciding what
to do.'

Related, as a matter of practice if not of theory, to the degree
of generality of the subject is the distinction between micro- and
macro-policy. Much more of the pure principle approach to the
subject appears to have relevance in a microeconomic context,
whereas specific policies especially of a quantitative kind occur more
frequently at the macro-level. Thus, the highly general discussions
of optimal pricing and investment policies for nationalised industries
may be contrasted with the analysis of specific expenditure tax
changes for national income purposes. The latter are more characteristic of this book, but we shall pay attention to some questions of
the former type.

It is also true that a great many of the general principles and
methods of analysis that arise in the economic analysis of policy
problems are not easily applied in practice. This is most true at the
micro-level. The incidence of particular taxes, the allocative effects
of monopoly behaviour, the introduction of an import quota, all
require for a full assessment of their consequences a knowledge of
the fine details of the economic system which is not available at the
present time and may, in the eyes of even the more optimistic
members of the profession, never be available. Even fairly elementary
micro-theory gives rise to a degree of complexity much beyond what
the applied economist can deal with even without taking note of
dynamics, uncertainty, and that kind of thing. It will also be apparent
that serious difficulties of application also arise at the macro-level,
especially when an attempt is made to apply principles of dynamic
control to the whole economy. It will be apparent, therefore, that
as a general rule only the first-order effects of particular actions can
actually be taken into account in predictions and evaluations, and
even then a broad brush and highly aggregative treatment is more
frequently the rule than not.

The only general conclusion from all this is surely that a complete, unified treatment of economic policy is not possible at this
stage in the development of economics. Instead, one can deal with
a wide variety of different matters pertaining to several of the

different models and approaches we have discussed. Sometimes, therefore, a static analogue of consumer theory or the theory of the firm will be used. At other times, conflict, dynamics and uncertainty will be taken into account. But at all times, what should be uppermost in the student's mind, as in the practitioner's, is the likelihood of error and the necessity for caution.

### Appendix: Group decision making

We have looked at individual decision making and have argued that this theory may still be applicable to groups or organisations because frequently they act or may be interpreted to act as if they were individuals. Now, however, we wish to look at groups made up of many individuals not all of whose interests are precisely the same, but who are obliged for some reason or other to act jointly. The whole of a country may be one such group.

Consider, therefore, some alternatives that pertain to several people. By this is meant that the presence or absence of these alternatives affects each of them (although not necessarily equally). The alternatives are available to them jointly. Can any sense be made of the idea of preference between these alternatives where preference refers to them as a group?

Let two alternatives be $X$ and $Y$ : $XP_iY$ means person $i$ prefers $X$ to $Y$. $XI_iY$ means person $i$ is indifferent between $X$ and $Y$. Suppose for all decision makers $XP_iY$; it seems reasonable to say $XPY$, where $P$ refers to society's preferences. Suppose for some decision makers $XP_iY$ and for no decision maker $XP_iX$, it also seems reasonable to say $XPY$. In other words, if some people prefer $X$ to $Y$ and the remainder are indifferent between $X$ and $Y$, we may say that the group prefer $X$ to $Y$. Note that $X$ and $Y$ pertain to all individuals. We are not discussing differences of opinion as to whether chocolate ice-cream is preferable to strawberry where each person can have what he wants. The kind of case we are discussing is where there are several people in a room listening to music and they may have to decide which records to play and in which order. The records played affect all of them unless there are as many record players as people as well as earphones and earplugs. As another example, if three musicians live in separate rooms with thin walls, a group decision problem is involved in determining the practice times available to each. In the present context more realistic problems arise from the fact that many individuals in our society have preferences about the distribution of

income, or the rate of price inflation, or the rate of unemployment,
all of which are group phenomena in the sense that their effects on
any one person may be seen by another person to be relevant to his
own welfare. The difficulties arise, obviously, when some people
prefer $X$ to $Y$ and some $Y$ to $X$, e.g. some prefer more unemployment
and less inflation, others less unemployment and more inflation.

Now it is an interesting and important part of economics to
consider how these differences are dealt with and reconciled, and
what their consequences are. Here, however, we are considering only
the much simpler question of whether given individual differences
in preferences we can make sense of the concept of group or social
preference. One possible answer is to say we cannot, i.e. if $XP_iY$ and
$YP_iX$, then no meaning can be attached to $XPY$ or $YPX$ or $XIY$.

This means that, if individual members of the group disagree
about the relative merits of group situations $X$ and $Y$, no meaning
can be attached to group preference between $X$ and $Y$. A possible
difficulty about this point of view is that it may happen that the
group is *obliged* to choose between $X$ and $Y$ so that one would then
have to analyse their choice in terms other than those of group preference. In addition, sometimes groups do manage to choose even
when they disagree. Economists have, therefore, attempted to
explore the possibility of group preference even where there is disagreement among individuals.

One idea they have employed is that of a social welfare function,
which for present purposes may also be called a social preference
function or a social utility function. This relates individual preferences
to social preference, the former being the independent variables and
the latter the dependent variable. For simplicity suppose, for
example, that there are three individuals 1, 2 and 3 and two situations, $X$ and $Y$. (The situations are sometimes referred to as *social
states*.) The possible preferences are $XPY$, $XIY$, $YPX$, for each
individual and society. This means that there are 27 possible combinations of individual preferences within society. These are listed
in the table opposite (ignore for the moment the last column under
'Society').

For each of these combinations of individual preferences we
must attach some social preferences. It is obvious that there are a
great many possibilities. One is to make society's preferences
exactly the same as those of a particular individual. This is to make
that individual equivalent to a dictator and it may perhaps be

|  | Individual: | | | |
|---|---|---|---|---|
|  | 1 | 2 | 3 | Society |
| 1 | *XIY* | *XIY* | *XIY* | *XIY* |
| 2 | *XIY* | *XIY* | *XPY* | *XPY* |
| 3 | *XIY* | *XIY* | *YPX* | *YPX* |
| 4 | *XIY* | *XPY* | *XIY* | *XPY* |
| 5 | *XIY* | *XPY* | *XPY* | *XPY* |
| 6 | *XIY* | *XPY* | *YPX* |  |
| 7 | *XIY* | *YPX* | *XIY* | *YPX* |
| 8 | *XIY* | *YPX* | *XPY* |  |
| 9 | *XIY* | *YPX* | *YPX* | *YPX* |
| 10 | *XPY* | *XIY* | *XIY* | *XPY* |
| 11 | *XPY* | *XIY* | *XPY* | *XPY* |
| 12 | *XPY* | *XIY* | *YPX* |  |
| 13 | *XPY* | *XPY* | *XIY* | *XPY* |
| 14 | *XPY* | *XPY* | *XPY* | *XPY* |
| 15 | *XPY* | *XPY* | *YPX* |  |
| 16 | *XPY* | *YPX* | *XIY* |  |
| 17 | *XPY* | *YPX* | *XPY* |  |
| 18 | *XPY* | *YPX* | *YPX* |  |
| 19 | *YPX* | *XIY* | *XIY* | *YPX* |
| 20 | *YPX* | *XIY* | *XPY* |  |
| 21 | *YPX* | *XIY* | *YPX* | *YPX* |
| 22 | *YPX* | *XPY* | *XIY* |  |
| 23 | *YPX* | *XPY* | *XPY* |  |
| 24 | *YPX* | *XPY* | *YPX* |  |
| 25 | *YPX* | *YPX* | *XIY* | *YPX* |
| 26 | *YPX* | *YPX* | *XPY* |  |
| 27 | *YPX* | *YPX* | *YPX* | *YPX* |

rejected on that ground. A second possibility is to make society's preferences independent of individual preference by, for example, writing *XIY* all the time. This seems to be rather pointless and also rejects some cases where there is no individual disagreement in the sense that no individual prefers *X* to *Y* and another individual prefers *Y* to *X*. Let us fill in these cases. They are 15 in number, leaving 12 where there is disagreement. Can we make any progress with this 12?

Consider the following rule. Suppose corresponding to some set of individual preferences we had solved the problem of social preference and determined that society prefers $X$ to $Y$. Now let the preferences of one individual who preferred $Y$ to $X$ or was indifferent between $X$ and $Y$ now change to preferring $X$ to $Y$, i.e. having not had the same preferences as society he moves towards society's ranking of the alternatives. It seems reasonable that, if no other individual changes in the opposite direction, society should continue to prefer $X$ to $Y$. Thus, if corresponding to case 12 we had for society $XPY$, we should certainly have for society $XPY$ in case 15 because individual 2 had switched to $XPY$ without anybody else changing his preferences. Equally, if in case 12 we had for society $XPY$, then we must have $YPX$ for society in case 18. We may go a little further in this direction by supposing that in some cases society is indifferent between $X$ and $Y$. If now some individual who previously preferred $Y$ to $X$ or was indifferent between the two, shifts to preferring $X$ to $Y$, society should continue to be indifferent between $X$ and $Y$ or should now prefer $X$ to $Y$. Equally, if some individual who previously preferred $Y$ to $X$ becomes indifferent between the two, society should continue to be indifferent between the two or should now prefer $X$ to $Y$. Thus, if in case 12 we had for society $XIY$, in case 15 we must have for society $XIY$ or $XPY$. What all this amounts to is that there should be some positive relationship between individual preferences and social preferences.

All that we have said so far is intended to indicate how economists have approached in general theoretical terms the problem of social welfare and social choice. What they have done is to lay down certain rules or criteria which it seems reasonable that a social welfare function should meet. The chief of these we have considered already, namely that social welfare should reflect individual preferences, and that it should not simply reflect the preferences of one person. A third criterion which is often put forward is much more controversial, namely that social welfare should reflect only individual *orderings* and not possess any qualities pertaining to cardinal utility. This means essentially that *how much* a person prefers $X$ to $Y$ is irrelevant to social welfare.

These conditions on the whole appear fairly innocuous. It is interesting to note, therefore, that it is possible to prove that they cannot be fulfilled in any group with at least two members confronted

with at least three alternatives. This theorem is attributable to
Kenneth Arrow and is too difficult to prove here. Some of its
flavour, however, may be seen by considering the so-called paradox
of majority voting which lies at its heart. Suppose there are three
individuals and three alternatives. Let the preferences of the individuals be as follows:

| 1 | 2 | 3 |
|---|---|---|
| $XPY$ | $ZPX$ | $YPZ$ |
| $YPZ$ | $XPY$ | $ZPX$ |
| $XPZ$ | $ZPY$ | $YPX$ |

Suppose these three people decide their group choices by
majority voting. If they vote on $X$ versus $Y$, two of them (1 and 2)
prefer $X$ to $Y$, and one of them (3) prefers $Y$ to $X$. It follows that
the social choice is $XPY$. If they vote between $Y$ and $Z$, two of
them (1 and 3) prefer $Y$ to $Z$, and one of them (2) prefers $Z$ to $Y$.
It follows that the social choice is $YPZ$. By transitivity, society must
now prefer $X$ to $Z$, but if $X$ and $Z$ are voted on, two of them (2 and
3) prefer $Z$ to $X$ and only one (1) $X$ to $Z$. In other words, there is
also a majority for $Z$ against $X$. What this means is that if social
preference is determined by majority rule, the transitivity principle
may cease to hold. Another way of interpreting this is to note that
the order in which the issues are put before the society may be of
crucial importance.

There are important special cases in which the paradox of
majority voting does not arise. One is the obvious one in which
individual preferences are identical. In this case social preference
will obviously correspond to these identical individual preferences.
A second possibility is when the individuals in society may be
paired, with one individual left over. Assume that the pairings are
arranged so that the preferences of one individual in each pair are
exactly the opposite of the other individual. On all voting, therefore,
all these individuals will cancel each other out leaving the odd
person's preferences to determine social preferences.

There is a third possibility which requires rather more analysis.
Assume that the alternative social choices can be arranged on a line
as illustrated in figure 2.6. Let the preferences of individuals be such

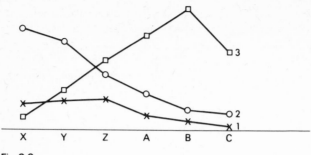

**Fig. 2.6**

as are illustrated in the figure, a higher point corresponding to a
more preferred position, a lower point to a less preferred position.
Thus, the figure illustrates the following preferences:

| 1 | 2 | 3 |
|---|---|---|
| Z | X | B |
| Y | Y | A |
| X | Z | C |
| A | A | Z |
| B | B | Y |
| C | C | X |

Now, the significant characteristic of these preferences is that,
given the horizontal arrangement of the alternatives, each person's
preference representation has a single peak. By this is meant that
starting from the left, utility either falls continuously or rises continuously or rises and then falls. In no case is a fall followed by a
rise. If the alternatives can be arranged on a line so that this single
peakedness characteristic holds for all individuals, there will be a
unique alternative which a majority of individuals will select over
all other alternatives. Starting from the left this alternative will be
the most preferred position of the median person, i.e. it will be the
$[(n + 1)/2]$ th peak. (We assume that there is an odd number of voters.)
In figure 2.6, $Z$ is the point chosen by majority rule. For any move
to the left individuals 1 and 3 will vote against. For any move to the
right individuals 1 and 2 will vote against. Individuals 1 and 2 will
vote in favour of moving to the left from B. Individuals 1 and 3
will vote in favour of moving to the right from $X$.

An example of the applicability of this discussion arises in the choice between unemployment and inflation. In figure 2.7 we have a Phillips curve and the indifference curves of an individual person.

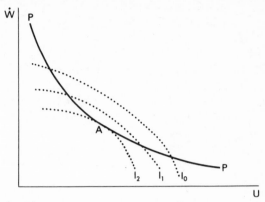

Fig. 2.7

Given the Phillips curve P P, A in his view is the best point on it. An examination of his indifference curves shows that, as he moves away from A towards either end of P P, he gets to less and less preferred positions. Thus, the ranking of available policies arranged along P P can be thought of as single peaked.

On the assumption that the position of everybody in society is typified by figure 2.7 all will have single peaked preferences. Their indifference curves may differ, as may their best position, but each

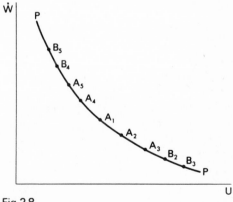

Fig. 2.8

ranking along P P, whatever it is, will be single peaked. It follows
that macroeconomic policy determined by majority rule will lead
to a unique outcome, namely the most preferred position of the
median voter. Moreover, only changes in preferences that affect
the median will lead to changes in policy. Thus, shifts to the
extremes may have no influence whatsoever.

In figure 2.8, we assume we are dealing with five people whose
best positions are $A_1$, $A_2$, $A_3$, $A_4$, $A_5$. The best position of the
median voter is $A_1$, which will be chosen by majority vote. Any
move to the left from $A_1$ will be welcomed by individuals 4 and 5,
but will be opposed by 1, 2, and 3. Any move to the right from A,
will be welcomed by individuals 2 and 3, but opposed by 1, 4, and
5. Thus, $A_1$ will gain a majority over all other alternatives. This
will continue to be the case if $B_2$, $B_3$, $B_4$, or $B_5$ replace any of $A_2$,
$A_3$, $A_4$ or $A_5$.

THE SCRIPT SYSTEM IS A LONG RUN PLAN.
WE CAN LOCK PRICES AND SUBSIDISE THEM DOWN
AND THEN SUBSIDISE FULL EMPLOYMENT. WE CAN
INTRODUCE RIGHTS AND IF PEOPLE HAVE A ONE CHILD
FAMILY FOR 5 GENERATIONS THE POPULATION WILL
FALL TO 3½ MILLION WITHIN 150 YEARS AND WE CAN
BUILD EVERYBODY BUCKINGHAM PALACE EACH. THERE
ARE NO FASHION MODELS IN THE SCHOOLS AND THE
STATE PLAN IS POOR.

HOUSE SIZE

TIME

# 3
# The objectives of macroeconomic policy

The most frequently mentioned objectives of macroeconomic policy are a high, stable and growing level of real income, stable or slowly increasing prices, a balance of payments surplus, full employment, and a fair distribution of income between people and between regions. It is also apparent that policy makers are not unconcerned about the instruments that they use in the sense of regarding them as existing solely to serve other policy objectives. Indeed, stability of the rate of interest and a high, stable and growing level of public expenditure and taxes (or a low and falling level of government expenditure and taxes) have certainly been seen as ends in their own right. It is no easier here than in any other part of economics to maintain a rigid distinction between means and ends, targets and instruments, or what have you. As we have remarked already exchange rates, although they are often treated as means in economics books, are very much regarded as ends by politicians, especially when the issue is one of devaluation.

The specification of the sorts of variables that need to be considered as ends in economic policy making does not take us very far. Something much more precise is required than 'a high, stable, and growing level of real income'. What exactly are 'high' or 'stable' or 'growing'? What sort of period of time are we talking about? What is our response to uncertainty about our ability to reach this end? Suppose the choice is between higher but less stable and lower but more stable, what then? If there are trade-off problems within the income objective, so to speak, are there not trade-offs between the income objective and (say) the balance of payments objective?

(For the purist there is even the problem of what is meant by real income and how it is to be measured.) In solving a problem of economic policy in theory or in deciding in practice what to do, all these questions must be answered, even if the answers are frequently given by default. In this chapter we shall explore some of them to show how deceptively simple they are and utter some words of caution on pitfalls that lie in the path of the unwary.

### Real Income

In any period of time, say a quarter, it may be agreed that, other things being equal, more income is better than less. This is not to say that it is income that is itself desirable, but income may be taken as a measure of the ability to achieve what is desirable within the economic sphere. This does not mean that in any quarter the correct policy is to maximise income, the reason being, of course, that other things are not equal and there may be adverse consequences that result from such a policy, especially if by 'real income' we mean 'real income as measured'. Thus, by a sudden influx of housewives and schoolchildren into the labour force, a drastic rearrangement of methods of working, increased overtime, and reduction of holidays, a substantial increase in gross and even net national product could be achieved. This might well have an adverse effect on ability to produce in the future, however, and in normal peacetime conditions the extra income itself might not be worth the effort required to produce it. If the analysis of economic policy takes into account the future consequences of present actions, there may be no danger of pursuing present ends which incur future costs. But sometimes in theory and almost always in practice we work with a limited time horizon. We are concerned with optimal policy from now until the end of next year or at most five years ahead. It is necessary, therefore, explicitly or at least at the back of one's mind to understand that 'optimal' includes 'leaving the economy in a satisfactory state at the end of the period'.

The question of maximum income is rather difficult if the time dimension is taken into account. Is it valid to add up this year's national income and next and treat that as a measure of our achievement, or should we discount next year's income by a rate of interest? In economics we emphasise the significance of the time

dimension in defining a commodity and say that it is just as invalid
to add up sums of money at different times as it is to add up apples
and pears. It would seem, therefore, that we must use an interest rate
in this sort of work. In practice, however, this has not been done,
especially in stabilisation policy, the reason being presumably that
the time periods are so short and the changes due to policy so large
that whether or not we discount next year or the year after relative
to the present hardly matters. Nonetheless it remains true that a
reduction of real income this year by £1,000m. must be justified by
the generation of £1,100m. extra income or the equivalent next
year (assuming a public sector discount rate of 10% per annum).

A related question concerns the stability of income. Ignoring
time discounting for the moment, is there any other reason why an
income stream of £43th.m., £43th.m., £43th.m. should be preferred
to £40th.m., £49th.m., £40th.m.?

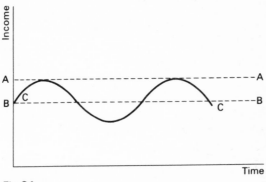

**Fig. 3.1**

In figure 3.1 it may be agreed that the stable path A A is
preferred to the cyclical path C C simply on the grounds that it
generates more income. But what of B B? If total income over some
period is the same, why is B B to be preferred to C C? If it is preferred, how much is it preferred? The last question also involves the
question of how much total income are we willing to give up for a
more stable income?

It is important in answering these questions not to confuse
instability with uncertainty. As we shall see, it may be that a more
certain national income is to be desired more than a less certain one
of equal expected value, but here we are assuming that the cylical
path is just as certain as the constant one.

One answer that might be given is that unstable income implies unstable employment and the latter is less desirable than stable employment. Another answer is that unstable income is less satisfactory from the equity standpoint than stable income. Yet a third answer might refer to instability of the balance of payments. What all three answers have in common is they shift the burden of proof to some other variable. They can, therefore, be considered subsequently. We are looking for an answer in terms of income itself.

It is, in fact, extremely difficult to think of such an answer. The nearest is to argue that cyclically varying income will go hand in hand with cyclical consumer expenditure, and that the latter is inferior from the household standpoint to stable consumer expenditure. Even here, of course, we have switched variables, but this might be justified by the proposition that it is consumer expenditure that measures the significance of economic activity.

For the rest, the undesirability of cyclical investment and the optimum use of existing equipment really pertain to the generation of income itself, and lead to the conclusion that instability is bad because income itself would be lower. In other words, the desirability of stable incomes simply stems from the initial assumption that more real income is better than less. If we can stabilise income, we can produce the same at a lower cost or more at the same cost. Otherwise the advantages of stable real income stem from the advantages of stabilising the components of real income or other related variables.

Let us now return to the problem of time discounting. A rather curious point to note is that time discounting does not necessarily favour a constant income over a varying one of equal total magnitude. Although this is trivially obvious once it is explained, it does sometimes tend to be misunderstood. Consider the following three income streams:

| Year: | 1 | 2 | 3 | 4 |
|---|---|---|---|---|
| 1 | 100 | 100 | 100 | 100 |
| 2 | 150 | 50 | 50 | 150 |
| 3 | 50 | 150 | 150 | 50 |

Let $i$ be the rate of interest and $d$ $[= 1/(1 + i)]$ be the discount factor. The difference between the present value of income streams 1 and 2 is

$$50 - 50d - 50d^2 + 50d^3$$

The difference between the present value of income streams 1 and 3 is

$$-50 + 50d + 50d^2 - 50d^3$$

The first of these amounts is equal to $50(1 - d^2)(1 - d)$ which is positive; the second is equal to $-50(1 - d^2)(1 - d)$. Thus, cyclical stream 2 is preferred to steady stream 1 which in turn is preferred to cyclical stream 3, although total income in all three cases is the same. In other words, simply taking time discounting into account does not help us to decide between stable and varying incomes.

This leads us on to the very difficult and deep question of risk and uncertainty in public sector decision making, but with special reference naturally to macroeconomic policy. Risk and uncertainty are dealt with in many parts of this book, mostly in terms of how it affects actual policy making and the interpretation of past policy making. Here we wish to mention rather briefly the fundamental question of what ought the government's attitude to risk be. In particular, should it be 'risk averse' in the sense of willing to pay something to avoid some of the risks of its policies? Put another way, should it regard all policies with the same returns on average (i.e. the same expected value) as equally desirable or should it prefer those with less risk (i.e. with a lower variance)?

At the present time economists are not in complete agreement in their answers to these questions. One answer is that individual people are risk averse and, since the consequences of government policy fall on individuals, governments should take account of that and also be risk averse. In other words, if the government has a choice between a policy which gives rise for certain to a national income of £40th.m. and a policy which gives rise to £39th.m. with a probability of 0.9 and £49th.m. with a probability of 0.1, it should choose the former with the certain payoff. The $\frac{1}{10}$ chance of an extra £9th.m. does not compensate for the $\frac{9}{10}$ chance of losing £1th.m. If no risk aversion exists, the two policies would be regarded as equivalent, and a small increase to the payoffs of everyone could cause it to be selected.

An opposite argument to this is based on the proposition that the risks incurred as a result of government activity are spread over the entire population. For a large population the cost of the risk falling on any individual tends pretty well to be zero. This is especially so if what happens to him anyway is independent of what happens as a result of the government's policy. Since the risk premiums required by individuals tend to zero, the government has no need to take risk into account in deciding its policies. It is also worth noting that all possible government policies are likely to involve risk so that any relevant allowances would be for differences in risk which might be rather small.

Now, if this second view is the correct one it could still be true that some policies that the government engages in are not small so that their risks appear large even when spread over the whole population. This could be the case in macroeconomic policy where differences of three to five per cent of national income may be involved. It is not obvious that these are sufficiently small so that their impact on each individual may be treated as negligible. It is equally true that their impact on all people will not be the same or that the independence assumption holds. For some people the possible direct impact of a particular policy may be very large relative to the status quo, for others it may be non-existent. The chance of national income falling 1 per cent could be transformed for some individuals into the chance of their own income disappearing altogether. Nonetheless, for a great many policies the differences in risk between them may not be large and when spread over the whole population can be treated as zero.

(It is, perhaps, worth mentioning here that there exists a second best problem for the government in its treatment of risk. The private sector may discount projects for risk because individual firms do not regard them as small relative to the number of their shareholders and are also unable to insure against them possibly because of market failure. In that case a project rejected at the margin in the private sector could be accepted in the public sector thus distorting the allocation of resources.)

Although our discussion has been in terms of national income the argument applies to other variables too. We may be concerned with the chances of particular levels of unemployment, or the balance of payments, or rates of price inflation. Certainly, with the first and

Each policy involves us in the same expected cost of unemployment, namely £200m.

In practice we may not actually transform other variables into equivalent units of income. In that case we may get much the same result by appearing to use a discounting factor for risk. In our example on numbers of unemployed we may reject the second policy because it is riskier than the first although it has the same return on average.

If discounting for risk is to be introduced for one reason or other in macro-policy making, the natural way to do it is to work in terms of the significance or utility of the payoffs rather than the payoffs themselves. Risk aversion is then about the diminishing marginal utility (or increasing marginal disutility) of such payoffs as income or unemployment. In our first example on income the gain in utility by raising income from £40th.m. to £49th.m. is less than 9 times the loss of utility by reducing income from £40th.m. to £39th.m. Sometimes this is regarded as too elaborate an approach and a more direct measure of risk such as the variance of the outcomes or even simply their range is used. Although this may appear satisfactory from a practical standpoint, the reader should be aware that some theoretical difficulties arise even though we will not pursue them here.

This section is really meant to be about income and before ending it reference must be made to growth and to income distribution. If we have a criterion that more real income is better than less, why mention growth at all? Indeed, is not growth a misleading criterion in that it takes no explicit account of income in the intervening period but is measured simply by comparing income at a later date with income at an earlier date? Assume income in year zero is £30th.m. and in year $t_{10}$ is £38.4th.m. If the degree of capacity utilisation is the same, we say that the growth rate is 2.5 per cent per annum. But this is compatible with an infinite variety of income paths in the intervening years as figure 3.2 illustrates.

Path A represents a constant rate of growth of income throughout the period. Path B is clearly superior to it and path C clearly inferior to it, yet they all imply the same growth rate as conventionally calculated. Path D has a lower growth rate than path A over the ten-year period, but would usually be regarded as superior to path A.

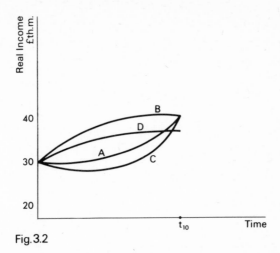

Fig. 3.2

As measures of economic performance on their own, growth rates are seriously misleading even if they are standardised for degree of capacity utilisation at the beginning and the end of the period (i.e. account is taken of the possibility that some of the output change from the beginning to the end of the period is due to changes in the rate of unemployment of labour or capital equipment). In particular, a high growth rate is compatible with low output, and may even be the result of some major force such as a revolution reducing the initial level of output. At the very least, therefore, in comparing streams of real income we must make an assumption that growth is at a constant rate throughout the period or differs from a constant in some constant way. Alternatively, apart from comparing growth rates we must also quote the average level of income in the period, but in that case the growth rates themselves are rather irrelevant.

There is one other reason why growth rates rather than total income may be considered valid measures of economic activity. In problems where the time horizon is finite and possibly rather short, say up to five years, one may also be interested in the likely path or potential path of the economy in subsequent years. The growth rate may be regarded as a reasonable approximation to prospective income at the end of the period.

This book's crap. Don't get it out.

Welfare may be influenced by relative income almost as much as by absolute income levels. The distribution of income really covers at least two quite different phenomena. Firstly, there is the functional distribution between wages and salaries on the one hand, and profits, interest, and rent on the other. Secondly, there is the distribution between income levels or persons, that is, between rich and poor. The two concepts are not the same. Their relationship revolves around the ability to earn income, and whether the distribution of the rights to profits, i.e. the ownership of capital, is itself much more unequal than the distribution of the capacity to earn wages and salaries. Because of the difficulty of including household income distribution in macro-models of the economy, the consequences for equity of macro-policy are usually dealt with approximately by looking at the functional distribution of income between 'wage earners' and 'capitalists'; but again it must be emphasised that this is at best a crude approximation and hides problems of inequality between different categories of wage earners.

A last point on real income as an objective is that sometimes we may regard aggregate real income as the appropriate measure, but for certain purposes policy may be directed at real income *per capita* as a measure of welfare and real income per worker as a measure of productivity. In the short run, population and the size of the working population may be regarded as constant, but again in the longer run these vary and may have to be taken into account.

### The components of real income

We have referred to some of these already but refer to them again in order to make some additional points of interest. We assume, however, that our earlier remarks on risk, growth, and measurements *per capita* apply equally here and will not repeat them.

It could be argued, following Adam Smith, and reiterated by Keynes, that consumption is the sole end of economic activity, and that it is a more appropriate objective than income for macro-policy, or at least should be considered as an additional objective. In fact, consumption would have to be treated in its broadest sense to include public sector consumption such as education and health, and possibly also leisure; but, given that, how strong is the case for consumption, more preferred to less, as the major objective of economic policy?

The answer again seems to revolve around the question of the time horizon. If the time horizon that is actually taken into account is infinite or at least very long, the appropriate objective for policy could well be expressed in terms of consumption. Where, however, it is short some account must be taken of consumption beyond the time horizon, so to speak, by including capital investment (public and private) as an objective on its own.

We have noted already that in many cases for the sake of simplicity it may be sufficient to concentrate on the level of income as the objective of economic policy. Consideration of the growth of income encompasses some more possibilities. Alternatively, growth may be dealt with by treating the level of investment, which is conducive to growth, as an objective, and yet a further combination could be consumption and investment as objectives.

As far as government expenditure is concerned this may be seen as an objective in its own right, as something desirable to meet social ends either of a consumption or investment nature. It may also be thought of as a variable affecting the future capacity to produce income, positively or negatively. Similarly, taxation may be viewed as something which disturbs the allocation of resources and affects the total utility to be got from a given level of income. Alternatively, it too may be treated as something affecting the capacity to produce income.

Government expenditure and taxation is an area of great political controversy so that it cannot be taken for granted how these figure as objectives of policy. While there is some debate as to whether more real income is to be preferred to less, this is quite minor compared with the arguments as to whether more public expenditure is to be preferred to less or whether taxation seriously distorts the allocation of resources or affects the supply of factors of production. Such controversy is not restricted to the conflict between the political parties; it occurs also within parties and gives rise (as we have noted in chapter 1) to policy making which appears to be self contradictory even at the macro-level.

It is for this reason too that it would frequently be incorrect to add private consumption spending to government consumption spending and just treat total consumption spending as an (or the) end of economic policy. Neither people nor politicians are indifferent about the private/public mix of consumer spending, and in many problems it is important to make the distinction quite clear. In particular, if it can be taken for granted that the mix is right, policy may then aim to maximise total consumption or real income, but if the mix is not right, the question of substitution arises, of whether it would be preferable to sacrifice some income in order to increase public expenditure.

### The balance of payments

Economists are generally agreed that the state of the balance of payments does not represent an objective in its own right, but is a constraint on behaviour and a means of reaching other objectives. At the same time, for practical purposes a specific level of surplus or deficit may appear as an objective of policy following from the way a problem has been formulated.

What is of great importance in treating the state of the balance of payments as a target is to get the formulation of the objective right, and to be clear which balance of payments is being referred to. There are such questions to be taken into account as the time horizon over which a particular surplus is to be earned, the rate of change of the surplus at the end of the time period, the state of the resources, the ability to borrow foreign funds, and the ownership of foreign assets. The objective 'the balance of payments must balance' requires the answers to all those questions before policies can be devised to achieve it. Does it mean the current account must balance, or the current and capital account must balance or that only such deficits can be incurred as can be finanaced by previous agreed borrowing arrangements? Does it mean balance every day, every week, every year, or every five years?

It is important to bear in mind that a surplus or an increase in surplus is not always a good thing or a deficit or increase in deficit a bad thing. A poor country able to borrow or with large resources might invest in the purchase of machinery on which future prosperity will be based. For several years, therefore, its desired state of balance of payments on capital account will be one of deficit. At the other extreme, a country anxious to enter the world banking business and see its own currency held in the form of reserves by foreigners might aim at a balance of payments surplus for a great many years.

In analysing the foreign trade and currency position of a country it is also worth realising that this is not solely a matter of the balance of payments, but also concerns the whole structure of its international credit and indebtedness. A country whose inhabitants have a great deal of short-term international debt matched largely by long-term assets can be subject to the difficulties of international currency speculations even with what otherwise might appear to be a satisfactory balance of payments.

This, of course, leads on to the whole question of the rate of exchange as an objective of policy. There are people who view this as an end in its own right, as a form of international prestige. Of course, it is true that, in so far as countries' incomes *per capita* are compared using the exchange rate to convert them into common units, a devaluation does appear to lower a country's relative standard of living. At the other extreme, an attempt to hold the rate of exchange constant may have such a large adverse effect on domestic output and employment that the standard of living falls absolutely and relatively. Between these views the merits of fixed and variable exchange rates are discussed in terms of their effects on the risks, uncertainties and general orderliness of world trade, and the ability of a nation to engage in international banking and to earn an income from invisible exports. At the present time no set of opinions has emerged as the dominant one so that the student of economic policy must content himself with recognising that sometimes a given level of the rate of exchange is a policy objective and must examine whether it can be met and what the consequences are for other objectives.

### Unemployment

To some extent the reduction of unemployment is a policy objective derived from the desire to produce more income rather than less. It is a measure of the degree of capacity utilisation so that less unemployment would be regarded as a good thing because it meant getting more output. It would also be argued on these grounds that too little unemployment was a bad thing in that it was indicative of too little economic change and implied that the economy was not responding sufficiently to varying consumer demands. In other words, too little unemployment could be interpreted as yielding lower national income or a less desirable structure of national income. But this is not the whole story, and up to a point less unemployment is considered by many to be a desirable thing even if it leads to a lower level of total real income over a period. In possibly extreme circumstances this might mean using more labour than is necessary to produce a given output, that is by work sharing, banning overtime, and the like. (It could well be that the three-day week introduced in the UK in 1974 was based on this view.) It could mean adjusting the economy so that more labour intensive procedures are used in individual firms, or it could mean adjusting the structure of demand so that industries which were labour intensive were subsidised and encouraged to expand. In other words, there is a psychic cost to unemployment which cannot be compensated for by producing more income and transferring some of it to the unemployed. The creation of a dependent part of the adult population is not good for them and is not socially desirable.

This returns us to the problem of the stability of employment. While fluctuations in employment are largely undesirable because they involve periods of unemployment instead of permanent full employment, it is also suggested that they are undesirable in their own right. By this is meant that a constant level of unemployment is better than alternating periods of high and low unemployment with the same average.

From the point of view of the individual this could well be, but is not necessarily, the case. If his average period of unemployment is given, he may then prefer to be out of work a given number of days each year rather than more one year and less the other. Viewed from the point of view of society as a whole, if unemployment is constant some people may be unemployed a great deal and some not at all, while if unemployment fluctuates it might be that the experience of unemployment could be spread more fairly over all people. In fact, an unemployment rate of $x\%$ does not mean that everybody is out of work $x\%$ of the time or that $x\%$ of the people are out of work all the time. Some people are out of work various percentages of the time, the average coming out at $x$, but in the general case most people are not out of work at all. If the unemployment percentage increases to $y\%$, this shows itself in those people who were in the past unemployed experiencing some more unemployment together with an entirely new set of people being unemployed for the first time. It then becomes a matter of fact which effect occurs to a greater extent. If fluctuating unemployment led to a fairer division of the given unemployment rate among the population, it could even be that a desirable end of policy was not to stabilise employment at a given level but to destabilise it around that average.

The same national level of unemployment is compatible with many different regional compositions. On grounds of equity it could then even be argued that a higher unemployment rate more fairly borne regionally is more acceptable than a lower unemployment rate less fairly borne. In analysing this argument assume the country has only two regions of roughly equal size called north and south and consider the following possibilities:

| Region: | North | South | Whole country |
|---|---|---|---|
| Situation 1 | 3% | 1% | 2% |
| 2 | 3.5% | 1.5% | 2.5% |
| 3 | 2.5% | 2.5% | 2.5% |

In rising from situation 1 to either 2 or 3 the national unemployment rate goes up by the same amount. Comparing situations 2 and 3 unemployment is distributed more equally in the latter which may be judged to be superior on that count. The question is, could it make sense to assert that either 2 or 3 is superior to 1. In both 2 and 3 the ratio of the northern unemployment rate to the southern is lower than in 1; but in 2 the unemployment rate is higher for both regions while in 3 it is lower for the northern region. It could well be that case 3 would be deemed superior to case 1. The more difficult example is 2 which, presumably, depends on the assumption that the psychic cost from unemployment diminishes for each individual as more individuals are out of work. The unemployed individual feels less ashamed, less of a failure, not so different from his fellow men.

### Prices

We turn lastly to the question of the behaviour of the general level of prices. High or low prices have no meaning as such; what is important is the level of prices at one time compared with another or, more generally, the rate of change of prices. It is for this reason that the static analysis of the problem of inflation is so limited and must be interpreted cautiously.

Like so many other objectives that have been discussed, the price level must also be seen as an indicator of real income or a means of getting a higher aggregate real income. Increases in the price level are said to interfere with the allocative mechanism in the economy either because they introduce unnecessary uncertainty or because means do not exist to offset them perfectly for people who do not care for them. A man who wishes to make certain of having a given amount of real purchasing power at his disposal may find it impossible or at least excessively expensive to do so, no matter what his present circumstances are. Perfect hedges against inflation do not exist, and good hedges may be too dear. To set against this is the view that rising prices up to a point are good for business confidence and private investment. In this case the price inflation is usually taken to be a reflection of a good or improving business situation, of sellers' markets.

Other essential aspects of price inflation are its effects on the balance of payments and its effects on the distribution of income. If domestic prices rise relative to foreign prices, in the long run the balance of payments will deteriorate. This may be offset by a devaluation of the same magnitude so that UK prices appear constant to foreigners and foreign prices appear to rise at the same rate as home prices to UK citizens. The issue then turns around the desirability of fixed versus varying exchange rates, whether the variations are smooth, whether they are automatic, and what sort of speculation will occur in foreign exchange markets in the latter regime compared with the former. It is not our purpose to pursue these matters here. Instead it is to emphasise that domestic price inflation can have an adverse impact on the foreign trade situation of a country and, therefore, its removal may legitimately be included in a list of the objectives of economic policy.

On the distribution of income, price inflation is said to be an arbitrary tax on savers and lenders and an arbitrary subsidy to borrowers. The circumstances that bring it about also involve an arbitrary shift in economic power towards certain sorts of workers

and certain sorts of capitalists, and in that way also arbitrarily shift
the distribution of income. Now, that being the case adds to the
legitimacy of the rate of change of the price level (in either direction)
as a concern of the economic policy maker, but again a word of
caution must be uttered. It is that the arbitrariness of the effects
of price inflation can be exaggerated. The retired people of today are
the wage earners and capitalists of yesterday. The wage earners and
capitalists of today are the retired people of tomorrow. In conditions
of constant price inflation the real income losses during retirement
will only be offsetting real income gains during working life. If we
consider larger units such as whole families or the extended family,
the income redistribution may be internal to them and can itself be
offset in whole or part. Similarly, the same man may be both a
creditor and a debtor, simultaneously or seriatim, so that again his
gain in one role may be offset by a loss in another.

In sum, we are not arguing that changes in the general level of
prices are a good thing. Far from it — the removal of fluctuations in
the general level of prices and of inflationary or deflationary trends is
a legitimate concern of policy. The important question for this and
every other objective is what weight it is to be given in the general
welfare function that guides the use of the instruments available
to the government.

Having explored, albeit rather briefly, some of the main objectives of macroeconomic policy, we must now go on to consider
how they are related to each other. We have already argued that
some of these objectives are convenient proxies for other objectives
and, in particular, derive from the general criterion that more real
income is better than less. It is more usual, however, to look at
objectives in terms of a preference function or a utility function
from which specific targets may be derived in individual cases. In
one problem the government may be supposed to have a utility
function involving real output and the balance of payments; in
another, preference may concern unemployment and the rate of
change of prices; in yet another, the relevant variables may be real
income *per capita* in this period compared with real income *per
capita* in the next. In the general case all the variables we have considered, suitably dated to refer to the time periods at which they
recur, may appear in the government's preference function (except

for the obvious point of avoiding duplication, that is, that there is
no need to include a variable together with a proxy for it!).

In consumer theory the household's utility function has a
number of important characteristics. One of them is the law of
diminishing marginal utility of a good, or the related law of
diminishing marginal rate of substitution between goods. The
addition to total utility resulting from a small increase in the
quantity of a good is its marginal utility. Positive marginal utility
means more of the good is a good thing. Diminishing marginal
utility mean that these additions to utility get smaller.

Certain phenomena are not goods but 'bads': as the consumer
gets more of them, he regards himself as worse off — his utility falls.
An equivalent law applies here, but is usually expressed in a different
way. It is that the rate at which utility falls increases, i.e. it is a
law of increasing marginal disutility. If we regard the decrease in
the quantity of a 'bad' as the same sort of thing as an increase in the
quantity of a 'good', the two versions of the law may be seen to be
the same. In each case utility rises, and in each case it rises at a
smaller rate; the only difference being that in one case the change
in quantity is negative, a decrease, and in the other is positive, an
increase.

In the form of diminishing marginal rate of substitution the law
concentrates on the increase of one good and reduction in the
quantity of the other holding utility constant. If we increase $X$
by one unit, the marginal rate of substitution of $Y$ for $X$ is how
much we have to reduce $Y$ to hold utility constant. As we go on
making this substitution, the law of diminishing marginal rate of
substitution says that the decrements of $Y$ fall for unit increments
of $X$. Similarly, if $X$ and $Y$ yield disutility or are 'bads', the law
states that as we reduce $X$, the increments of $Y$ which yield constant utility diminish.

All this is illustrated below. In figure 3.3, $X$ and $Y$ are goods.
A typical indifference curve is $I_0$ which gets flatter as we go along
it from left to right. Total utility increases in the direction of the
arrow. In figure 3.4, $X$ and $Y$ are bads. A typical indifference curve
is $I_0$ which gets steeper as we curve along it from left to right. Total
utility increases in the direction of the arrow which is the reverse
of that in figure 3.3.

The question then arises of how these ideas are to be applied to

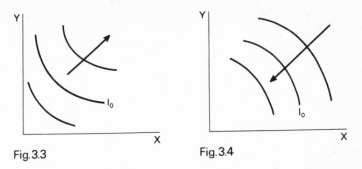

Fig.3.3                          Fig.3.4

the analysis of the objectives of public policy. There are at least
three important matters to be investigated. Firstly, it is assumed that
the quantities of the goods, or in our case the magnitudes of the
policies, are continuously variable, that indivisibilities are not
important. It is clear that in all our discussion of objectives we have
made precisely that assumption about them so need pause no longer
over that. Secondly, it is assumed that substitution is meaningful.
This is altogether a much more controversial assumption and one
that is not applicable in all cases. The best way to understand the
problem is to examine an alternative assumption. Consider a simple
case in which policy is concerned solely with the number of unemployed and the rate of change of prices, increases in either being
thought to be bad. It is possible that the policy maker's preferences
are such that he always gives a reduction in unemployment priority
over a reduction in inflation. Thus, in comparing two alternatives
each with an unemployment component and a price change component, so to speak, he ranks them by first examining the unemployment component, regarding as superior the one with less
unemployment. It is only if the alternatives have the same
numbers unemployed, that he goes on to examine the price component. What this means is that, if one alternative has less unemployment than another, no degree of reduction in the rate of
inflation can offset that fact. In other words, no substitution is
possible.
    More generally, given objectives $X$, $Y$, $Z$, etc., each policy will
have consequences for each of them, and may be thought of as a
package made up of a level of $X$, a level of $Y$, and so on. The
decision maker's preferences enable him to rank $X$, $Y$, $Z$ as such.

Each policy package is then ranked according to the level of its most important component. It is only when this is the same for two or more packages that the second component is looked at, and it is only when the first and second components are the same that the third component is looked at.

Assume, for example, that we are choosing a policy which has an effect on unemployment, prices, and the balance of payments. Some possibilities are as follows:

| Policy | Unemployment | Prices | Balance of payments surplus |
|---|---|---|---|
| 1 | 300th.m. | 5% p.a. | £200m. |
| 2 | 300th.m. | 4% p.a. | £300m. |
| 3 | 400th.m. | 4% p.a. | £600m. |
| 4 | 500th.m. | 2% p.a. | £1200m. |

Assume the policy maker gives first priority to unemployment, second to prices, and third to the balance of payments. In choosing between policies, therefore, he will start by examining their first component, and in this case he will rank both 1 and 2 superior to 3 or 4. Since 1 and 2 lead to the same level of unemployment, he now looks at the second component. In this case policy 2 is superior, and thus this is chosen regardless of what the third component is. Altogether, he would rank the policies in the order 2, 1, 3, 4. In no case did the ranking depend on the third component and except for the first ranking no attention was paid to the second component. No increase in the balance of payments surplus can act as a substitute for an increase in the numbers of unemployed.

A little reflection will show that this kind of ranking is not at all uncommon. Consider the appearance of words in a dictionary. The position of a word depends on the letters of the alphabet of which it is comprised. Firstly, the initial letter is examined, all words beginning with A appearing before all words beginning with B, etc. Next, all the A's are ranked according to their second letter, words beginning with A A occurring before those beginning with A B, and so on. There is never any doubt about where a word goes, and no later letter can act as a substitute for an earlier letter. (B A A cannot precede A X E, despite the X coming so much later in the alphabet than the second A). Because of the dictionary connotation this kind of ordering is called lexicographic and, as far as economics is concerned, a lexicographic ordering is perfectly possible and meaningful, at least for some levels of the objectives to be pursued. It is then an empirical matter whether it is the correct assumption to be made about preferences in any individual decision situation.

Turning back to the more usual utility function, the question is now whether it also makes sense, given that substitution is relevant, to posit the law of diminishing marginal utility. One argument would be that as national income is increased, the income of each individual is increased and, since they experience diminishing marginal utility, this must be deemed to hold at the macro level too. Against this it would be said that not all individuals gain as income increases. It could be that a given increase in income accrues largely to rich people and that a subsequent increase accrues a little more to poorer people. An appropriate preference function might then exhibit a range of increasing marginal utility and a range of constant marginal utility of income.

·A similar point may be made about unemployment. We have already noted that a reduction of unemployment may be interpreted sometimes in terms of the number of people actually out of work and sometimes in terms of the probability of various people being out of work. As unemployment is reduced those who find jobs later are not necessarily to be regarded as less meritorious than those who find jobs earlier; and those whose probability of being unemployed only falls when unemployment is low are not necessarily to be regarded as less meritorious than those for whom the probability falls when the reduction occurs at a high level of unemployment. For this reason it cannot be taken for granted that the gain from reducing unemployment from 1m. to 900,000 is greater than the gain from reducing it from 500,000 to 400,000.

A rather different but related comment may be made about the balance of payments. It could well be that special significance is attached to whether this is in surplus or deficit, and that there is a great leap in utility as the account shifts from one state to another. While the state of the balance of payments itself may be considered to vary continuously, its utility may possess a discontinuity. This is illustrated in figure 3.5. We have drawn this figure so that there is increasing marginal utility as the deficit is

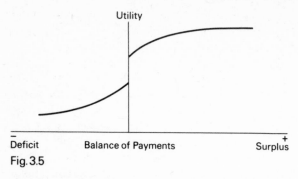

Fig. 3.5

reduced to zero, then a jump in utility, and then diminishing
marginal utility as the surplus is increased.

If we assume that there is diminishing marginal utility of, say,
the income variable, the indifference curves between income and
the balance of payments would be as in figure 3.6. A B C D is a
possible indifference curve, while E F G H is a higher indifference
curve. In the range of A B there is increasing marginal rate of substitution, there is a discontinuity B C, and then the normal range of
diminishing marginal rate of substitution C D.

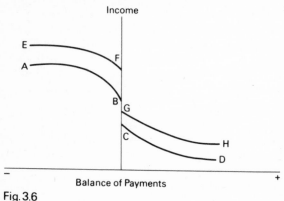

Fig. 3.6

The purpose of this argument has not been to reach the conclusion that the law of diminishing marginal rate of substitution
does not hold at all, but that it may not hold in all cases. It is
again necessary, therefore, to examine each actual case of policy
making on its own merits but, in particular, the 'normal' shape of

indifference curves must not be taken for granted.

Before concluding this chapter it is of interest to add how the analysis of objectives in terms of a utility function relates to the analysis of objectives in terms of specific targets. One possibility that may be looked at is that the target is merely a special case of the utility function. Thus, the specification of a particular level of each variable might mean that there are only two states of utility — achievement of all targets and non-achievement of all targets, the first to be scaled with a utility of unity, the second with a utility of zero. A slightly less extreme view would consider the targets to define a minimum level of achievement. Utility is zero if all the targets are not achieved but, once they are all reached, it rises for over-achievements.

The difficulty with these views is that they are not very helpful when it comes to decision making in situations in which under-achievement of targets is necessary. Although there may be situations in which the ideal levels of all target variables can be reached, in practice there will be many more when inferior levels are the best available. What is more, to concentrate on what is thought to be satisfactory presupposes that the decision maker always knows what that is and that it can be defined independently of what turns out to be feasible. There is also the danger that concentrating on what one is pretty sure is feasible may involve undue caution and the missing of much better opportunities. This is not to say that a first approach to see whether we can achieve a minimal set of ends is unhelpful, but ultimately the problem of choice is not simply the technological one of deciding the means to bring about a particular set of ends, but of choosing the ends themselves together with the appropriate means.

This leads to a different interpretation of targets as an intermediate stage of discovering the appropriate policy and of putting that policy into practice. In many problems a preference function of the sort we have discussed is hard to find and may not even exist. Instead, the decision maker may have some idea of the ends which he would like to achieve, and these will be the targets for a first analysis of a particular problem. These targets may be tested for feasibility and the resulting instruments determined. If they are feasible, further exploration may lead to the discovery of alternative targets which the decision maker may prefer. If they are not feasible, small reductions in one or all may lead to a feasible set which is at least initially satisfactory. The decision maker may make sense of this approach where he may reject the idea of a preference function or an explicit statement about marginal rates of substitution. Of course, if an optimum is reached by such an iterative procedure, he must at some stage or another have answered questions like: 'How much extra on the balance of payments will compensate for 100,000 more people unemployed?' But he will have done this implicitly, in terms of questions like: 'Can we achieve this set of targets?' and 'What happens if we raise the target level of that variable?'

This is the role of targets in the analysis of policy. There is also the role of targets in the carrying out of policy which is something the economist tends to forget. A decision on policy is really an intention to go for certain ends by the use of particular means. A precondition of achieving those ends will generally be their precise specification in the form of targets. A general exhortation to maximise utility will not do even if in some future economic utopia the public sector utility function were specified in an exact mathematical form. Instead the role of analysis is to give rise to statements of the kind: 'Our objective is to lower unemployment by 200,000, allow price inflation at 8% per annum, and have a surplus on the balance of payments on current account of £400m. next year.'

# 4
# Targets and instruments

In our simple example we considered three variables: the target, national income; the instrument, government expenditure; and the uncontrolled variable, investment. Let us look at this equation further; to start with as if it were merely to do with elementary mathematics. It consists of one equation in three variables. If we fix the values of any two of them, the third is determined. We are not free to choose all three of them as we like because the equation itself acts as a restraint on our choice. Conversely, if we set the value of only one variable, the single equation is not sufficient to determine unique values for the other two.

If we had two equations in these three variables, the position would be changed. In what might be called the normal case we would be free to choose the value of one of the variables and the values of the other two would be determined by the equations themselves. (There are also special cases where no solution or no unique solution for two variables results from specifying the value of the third one, but we shall ignore them for the time being.) The effect of the additional equation is to make the system more determinate, that is, to restrict our freedom of choice.

Let us now concentrate on the economics. In discussing the multiplier we did not assume that we could treat all the economic variables in the same way. We took it for granted that a variable such as national income was the target and a variable such as government expenditure was the instrument. We did not interpret the model as one in which national income was fixed extraneously and we used investment as an instrument to control government expenditure. Clearly, there was nothing in the algebra that prevented our doing this; rather it was our economic theory or our interpretation of the way the economy works.

The same general equation between $Y$, $I$, and $G$ could have at least three interpretations:

(a) national income determined by investment and government spending which is the form we have been discussing:

(b) investment determined by national income and government spending which is a form of investment equation;

(c) government spending determined by national income and investment, which is a possible behavioural equation for the public sector.

It could be that our theory includes all or only some of these equations, but our interpretation of any general, implicit equation of the form, $f(Y, I, G) = 0$, (i.e. income, investment, and government expenditure are related to each other) depends on the specific economic meaning given to it.

If equation (2.1) were all our economic theory it would amount to saying firstly that we have no theory of investment. Investment is determined outside the system, is *exogenous* to it. Secondly, national income is determined by investment and government expenditure. There is a causal connection *from* the latter *to* the former. This means that given the value of investment we can choose a desired value of national income. From this we can infer the appropriate value for government expenditure. Our theory then tells us that if we set government expenditure at that level, and that the given value of investment actually occurs, national income will be at its desired level.

Note immediately that we cannot go further than this. Although mathematically we can choose any pair of values of $Y$ and $I$ and then solve equation (2.1) for the resulting value of $G$, we cannot then interpret that value of $G$ as an instrument which will enable us to arrive at the preselected values of $Y$ and $I$.

We are also not free, with $I$ as given, to set $G$ as our target and then interpret equation (2.1) as telling us the level at which to set national income. One reason for this we have already remarked on — equation (2.1) does not postulate a causal connection from $Y$ to $G$. There is, however, a second reason which now must be considered. Lying behind our discussion of policy in chapter 2 there was not only the assumption of a causal connection from $G$ to $Y$, but also the assumption that $G$ was under the direct control of the policy makers. It was assumed to be an instrument the value of which they could set more or less directly. National income may not be able to be treated as an instrument in the same sense.

Consider, for example, the following equally elementary multiplier model

$$Y = M_1 A + M_2 T \qquad (4.1)$$

where $Y$ is national income, $A$ is exogenous spending (i.e. investment plus government expenditure), $T$ is total taxes, $M_1$ is the spending multiplier, $M_2$ is the taxation multiplier.

It is easy to show that $M_2$ is negative and in elementary cases less than $M_1$ in absolute value. (Many such multipliers will appear in subsequent chapters.) We may now analyse equation (4.1) as we did equation (2.1), with $Y$ as the target variable, but this time $A$ will be exogenous spending and $T$ will be the instrument.

Is it right, however, to treat total taxes as an instrument if by that we mean a variable under the direct control of the government? Surely, it could be argued, the government fixes tax rates and $T$ itself is only indirectly determined via the resulting levels of income and expenditure?

This is, of course, a perfectly valid comment, and while it does not detract from the view of an instrument as being a variable which the government is able to control more or less directly, it does show that the definition is by no means as simple as appears at first sight. In theory, at least, whether a variable is an instrument depends on the point of view adopted and the kind of economic model under investigation. Thus, for certain purposes it is satisfactory to treat total taxes as an instrument, but for other purposes it is necessary to work in terms of tax rates. There can be problems at a more micro level where it would be misleading to think of the government as directly controlling public expenditure, and instead individual programmes must be looked at. At the other extreme there are problems of economic policy where it is perfectly all right to assume that the government is so well in control of national income that we can treat that itself as an instrument in trying to reach other targets.

Having said all that, it remains true in the elementary multiplier

model that it is incorrect to treat $Y$ as an instrument, because it is
not directly under control nor is it assumed to have a causal effect
on $I$ and $G$. Similarly, $I$ is not an instrument because it is not
directly under control and is not assumed to have a causal effect on
$G$. In addition, while $G$ is an instrument that affects $Y$, the model
as it stands does not allow us to treat it as an instrument which
affects $I$.

There is one other comment that can be made about $G$. Apart
from being a variable under our control which we can use to
influence other variables, it may also be something the level of
which is of interest to us in its own right. In other words, it could
itself be the target variable as well as the instrument, so to speak.
Instead of using $G$ to control $Y$, we could use $G$ to control $G$,
leaving $Y$ to change as $I$ changes. While national income may be a
target, government expenditure may be either a target or an
instrument. (Naturally, in a larger discussion we might say that
national income is a target in the macro-model because it is an
instrument in some model of social policy aiming at such more
general targets as welfare or equality.)

We are now in a position to begin to classify the variables in a
model of the economy.

(a) There are *purely exogenous variables* the values of which are
taken to be determined outside the model or system of anaysis
under consideration. These same variables may be endogenous
in a different system; thus, while in our first simple example
private investment is exogenous, there is no difficulty in
constructing a theory in which it is endogenous. Government
spending is not exogenous in equation (2.1), but it is exogenous
as part of $A$ in equation (4.1). Specifying a variable as exogenous
still leaves us with the question of how its value is to be ascer-
tained for policy purposes, or what the consequences for policy
are of not being able to ascertain its value. In this connection it
is worth noting that a variable that is exogenous to a policy
model of the UK economy may be an instrument in another
economy. Thus, the UK balance of payments on capital account
will be influenced by the US Treasury Bill rate which is a
policy instrument in that country.

(b) There are variables which are exogenous in the sense that
their values are not determined inside the system, but instead

they are determined by the government. Their values are not
influenced by other variables within the model. If equation
(2.1) were our whole system, government spending would be
an example of this kind of variable. Such instruments of this
kind may also have their values set as targets. Alternatively,
they may only be used as instruments, in which case they might
also be called *pure instruments.*

(c) There are variables which may or may not be endogenous
depending on how the government approaches them. There
may be a monetary equation, for example, relating the quantity
of money to the rate of interest:

$$L = f(i) \tag{4.2}$$

where $L$ is the quantity of money and $i$ is the rate of interest.
Both variables are potentially instruments in that either may be
directly controlled by the government. If equation (4.2) holds,
each cannot be set independently of the other. If, for example,
$L$ is the instrument, the value of $i$ will follow. $L$ will be exogenous and an instrument, while $i$ will just be an endogenous
variable which might in other circumstances be treated as
exogenous and an instrument. In this case too the fact that
a variable is a target does not preclude its being an instrument.

(d) There are variables which are *endogenous* to the system
under discussion, the values of which may or are likely to be
chosen as targets by the policy makers and which cannot be
used as instruments. We may refer to those as *pure target
variables.* Within a dynamic analysis these target variables must
be the current or future values of economic variables. Past
values of these variables are given (or *predetermined*) and
except possibly for a 1984 sort of society cannot be controlled
by present or future policy.

(e) Lastly, there may be endogenous variables which are never
selected as targets by the government. They are not under the
direct control of the government and are not available as
instruments. They are neither targets nor instruments.

Let us now consider what are likely to be the characteristics of
a model of the economy. One way of thinking of this is as a system
of equations although it is quite usual in economics not to be able
to specify the precise form of all the equations or their coefficients.

In other words, we may not possess much quantitative information but can still formulate our theory in mathematical terms. Thus, the proposition that the quantity of money is determined by the rate of interest can be expressed in the form of equation (4.2). (In case of doubt, we cannot always be confident that our view of the economy can be expressed in quite this way mathematically. It can happen that our knowledge is limited to statements of the kind 'sometimes the quantity of money is determined by the rate of interest and sometimes it is not and we are not sure which times are which.' We shall ignore such a complication although it may readily be agreed that it is not uncharacteristic of economics.)

Our theoretical model will contain both endogenous and exogenous variables, and of the former some will refer to past moments of time. Suppose the values of all the exogenous variables are given as well as the earlier or lagged values of the endogenous variables. What are left are present and, in the case of dynamic models, future values of the endogenous variables. It seems reasonable to say that if our theory is to be regarded as complete it must explain or predict the behaviour of these remaining endogenous variables.

Another way of looking at this is to say that the purpose of the theory or model is to explain or account for the behaviour of certain variables. These are the endogenous variables. Their behaviour is determined in part by their own earlier values and in part by other variables called exogenous. They are also interrelated amongst themselves. What we are saying is, given what is determined outside the model and before the model begins, the theory or equations must account for the variables which are left.

In a crude sense what this amounts to is that the equations which make up the model should usually be as many in number as the endogenous variables. In fact, there is often more to the solution of a system than the mere counting of equations and unknowns, but that will do for the simplest and normal cases. (It is certainly what is taken for granted in elementary economics.) What we must end up with, therefore, if we have $n$ endogenous variables, is $n$ equations.

Now, as far as possible policy making is concerned, the purely exogenous variables of type (a) above and the values of all variables at previous dates are given. What are left are the $n$ endogenous variables together with the potential instruments of the present and future. Let the latter be $m$ in number. What we have, therefore, is $n + m$ variables and $n$ equations.

In principle, what we can now say is that if we have $n$ variables and $n + m$ equations we can select the values of $m$ of those variables and solve for the remaining $n$. What is more, ignoring all sorts of complications which we shall have to face up to soon, the $m$ that we select can be any $m$.

Now, the variables the values of which the government can select are the target variables, so what we have been able to show is that the number of targets the government can set is $m$. But this is precisely the number of instruments under its control. Thus, we have arrived at the well-known theorem that the number of targets that can be set is equal to the number of instruments at the disposal of the policy makers.

We shall later on indicate some special cases where this is not true, but let us accept it at its face value temporarily. How is it to be interpreted? Recall that the instruments are variables the values of which the policy makers set directly, while the remaining variables are determined by the economic system. Our theorem does not change that distinction. What it does tell us is the values at which the instruments are to be set. Some of these instruments could also be targets, and some of the endogenous variables will be targets. Together these will total $m$ in number. Given these $m$ values the equations of the model can then be solved for the values of the $n$ remaining variables, some of which will be instruments and some neither targets nor instruments. This solution tells the government at what value to set its instruments. In other words, it will set the values of some instruments immediately because they are also targets. It will set the values of other instruments as they have been derived in order to reach the remaining targets. When all the instruments are fixed in value as a result of economic policy, the system will work to determine the values of the endogenous variables some of which are targets.

The vital distinction to bear in mind here is between (a) the analysis of the model of the economy and its solution by the government or its advisers to determine the value of the instruments, and (b) the solution generated by the economy for the endogenous variables given the values set for the instruments by the government.

Let us illustrate all of this with a simple model. We have a modified version of equation (2.1):

$$Y = M(I_1 + I_2 + G) \tag{4.3}$$

where $I_1$ is exogenous investment and $I_2$ is endogenous investment.

$$I_2 = g(i) \tag{4.4}$$

Government spending and the rate of interest are possible instruments; national income and endogenous investment are endogenous! Exogenous investment is taken as given. We have four variables altogether, two endogenous ($n = 2$), and two instruments ($m = 2$) and two equations. Once the government has chosen $i$ and $G$, the economic system will work to determine $Y$ and $I_2$. The problem of economic policy is about how $i$ and $G$ are to be chosen.

One possibility is that the government will set particular values of $Y$ and $I_2$ as its targets. The value of $I_2$ may then be inserted into equation (4.4) to give the relevant value of $i$. The values of $I_2$ and $Y$ may also be inserted into equation (4.3) which, given $I_1$, enables us to arrive at the relevant value of $G$. The government then sets $i$ and $G$ equal to these values and, if the economic system is as in equations (4.3) and (4.4), the target values of $Y$ and $I_2$ will be reached. Note the four stages:

(a) The setting of the targets.

(b) The derivation of the values of the instruments.

(c) The setting of the instruments.

(d) The achieving of the targets.

A second possibility is that the government wishes to set $G$ at a particular value in order to achieve some social end. Its second target variable may be $Y$. Putting these values in equation (4.3) results in a particular value for endogenous investment, $I_2$. Equation (4.4) may then be examined to infer the necessary value of $i$. Once again the government now sets $G$ and $i$, the former at its target value since it is a target and an instrument, the latter at the value necessary to achieve the target value of $Y$.

It is easy to see that we can go through the same process if we choose to set values of $I_2$ and $G$ or $Y$ and $i$ or $G$ and $i$ as our targets. What is more important to recognise is that the nature of the model prevents our setting values of $I_2$ and $i$ independently as targets. Once one is given, the value of the other follows. In other words, if $I_2$ and $i$ were the only variables we are interested in as targets, the fact that last of these it is important to remember the heterogeneity of individual experience. There is, however, a further complication. We argued that, when national income was the objective, in many cases it might be correct to compare policies by means of their effect on national income on average. Does this mean that we should do the same with other variables such as unemployment? If, for example, we have a choice between a policy which has half a chance of reducing unemployment by 100,000 people and half a chance of reducing it by 300,000 people and a policy which has half a chance of reducing unemployment by 50,000 people and half a chance of reducing it by 350,000, do we consider the two of them to be equivalent? On average they both reduce unemployment by 200,000, but the former has a smaller range about this average. Are the 50,000 fewer unemployed when unemployment is 100,000 to be treated as the same as 50,000 fewer when unemployment is 350,000? (Note that we are concentrating on the unemployment as such and not treating it as a proxy for some other economic variable. In addition, our concern is with risk not instability.) One answer is that an unemployed man is an unemployed man no matter how many others are unemployed. In that case there would be no need to invent a unit of measurement of the significance of the numbers unemployed, a 'disutility of unemployment function'. It could be argued, however, that the economic and social composition of the unemployed varies with total numbers as does the general impact of unemployment on the nation at large. In that case, the increase in the maximum numbers that might be unemployed will not necessarily be offset by an equal decrease in the minimum numbers that might be unemployed.

What this means is that it would be correct to transform the unemployment (or price inflation) figures into different units measuring their relative economic significance. The obvious candidate would be a measure of cost or income lost. We would then apply our probabilities to those transformed figures; thus we might be indifferent between the following two policies each of which gave rise to some unemployment:

Policy 1    $\frac{1}{2}$ chance of unemployment valued at £100m and
            $\frac{1}{2}$ chance of unemployment valued at £300m.
Policy 2    $\frac{1}{2}$ chance of unemployment valued at £50m. and
            $\frac{1}{2}$ chance of unemployment valued at £350m.

formally we have enough instruments to achieve two targets is over-ridden by the particular form of equation (4.4). What this means is that we now have a spare instrument, but one which is of no use to us. We illustrate all this in figure 4.1

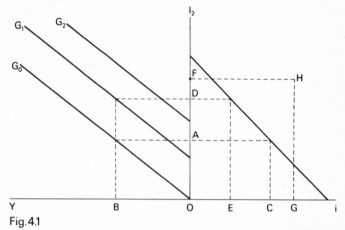

Fig. 4.1

In the right-hand side of figure 4.1 we illustrate the relationship between $I_2$ and $i$ given by equation (4.4). In the left-hand side we show the relationship between $I_2$ and $Y$ for different values of $G(G_0 > G_1 < G_2)$ assuming $I_1$ to be given.

If $I_2$ is set at a value of $A$ and $Y$ at $B$, this means that to achieve these targets the rate of interest must be equal to $C$ and government spending to $G_0$. If government spending were set at $G_1$ and national income were still desired to be at $B$, the only possible value of $I_2$ is $D$ which requires an interest rate of $E$. Lastly, because we are con-strained by the relationship between $I_2$ and $i$ we cannot set their values independently at, say, $F$ and $G$ because the resulting point $H$ is not achievable.

To illustrate the problem much more fully consider the following macro-model of the economy.

$$I = f_1(Y) \tag{4.5}$$

$$E = f_2(Y, P_h, P_f, r, W, T_2) \tag{4.6}$$

$$M = f_3(Y, P_h, P_f, r, W, T_2) \tag{4.7}$$

$$U = f_4(Y) \tag{4.8}$$

$$P_h = f_5(P_f, r, U) \tag{4.9}$$

$$C = f_6(Y, T_1, T_2) \tag{4.10}$$

$$Y = I + C + E - M + A \tag{4.11}$$

where $I$ = private industry gross fixed investment, $Y$ = gross national income at factor cost, $E$ = exports, $M$ = imports, $C$ = consumption, $A$ = the remaining components of national income. (All these are in constant prices.) $P_h$ = index of home prices at factor cost, $P_f$ = index of foreign prices, $W$ = a measure of world economic activity, $r$ = the rate of exchange, $T_1$ = taxes on income, $T_2$ = taxes on expenditure, $U$ = percentage unemployment.

The model is set out in diagrammatic terms in figure 4.2.

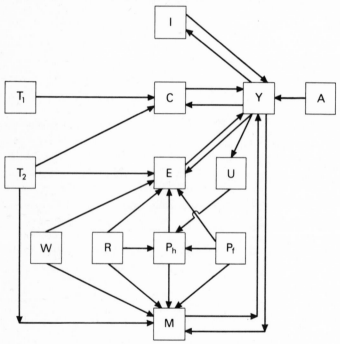

Fig. 4.2

An arrow going from one box to another indicates that the variable where it starts has a direct influence on the variable where it ends. The arrow from $Y$ to $U$, for example, indicates that real national income (in this model) determines the rate of unemployment, i.e. equation (4.8). Between some boxes there are arrows going in both directions indicating that each variable has a direct influence on the other. Thus, there is an arrow from $Y$ to $I$ corresponding to equation (4.5) and from $I$ to $Y$ corresponding to equation (4.11).

The dependent variables on the left-hand side of the equations are all measured at time $t$. In the simplest form this will also be true of the independent variables. We could, however, also go on to consider lagged values of these, if we wanted to.

We have here seven equations in thirteen unknowns. Of these we assume $P_f$ and $W$ are fixed exogenously by forces outside the system. We also assume that $A$, which is equal to the current expenditure and capital expenditure of the public authorities plus inventory accumulation and housing investment, is fixed exogenously. (They can be interpreted as instruments set outside this model to reach various social targets.) That leaves ten variables, of which three, $r$, $T_1$, and $T_2$ are taken to be policy instruments. Note that we have assumed that the government can set tax totals as policy instruments rather than tax rates.

According to our theorem, since we have three policy instruments, we can set values of three of the variables as objectives and then determine the values of the remaining seven from the seven equations. Remember that all this is contingent on the given values of the exogenous variables, $P_f$, $W$, and $A$.

The government might, for example, choose $Y$, $P_h$, and $E$ as its targets. We can see immediately that, once $Y$ is set, from equation (4.5), $I$ is determined, and from equation (4.7) $U$ is determined. Once $U$ is determined, from equation (4.9), since $P_f$ is given and $P_h$ is set as a target, $r$ is determined. We are now left with four equations, (4.6), (4.7), (4.10), and (4.11) to determine $C$, $M$, $T_1$ and $T_2$. All the variables in equation (4.6) are now set one way or other except for $T_2$ so we may use that equation to determine $T_2$. The insertion of this value of $T_2$ into equation (4.7) will give us a value for imports, $M$. All the variables in equation (4.11) are now set except for $C$, so that we can now get a value for $C$ from that equation. We can then work out from equation (4.10) the taxes on income $T_1$ which will give rise to this same value of $C$.

We may regard what we have just done as purely a matter of

logic. This would involve the interpretation of the equations as 'the right-hand side variables have an influence on the left-hand side variables.' Alternatively, we may interpret $f_1, f_2$, etc. as functional equations, and our argument as being an (albeit rather casual) analysis of their solution. Either way the existence of the instruments is what gives us the freedom to control other variables as targets, this freedom being partly to do with the number of the instruments.

We must now go on to consider various complications. One we have noted already, namely, that certain variables cannot be set independently of each other. This is true of $I$ and $Y$ because of equation (4.5) and $U$ and $Y$ because of equation (4.8). This also means that $I$ and $U$ cannot be set independently of each other.

If investment were influenced not only by national income but also by direct taxes, we would be much less constrained. Having set $Y$ at one value we are still free to choose a target value for $I$. Similarly, unemployment might not be a function of national income but of the components of expenditure, $I, C, E$, and $A$. This too would give us a chance to set $U$ independent of $Y$. Thus, if the model were modified so that equations (4.5) and (4.8) were replaced by

$$I = f_1(Y, T_1) \tag{4.5*}$$

$$U = f_4(I, C, E, A) \tag{4.8*}$$

our freedom of maneouvre would be increased.

Note that this increased freedom of policy does not result from increasing the number of variables but rather, in one case, from changing how they work and, in another, from changing the structure of the model. Apparently, there is more to the theory of economic policy than the equating of the number of targets and the number of instruments. (Of course, if the rate of interest, $i$, were also at hand as a policy instrument that directly affected investment, we would be able to set a fourth target. This might, for example, be investment itself as a proxy for growth.)

There is a further limitation on targets that must be considered. It is the fairly obvious one that not all conceivable values of the variables can be met by individual equations. If equation (4.5) is considered, for example, it could be that, no matter how large income is, investment will not increase above a particular finite amount. Similarly, in equation (4.8) there may be a positive lower limit to the rate of unemployment. To set as targets quantities of investment above its absolute maximum or unemployment below its absolute minimum would be to impose a contradiction on the economic model.

Examples of what we have in mind are:

$$I = a_1 - \frac{a_2}{Y} \qquad (4.5**)$$

As $Y$ increases $I$ increases, but it is impossible for $I$ to rise above a level of $a_1$.

$$U = b_1 + \frac{b_2}{Y} \qquad (4.8**)$$

As $Y$ increases $U$ decreases, but it is impossible for $U$ to fall below $b_1$.

This is not necessarily a matter of shortage in the number of instruments. Assume that investment responds also to the rate of interest as in the following equation:

$$I = a_1 - \frac{a_2}{Y} - a_3 i \qquad (4.5***)$$

There may be advantages in the control of the economy resulting from such direct influence of interest on investment, but it will still be true in the example cited that a level of investment above $a_1$ cannot be reached.

What this leads to is the point that the effectiveness of the instruments in various ways may be just as important as, or even more important than, the number of instruments. Our argument may be thought of in terms of the set of possible solutions to our equation system. The introduction of an additional policy instrument, while it may in a formal sense increase by one the number of objectives we can set, may in practice add very little to the set of possibilities open to us. Put differently, the point may be made that an instrument may be available but still be pretty useless. In our model one way of directly affecting the balance of payments is via the influence of the indirect tax variable, $T_2$, on exports and imports. Suppose

we have set $Y$ as a target and thus determined $U$. If we also have a
policy objective for $P_h$, the only way to reach this will be by setting
the rate of exchange, $r$, at a particular level. Thus, given our objectives, $T_2$ is not merely one way of influencing the balance of payments, it is the only way. If it does not happen to be a very powerful
weapon to that end, the fact that it exists at all may be virtually
irrelevant to economic policy. What is more, if the balance of
payments is something that matters very much, the ability to introduce many more policy instruments will be of much less interest than
the power of any one of them.

What may be meant by the effectiveness of a policy instrument
is a rather difficult matter. There is, first of all, its influence on the
set of attainable values of likely target variables. Secondly, there is
the way in which any target variable changes as the instrument
changes. Here we must mention the alternative ways of measuring
the change in one thing with respect to another that economists are
used to: elasticity or slope. The advantage of the former is that it is
independent of the units in which the variables are measured, but
it is not easily applied directly to linear systems. If the latter is
used it is easily applied to linear models, since the relevant numbers
are the coefficients of the variables in the equation, but in comparing the effectiveness of different instruments it is important to
bear in mind the units of measurement.

Apart from the formula that is used for measuring effectiveness
there is also the question of the context within which the measure
is placed. Initially this may be thought of as the effect of an
instrument on a target in a single equation where the former is one
of the independent variables and the latter a dependent variable. In
practice, however, we shall be operating with a whole model. We
must consider, therefore, the effectiveness of an instrument on a
target via the complete system even though the two may not be
directly related within a single equation. This would be the case in
our model for income taxes and income. The former is not a direct
influence on the latter, but does influence it indirectly via consumption. We are interested in two sorts of questions:

(a) If we change the value of one target, holding all others
constant, how much do the individual instruments change?
(b) if we change one instrument, holding some or all other
things constant, how much does the particular target change?

As an example of the first sort of question let us assume that we try to reach a higher target level of exports while maintaining national income and the home price level constant. Because $Y$ and $P_h$ are constant it follows from equations (4.6) and (4.8) that the rate of exchange must be constant too. In this case it follows that the only way of increasing exports is by raising indirect taxes making the home market less profitable. The effect of this will be adverse on consumption necessitating a reduction in income taxes so that income does not fall. (We assume that while an increase in expenditure taxes may lower imports this is small relative to the effect on consumption and does not offset the need to increase that variable.) Our conclusion is that an increase in the target variable, exports, affects both sorts of taxes. It is then an empirical matter whether the changes in these instruments are absolutely large or small. In the former case we may regard them as sensitive to the particular instrumental change, in the latter insensitive. The third instrument, the rate of exchange, does not change at all so that for this case it is most insensitive to exports.

It is worth emphasising that this question of the sensitivity of an instrument to the change in a target depends on what other targets are set and what other instruments are available. In the present model if income were not set as a target but, say, consumer spending were instead, an increase in exports would have an effect on the rate of exchange. Indeed, it can be shown within the present model that, since an improved balance of payments must lead to an increase in income, it is necessary if increased exports imply such an improvement to revalue the currency in order that home prices at factor cost are to remain constant. This in turn means a reduction in expenditure taxes and an increase in income taxes to hold consumption constant. Such seemingly perverse results come both from the structure of the model and the targets which are set. They certainly underline the need for caution in predicting the effect of a change of objective.

Turning now to our second sort of question, the answer to this too depends on what is given and what is permitted to vary.

We have remarked that our model consists of $n$ equations in $n + m$ unknowns (ignoring all the given exogenous and predetermined variables). The earlier discussion was how we fixed $m$ targets and solved for the remaining variables. (This involved the assumption that the equation system could be solved in this way. In fact that cannot always be taken for granted and requires justification in individual cases.) Each of the remaining variables can then be investigated as a function of the target variables; and our first sort of question was about the nature of this functional relationship: as a target varies, other targets being held constant, what happens to the instruments? (We could also ask what happens to the other variables which are neither targets nor instruments.)

In our second sort of question we treat the instruments as independent variables and solve our equation system to give each one of the remaining variables as functions of them. (Again, in a more advanced treatment we could not take it for granted that such a solution was possible, but at the elementary level we can ignore these mathematical complexities.) Thus, what we have done is to convert our equation system into a form comprising $n$ equations each one of which has a non-instrument on the left-hand side and is a function of the $m$ instruments on the right-hand side. Our question is then about how variations in the independent variables, the instruments, lead to variations in particular target variables, the dependent variables. (In calculus terms we are discussing the partial derivatives of the latter with respect to the former.)

We have already remarked that in some cases the question of what are the instruments is not an easy one to answer. We cited an example in which we had the choice of regarding either the quantity of money or the rate of interest as an instrument. In this case it could happen that the influence of an instrument depends on which other variables are instruments. More generally, the influence of an instrument is likely to depend on the levels at which other instruments are set. For example, in percentage terms a given change in income taxes will have a larger effect on national income the larger is the level of expenditure tax revenue. The reason is that the larger the level of expenditure taxes the lower will be the level of national income, so that the given change in national income resulting from the change in income taxes will be a larger percentage change.

A simple algebraic example is as follows:

$$I = I_1 + a_1 Y + a_2 i + a_3 T_1; \qquad a_1 > 0, a_2 < 0, a_3 < 0 \qquad (4.12)$$

$$Y = M(I + A - bT_1) \qquad (4.13)$$

where $b$ is the marginal propensity to consume.

All the other variables are as we defined them before. Equation (4.12) concerns the determination of investment which, apart from its autonomous component, is positively related to income and negatively related to interest and income taxes. Equation (4.13) is of the multiplier form and will be explored in much more detail in the next chapter.

From these we derive the following seemingly rather complicated equations:

$$Y = \frac{M}{1 - a_1 M} [a_2 i + (a_3 - b)T_1 + I_1 + A] \tag{4.14}$$

$$I = \frac{a_2 i + (a_3 - a_1 bM)T_1 + I_1 + a_1 MA}{1 - a_1 M} \tag{4.15}$$

The coefficients of $i$ and $T_1$ in each equation tell us how the target variables change as the respective instruments change. Thus, if income taxes go up by one unit, income falls by $M(a_3 - b)/(1 - a_1 M)$. (Note that we usually assume that $a_1 M$ is less than unity so that the denominator of this expression is positive. We have already assumed that the numerator is negative.) The effect on investment will be $(a_3 - a_1 bM)/(1 - a_1 M)$. The assumptions usually made about the respective sizes of the coefficients in these expressions leads to the conclusion that the first one, the effect of taxes on income, is absolutely larger than the second, the effect of taxes on investment. Since, however, income is itself so much larger than investment, the same conclusion cannot be arrived at with respect to the proportionate effect or elasticity. This may be seen by means of an arithmetic example.

Assume $a_1 = 0.05$        $b_1 = 0.08$

      $a_2 = -100m.$      $M = 2$

      $a_3 = -0.05$

(The reason why the coefficient $a_2$ is so large is that we are measuring the interest rate as a number in the range $0 - 15\%$, while national income and investment are in thousands of millions of pounds.)

This gives a value for the change in $Y$ resulting from a change in $T_1$, $dY/dT_1$, of $-1.89$, and of a change in $I$ resulting from a change in $T_1$, $dI/dT_1$ of $-0.14$. If income taxes are raised by £1,000m.

national income will fall by £1,890m. and investment by £140m.
The fact that the latter is only 7.6 % of the former should be seen
in the context of investment itself being only about 20 % of national
income. The elasticity of income with respect to income taxes is
larger than the elasticity of investment, but the difference is smaller
than that between the absolute figures.

If we work out the appropriate formulae with respect to changes
in the rate of interest, we discover that $dY/di$ is $-222$m. and
$dI/di$ is $-111$m. If the interest rate is raised say from 4 % to 5 %
income will fall by £222m. and investment will fall by £111m. Once
again the absolute effect on income is larger than the absolute effect
on investment but, since the former is only about twice the latter,
the relative effect on income is less than the relative effect on
investment.

To get income to fall by £1,890m. would require the rate of
interest to rise from 4 % to 12.5 %, i.e. more than tripling it. If direct
taxes were at £1,000m. raising them by £1,000m. would only involve
a doubling. Although this is only an arithmetic example and the
actual numbers are not to be taken too seriously, they do lead to the
conclusion that instruments can be ranked in terms of their effectiveness to achieve (or in dynamic terms to control) different targets.
Thus, a doubling of direct taxes lowers investment by 140m. while
the same effect can be achieved by multiplying the interest rate by
only $1\frac{1}{4}$ times. This leads to the view that it may be that certain
policy variables should be assigned to particular targets, so that
income may be controlled by direct taxes and investment by the
interest rate. We explore this further in a more explicitly dynamic
context later on.

All this is based on the assumption that policy making is not a
costless activity, and that more frequent and larger changes in policy
variables are more expensive than smaller and less frequent changes.
(We may also want to consider the trade-off between frequency of
change and size of change.) Such changes may involve distortions
and upsets in various parts of the economy which, while we do not
look at them in detail at the macro-level, certainly exist and may have
to be taken into account formally or informally. Although in a static
model there is no obvious reason why setting the rate of interest at
one level has any greater significance for costs than setting it at
another level, dynamically it may be very important indeed. This

is yet another reason why it is unsafe to ignore the dynamics of
policy making even at an elementary level.

In essence this discussion of effectiveness has been concerned
with the exploration of possibilities. This is an extremely important
aspect of economic policy making and it is one where positive
economics has the greatest role to play. What sort of objectives can
we set? What happens if we change this objective? What happens if we
vary this instrument? These are crucial questions which may need
to be answered before the actual business of policy making begins.
The examination of what is feasible may come before the specification of what is desirable. Moreover, the attempt to pursue the
infeasible may lead to results which are not at all desirable.

Now, while there may be many good reasons why the formulation of the policy problem in terms of an economic model may be
objected to, there is one excellent reason in its favour, namely it
allows for this explicit analysis and discussion of possibilities. Such
a model may exhibit spurious precision, and there may be temptations
to treat it as more accurate and reliable than it is. But its precision
also exposes it to explicit criticism and its faults may be pinpointed.
It cannot shift its ground as can the implicit theorising of much
verbal economics and policy making. In addition, since it is clear
what the assumptions are, it is also clear how they have to be
changed when they are wrong.

This is not to deny that economic models are sometimes built
and left unanalysed and unexplored. It is also not to say that model
building solves all our problems and cannot in practice be damaging.
It is merely that a model, whether or not it is cast in a mathematical
form, has an objectivity and a lack of open endedness which other
approaches, whatever they may be, do not possess.

We are not saying that the economic system can or should be
expressed in a complete model with no loose ends whatsoever. It is
doubtful, even in a very general abstract sense, that this is possible.
It is certainly not the case if it is taken to imply that the precise form
and numerical coefficients of the equations are known. Instead, the
real situation is characterised by a great deal of uncertainty. By this
is not meant simply, that a random variable should be added to each
equation or that there exist exogenous variables the values of
which are hard to predict. It is rather that in many cases there are
no well-established equations, and lots of contenders. As an example,

consider the determination of fixed investment in private manu-
facturing industry in the UK quarter by quarter. It is not the case
that we know all the variables that determine this together with their
coefficients. It is also not the case that our limitations of knowledge
can be expressed by the addition of a random variable. It is rather
that there is a lot of evidence that is not decisive one way or
another about the relevant variables (instruments and non-instruments)
and the form of the equation. There are also lots of arguments that
this or that variable or combination of variables are the correct ones
to take into account. Of course, certain correlations exist, but they
still leave open to doubt the causal structure of this part of the
economy. It may even be the case that the dependent variable is not
in a suitable form and that, for example, some disaggregation is
necessary.

A correct formulation of economic policy must take into
account uncertainty due to the failures of economics as well as all
other forms of uncertainty. The sort of propositions that one can put
forward, therefore, are: 'if we assume the economy (including our
instruments) works this way, and if all the exogenous variables have
these values, then we can set the following targets and these imply
that we should fix our instruments at these values, but if we assume
the economy works this other way, or we make these other assumptions about the exogenous variable, then the following targets imply
the following values for the instruments'. Moreover, the values of
the targets which were feasible in the first place may not be feasible
in the second; they may even differ in number.

All this can be done, however, only if the assumptions and the
chain of reasoning are spelled out. In one form or another this is
the role of economic model building.

Reverting to our main theme of examining the complications
to our simple targets and instruments theorem, a typical economic
model as expressed in the form of equations tends to suppress
various constraints, notably inequality constraints, on the value of
the variables. Thus, most variables are defined in such a way that
their value cannot be negative. In the short run there is a full
employment upper limit to the value of real national income and
employment. The unemployment—output relation may be specified
with a positive minimum level to unemployment. Marginal tax
rates as a rule are not allowed to exceed unity. In a particular problem

government expenditure may have a lower limit defined by earlier commitments. In certain situations the rate of exchange, while variable, is restricted, between upper and lower limits. Some of those restraints are in the nature of things; others may be due to past decisions which could in principle be changed. Sometimes the constraint derives from the way a particular equation is formulated.

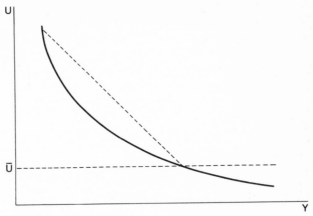

Fig. 4.3

In figure 4.3 we illustrate the unemployment–output relation. The continuous line may, strictly speaking, be the correct relationship. It may, however, sometimes be convenient to approximate it linearly by the broken line together with the constraint that unemployment must be above the level $\bar{U}$, i.e. $U = aY + b$ if $aY + b > \bar{U}$, otherwise $U = \bar{U}$.

The objectives of policy may also sometimes be specified using inequalities. Instead of setting government expenditure at a certain level as an objective, we may say that government expenditure must be no less than a certain level. This means that when our policies would anyway achieve that minimum level, we are in a position to achieve one additional target. An objective expressed as an inequality only counts as one of the targets when it is binding. It could even happen, of course, that an objective expressed in the ordinary way is not binding because it is automatically met whenever any other likely objectives are met. Usually, however, this is not the case. In our simple model if we set four objectives we are then left with seven equations in six variables. The system is overdetermined and this will involve contradictions (i.e. no solution) unless one of the equations is not independent of the others. In general, that will not be so and an attempt to pursue an impossible number of objectives will lead to some of them, possibly even all of them, not being reached. Certainly, economic policy cannot be based on a mathematical rarity.

Our treatment of objectives has so far concentrated on specifying the levels of individual variables. It applies just as well if we specify relationships between variables. An obvious example occurs in our model. We may set as an objective neither a level for exports nor a level for imports, but a level for their difference, modified by their respective price indices, i.e. the balance of payments. We may interpret the relationship as a means of expressing one variable in terms of the other and, thus, enabling us to get rid of it. Alternatively, it is an additional equation so that we have one fewer variables than equations.

We started with $n$ equations and $n + m$ variables and argued that we could set the values of $m$ variables as targets and solve for the remainder. What we are now saying is that we can instead add $m$ extra equations and solve for the $n + m$ variables. More generally, we can add equations or specify the levels of individual variables up to $m$ in all.

Referring earlier to taxes as an instrument we said that it is extremely important to specify them correctly. In the simple model we have $T_1$ as an instrument called total taxes on income. In fact, taxes on income tend to be related to income so that what the government controls is the basic tax (say the national insurance contribution) which everybody pays together with the tax rates as income varies. This may be expressed in the following equation:

$$T_1 = t_0 + t_1 Y \tag{4.16}$$

The model now contains eight equations, but in twelve variables rather than ten because $t_0$ and $t_1$ can now both be regarded as policy instruments. As a result we have an extra degree of freedom; we can set four objectives instead of three.

In most economic systems the marginal rate of income tax is not constant. There is a progressive income tax system with an increasing marginal rate. This may be expressed as a quadratic equation:

$$T_1 = t_0 + t_1 Y + t_2 Y^2 \tag{4.17}$$

We may now regard $t_0$, $t_1$, and $t_2$ as policy instruments so we have increased their number still further. This leads to the general observation that in so far as the government chooses functional relationships rather than values of single variables there is no shortage of instruments. The government has as many as it likes under its control. A similar remark could be made about public expenditure. Instead of taking this as fixed, the government could fix a relationship as a function of national income:

$$A = g_0 + g_1 Y \tag{4.18}$$

The first coefficient $g_0$ could be the basic level of expenditure, and $g_1$ could determine the income related part. Each can be interpreted as a policy instrument, but neither is of much use if unemployment or investment are variables we wish to treat as targets.

All this reinforces the view that the number of policy instruments as such may not be especially important. What matters is the number of effective instruments in terms of the set of possible solutions to our equation system. The introduction of an additional policy instrument may in a formal sense increase by one the number of objectives we can set, but as a more practical matter it may add very little to the set of possibilities open to us. In our simple model, unless we can introduce a policy instrument directly into equation (4.8) we are unable to vary $Y$ independently of $U$. The fact, therefore, that we have a whole variety of tax rates and expenditure programmes at our disposal may be of little value. If, having set $Y$ and determined $U$, we now wish to treat the price level, $P_h$, as a target this can only be done by fixing the rate of exchange, $r$, at some level. Our ability to influence the balance of payments will then depend on the effectiveness of $T_2$, indirect taxes. If that is not a very effective variable what we require is a policy instrument to replace it rather than an additional instrument as such.

Before ending this part of the argument it is worth reiterating how a change of objectives can also ease the problem of policy. If, instead of trying to set a level of home prices at factor cost as a target, we aim at home market prices, i.e. prices at factor cost plus net indirect taxes, we may find ourselves with more freedom for manoeuvre. The reason is simply that we can help to achieve our home price objective by using indirect taxes, and our balance of payments objective using the exchange rate. In our previous discussion the rate of exchange was fixed by the home price objective leaving a possibly ineffective tax rate for the balance of payments. A change of objective makes the indirect tax rate more useful, and releases the rate of exchange for other purposes. Again, therefore, the number of objectives or instruments has not varied, but economic policy making is eased.

On several occasions reference has been made to the possibility of the model being dynamic. If lagged values of the dependent variables appear as independent variables, decisions about objectives in any one period will influence possible objectives in later periods. This interdependence suggests that we must set our targets in terms of the values of variables through time.

Since, however, every equation repeats itself every time period, once we have correctly specified each equation the targets and instruments theorem still holds. Thus, equation (4.5) may be rewritten as follows:

$$I_t = f_1(Y_t, Y_{t-1}) \tag{4.19}$$

where all values are current values except for $Y_{t-1}$, which is income lagged one period. When considering policy in the current period, $Y_{t-1}$ is given. If our policy making extends over two periods we have 14 equations (i.e. each equation occurring twice). That is, apart from equation (4.19) we have equation (4.19*):

$$I_{t+1} = f_1(Y_{t+1}, Y_t) \tag{4.19*}$$

Similarly, equation (4.8) will be rewritten and we also have equation (4.8*)

$$U_t = f_4(Y_t) \tag{4.8}$$

$$U_{t+1} = f_4(Y_{t+1}) \tag{4.8*}$$

We also have 26 unknowns, assuming $Y_{t-1}$ is given and noticing the lagged value of income in period $+ 1$ is the income determined in the current period. The givens are now taken as such for two periods, making six predetermined values in all. We then have 14 equations in 20 unknowns. The difference of six results from the existence of three instruments for two periods.

What we might do, therefore, is to set the levels of three targets for two periods determining the value of six variables in all. If we make policy over $n$ periods we have $3n$ instrument values to set and can, therefore, choose $3n$ target values. The effect of dynamics, thus, is to complicate and extend matters, but not from this point of view to change them fundamentally. There is, however, an additional point to note which will be returned to later. Just because a particular variable is a target in one period it does not have to be a target in another period. Thus, we may aim to set income at a particular level $\tau$ periods ahead, i.e. make $Y_{t+\tau}$ a target, but not be concerned with intermediate values of income and instead set the balance of payments, say, as a target between the present and period $\tau$. This is an extremely important enlargement of the scope of the analysis which a purely static analysis has a tendency to miss.

Of course, a dynamic approach will remind us of a great many other significant matters. It causes us to think about problems of risk and uncertainty which otherwise might be ignored. It reminds us that we have to set time paths for things such as national income and prices, and concentrate on growth rates and rates of change rather than levels. We are obliged to recognise that our ability to vary some policy instruments may be limited by certain maximum frequencies of change (e.g. for some taxes once a year at budget time) or by maximum accounts (e.g. the ten per cent change of the regulator).

### Appendix 1: Targets and instruments

The usual analysis of targets and instruments pays little attention to the way in which the instruments themselves may be varied but concentrates instead on the number of targets and instruments. Our view is that this is not the only worthwhile consideration in this field and may sometimes not even be an important consideration. This appendix emphasises another aspect of the matter and discusses a problem where the variability of the instruments is important.

Assume we are trying to control a variable $X$ which is subject to random shocks $w$. We have a system equation:

$$X_t = f(u_t, w_t) \tag{4.20}$$

where $u_t$ is our control variable

$$\frac{\partial X}{\partial u}, \frac{\partial X}{\partial w} > 0$$

We assume that whatever process determines $w$ it is confined to a finite range:

$$w_- \leqslant w_t \leqslant w_+ \qquad (4.21)$$

We now wish to examine the consequences of restraint on the range of values open to $u$, i.e.

$$u_- \leqslant u_t \leqslant u_+ \qquad (4.22)$$

Examples of relevant problems in which constraints occur include the following:

(a) The permissible range of variation of the rate of exchange limits the use of that instrument as a means of controlling the balance of payments.

(b) The permissible range of variation of the rate of interest limits the use of that instrument as a means either of controlling the balance of payments or internal spending.

It may also be the case that in any short period of time, up to a year say, there may be constraints on the range of variations of government expenditure, total taxes, and the stock of money around their current levels.

We assume for simplicity that $u_t$ occurs later than we observe $w_t$ so that in principle we can control $X_t$ perfectly. (As is obvious to the mathematical reader, we would, of course, consider explicitly a general process that generates $w$ together with lags in $u$ to determine the optimal, albeit imperfect, control strategy for $u$, but this adds nothing to the substantive point we wish to make. We do, however, illustrate our argument with an elementary example in this area.)

Suppose we wish to keep $X$ at a value $X_1$. There will be a set of values of $u$ and $w$ which will lead to that value of $X$. A subset of those values will be defined by the range of $w$. To this will correspond a range of $u$. If the permitted range of $u$ includes this desired range, we can control $X$ perfectly at $X_1$. Otherwise $X$ itself will vary. This is illustrated in figure 4.4. The line $X$ is the locus of the desired combinations of $u$ and $w$. It is a sort of policy equiproduct curve for $u$ and $w$.

As long as $w$ is in the range $w_1$–$w_2$, $u$ can be adjusted to keep $X$ at $X_1$. Outside that range it cannot be adjusted.

Assume that it is always desirable to make $X$ as near as

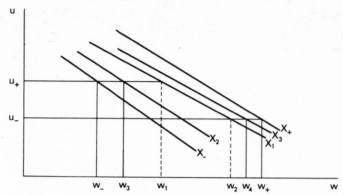

Fig. 4.4

possible to $X_1$. When, therefore, $w$ equals $w_3$, the best policy is to put $u$ equal to $u_+$ making $X = X_2$; and when $w$ equals $w_4$, the best policy is to put $u$ equal to $u_-$ making $X = X_3$. It can be seen therefore, that $X$ will fluctuate in the range $X_+$ to $X_-$.

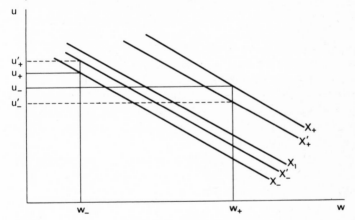

Fig. 4.5

Suppose now the permissible range of $u$ increases. It is then easy to see from figure 4.5 that the range of fluctuation of $X$ diminishes. Given the range of fluctuation of $w$, when $u$ is confined to the interval $u_+u_-$, $X$ varies in the interval $X_+X_-$. When $u$ is confined to the larger interval $u'_+ u'_-$, $X$ varies in the smaller interval $X'_+X'_-$.

It is easy to see similarly that as the range of variation of $w$ falls so does the range of variation of $X$.

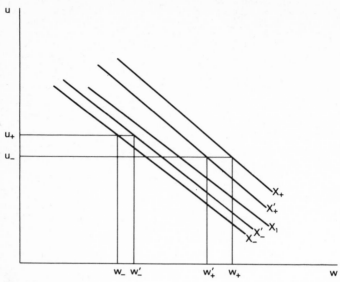

Fig. 4.6

In figure 4.6 the range of variation of $w$ is initially $w_+$ $w_-$ and the range of variation of $X$, $X_+$ $X_-$. When the range of $w$ is reduced to $w'_+$ $w'_-$, the range of variation of $X$ falls to $X'_+X'_-$.

To interpret what we have said so far in explicitly economic terms consider the balance of payments. Control of this has been discussed in terms of whether we have an instrument available to achieve the desired objective, or whether with a shortage of instruments we are obliged to consider the trade-off between balance of payments equilibrium and full employment. Our view is the presence or absence of an instrument corresponds to too narrow a view of the matter, and is the limit case, so to speak, of zero variability. As we widen the range of variability (for example, of the rate of exchange) we gain more control of the balance of payments, but restraints on that range still limit our control. Moreover, if the variability of the outside shocks increases (for example, foreign prices or incomes fluctuate to a larger extent) we may have to increase the permissible range of the rate of exchange to obtain the same control over the balance of payments.

This analysis can be extended in an obvious way to allow for more than one controlling instrument and also for more than one target. It may also be applied explicitly to the problem of optimum dynamic stochastic control policy to show that constraints on the controls lead to increased variance of the target.

In this case the existence of constraints on the controls mean that there will be periods of time when the system is essentially out of control compared with the unconstrained optimum. Thus, optimum control may require that occasionally to offset extreme variations in aggregate expenditure there be extreme variations in taxation. The government may prefer to reduce those variations in taxation and allow national income to vary more than would happen under maximum stabilisation.

To return to the non-stochastic case, a particularly relevant generalisation occurs when there are two instruments and one target, but where the range of one instrument is constrained. If the target is to be met, the more narrow the range of one instrument the wider the range of variation of the other.

Assume, for example, there is a balance of payments objective to be met. This may be achieved by varying the scale of activity of the domestic economy, $Y$, or by varying the rate of exchange $r$. Let $X$ be the state of the balance of payments so that we have

$$X_t = f(r_t, Y_t, w_t) \tag{4.23}$$

This equation assumed that imports and exports are a function of national income and the rate of exchange, but are also subject to some uncontrolled variable such as the state of world production designated by $w$. An increase in national income worsens the balance of payments which may be offset by a reduction in the rate of exchange, measured in terms of foreign currency per unit of home currency. (National income is not strictly speaking an instrument, but we assume that we have other instruments which can be used to control it. For our purposes, therefore, it may be interpreted as an instrument but the purist may prefer to interpret it as a proxy-instrument). Our analysis is, of course, altogether static. If explicit consideration were given to lags, the range of variation of the balance of payments would then also depend on the speed of response of the instruments to meet the desired target.

Given $w$ we have a set of effective combinations of $r$ and $Y$ which put $X$ at its desired value. It may be that the range of $r$ is such that we can put $Y$ at some desired level (e.g. full employment), and vary $r$ so as to determine $X$. If, however, the range of $r$ is more restricted, $Y$ must be permitted to vary to generate the desired value of $X$.

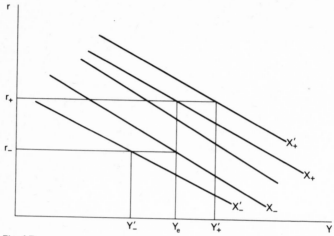

Fig. 4.7

In figure 4.7 if $w$ varies so that the policy locus between $r$ and $Y$ is restricted to the lines between $X_+$ and $X_-$ , $Y$ can be kept at $Y_e$ and $r$ allowed to vary between $r_+$ and $r_1$. If, however, external shocks increase so that we are dealing with loci in the range $X'_+ X'_-, Y$ will vary in the range $Y'_+ Y'_-$ . The wider the external shocks and the narrower the range of $r$, the greater the range in which $Y$ will have to vary. Alternatively, if $Y$ is also constrained it is easy to see that the range of variations of $X$ will increase.

### Appendix 2: The targets and instruments theorem in a stochastic model

Suppose the number of target variables is given and we already have an equal number of instruments. Is there any benefit to be gained from adding to the number of our instruments? In the main text we have indicated why the answer to this question is likely to be yes. The new instruments may be less costly to use, either in total or at the margin, than the existing ones. There may have been restraints on the use of the existing instruments or their effects may have been non-linear and, therefore, bounded, in either case limiting the range over which the targets can be set.

In this appendix we discuss another reason, namely that the effects of the instruments may be stochastic. For the sake of simplicity we consider a single target which is related linearly to a number of instruments which are themselves unconstrained.

$$Y = \sum_{i=1}^{n} a_i U_i + a_0 \qquad (4.24)$$

where $Y$ is the target variable, $U_i$ are the instruments, $a_0$ reflects the influence of all other factors and is assumed for the sake of simplicity to be an independent random variable. Thus, $Y$ might be the change in national income; $U_1$, the change in public expenditure; $U_2$, the change in income taxes; $U_3$, the change in the rate of interest, etc.

We assume that there is a desired value for the target variable, $Y^*$. The policy maker's criterion function is $W = (Y - Y^*)^2$ and he wishes to minimise the expected value of $W$.

If the $a_i(i = 1, ..., n)$ are known for certain, there is the standard result that the optimum policy is given by

$$\sum_{i=1}^{n} a_i U_i = Y^* \qquad (4.25)$$

In other words, the certainty equivalence theorem holds, and we have an excess of instruments. We lose nothing within the context of the present problem if we are limited to only one of them.

This is true as long as the stochastic side of the model consists solely of an additive disturbance (which, incidentally, does not have to be an independent random variable, but may follow any stationary stochastic process). Let us, therefore, drop the additive disturbance from the model and concentrate on the other co-efficients $a_i$ ($i = 1, ..., n$). These indicate the influence of the instruments on the target and are what the engineers call the gain. Suppose they are random variables. (In essence, we are making one of two assumptions, either (a) that we have no estimation problem, that the coefficients are *known* to be stochastic, and we know their probability densities, or (b) that we have used a Bayesian estimation method with known posterior distribution.)

The problem is then to minimise $E(W)$:

$$E(W) = E(\sum_{i=1}^{n} a_i U_i - Y^*)^2 \qquad (4.26)$$

Now, it will be seen immediately that this is quite analogous to the classic problem of least squares.

Let us rewrite (4.26) in matrix form where $\mathbf{U}$ is a vector with elements $U_i$; $\mathbf{C}$ is the matrix with elements $E(a_i a_j)$, which is assumed to be non-singular, it is also, of course, positive definite; $\mathbf{B}$ is a vector with elements $E(a_i)$. We then have

$$E(W) = Y^{*2} - 2\mathbf{U'BY^*} + \mathbf{U'CU} \qquad (4.27)$$

The optimum policy then consists of that vector $\mathbf{U}$ which minimises $E(W)$, that is:

$$-2\mathbf{Y^*B} + 2\mathbf{C\hat{U}} = 0 \qquad (4.28)$$

or

$$\mathbf{U} = \mathbf{C}^{-1} Y^* \mathbf{B}$$

The optimum policy depends on the covariance as well as the means of the coefficients.

Note that equation (4.28) determines all the elements of $\mathbf{U}$. None of the instruments is superfluous. If we insert this value in equation (4.27) we get an expression for the minimised value of $E(W)$.

$$\min E(W) = Y^{*2} - (Y^*, \mathbf{B})'\mathbf{C}^{-1}(Y^*\mathbf{B}) \qquad (4.29)$$
$$= Y^{*2} - \hat{\mathbf{U}}'(Y^*\mathbf{B})$$

We also have the standard result showing how the criterion is affected by sub-optimal policies. This may be written as

$$E(W) = \min E(W) + (\mathbf{U} - \hat{\mathbf{U}})'\mathbf{C}(\mathbf{U} - \hat{\mathbf{U}}) \qquad (4.30)$$

Note, in particular, that if all the elements of $\mathbf{U}$ are zero, the loss compared with the optimal situation is $\hat{\mathbf{U}}'\mathbf{C}\hat{\mathbf{U}}$. Another way of looking at this follows from equation (4.29). If the $U_i$ are all zero, the value of $E(W)$ is $Y^{*2}$. The benefit from following the optimal policies is then $\hat{\mathbf{U}}(Y^*\mathbf{B})$.

It is illuminating to examine these results in a little more detail assuming that there are two instruments, say government expenditure and taxation, and only one target, say national income.

$$Y = a_1 U_1 + a_2 U_2 \tag{4.31}$$

Suppose we fix $U_2$ arbitrarily and minimise $Y$ with respect to $U_1$ only. The value of $U_1$ which achieves this is

$$\hat{\hat{U}}_1 = \frac{Y^* Ea_1 - U_2 Ea_1 a_2}{Ea_1^2} \tag{4.32}$$

(Note that in general $a_1$ and $a_2$ will not be independent so that we cannot write $Ea_{1} a_2$ equal to $Ea_1 Ea_2$. If, for example, $a_1$ and $a_2$ are the public expenditure and tax multipliers, respectively, they will both depend on the same marginal propensity to consume, marginal propensity to import, etc.)

Let us compare $\hat{\hat{U}}_1$ with $\hat{U}_1$. Writing them out explicitly we obtain

$$\hat{\hat{U}}_1 - \hat{U}_1 = \frac{Y^*}{Ea_1^2}\left[ Ea_1 - \frac{U_2}{Y^*} Ea_1 a_2\right]$$
$$- Y^*\left[\frac{Ea_1 Ea_2^2 - Ea_2 Ea_1 a_2}{Ea_1^2 Ea_2^2 - (Ea_1 a_2)^2}\right] \tag{4.33}$$

This rather messy expression simplifies to

$$\hat{\hat{U}}_1 - \hat{U}_1 = -\frac{Ea_1 a_2}{Ea_1^2}[U_2 - \hat{U}_2] \tag{4.34}$$

In other words, the conditional optimal value of $U_1$ differs from its overall optimal value by an amount that depends on the deviation of $U_2$ from its optimal value. For the fiscal policy case we would expect $Ea_1 a_2$ to be negative. Our result is then the standard one that if taxation exceeds its optimal level the second best policy for public expenditure is that this should exceed its optimal level. If we insert the value of $\hat{\hat{U}}_1$ in equation (4.30) we obtain

$$E(\hat{\hat{W}}) = E(\hat{W}) + (U_2 - \hat{U}_2)^2 \frac{[Ea_1^2 Ea_2^2 - (Ea_1 a_2)^2]}{Ea_1^2} \tag{4.35}$$

where $E(\hat{W})$ is the value obtained when we minimise with respect to $U_1$ and $U_2$, and $E(\hat{\hat{W}})$ the value when we minimise only with respect to $U_1$. The loss of performance varies positively and at an increasing rate as $U_2$ deviates from its overall optimal level. (The positive definiteness of the matrix **A** guarantees that the expression $Ea_1^2 Ea_2^2 - E(a_1 a_2)^2$ is positive.)

Our result may be interpreted in two ways. One is that where we happen to have more instruments than targets, but the effect of each instrument is uncertain, we can improve performance by using all the instruments rather than restricting ourselves to the same number of instruments as targets. In a sense the uncertain effects offset each other to some extent. This corresponds to the explicit treatment we have presented.

But there is another equally interesting implication. Suppose we had started with only one instrument, $U_1$, and then invented and introduced a second instrument, $U_2$. This corresponds in our discussion to comparing what happens when $U_2$ is zero with what happens when $U_2$ is given its optimal value. What we have shown is that used optimally the additional instrument, despite its imperfections, will improve the performance of the economy. Indeed, we have demonstrated the more general point that performance may be improved by an additional imperfect instrument, even if it is used worse than optimally.

# 5
# The static theory of macro-policy

The static approach to macro-policy consists of the formulation of a static macro-model and the analysis within that of the consequences of varying certain policy instruments. In this chapter we shall give some examples of this approach, but it should be borne in mind that there is no limit to the number of models that can be constructed and we make no attempt to cover the subject completely. We shall concentrate on variables expressed in constant prices and will be concerned rather more with input and output than with price effects. We do make a few remarks about the effects on the price level of the policies under consideration, especially indirect taxes. As far as method is concerned, we mostly devote our attention to comparative statics which can, of course, be interpreted as a form of pseudo dynamics.

The chief policies we have in mind are:

(a) Changes in government expenditure. In this category we can distinguish current expenditure on goods and services from capital expenditure, and in turn these two may be distinguished from transfer payments.

(b) Changes in total taxes. In this category we shall sometimes consider the effect of changes in (aggregate) tax rates, such as 'the' rate of income tax and 'the' rate of sales tax.

(c) Changes in the quantity of money. Our approach to monetary policy will be simpliste in the extreme. We shall think in terms of the total supply of money or assume that the government has direct control of the interest rate. We shall not discuss monetary policy in the more general (and correct)

way, i.e. varying the asset composition of the private sector.
(d) Changes in the rate of exchange. We assume that an aggregate
rate of exchange of the UK relative to the rest of the world can
be defined.

The simplest model one can consider is as follows

$$Y = A + C + G \tag{5.1}$$

$$C = a(Y - T) \tag{5.2}$$

where $Y$ is gross domestic product, $C$ is consumption, $G$ is government
spending, $T$ is taxes on incomes net of transfers, $A$ is all other components of gross domestic product.

From these two equations we derive

$$Y = \frac{A + G - aT}{1 - a} \tag{5.3}$$

If we interpret $1/(1 - a)$ as the multiplier, the existence of government
activity leaves the multiplier unchanged.

We have the standard results:

(a) An increase of government spending, $\Delta G$, raises national
income by $\Delta G/(1 - a)$.

(b) An increase of taxation, $\Delta T$, lowers national income by
$a \Delta T_i/(1 - a)$.

(c) An increase of government spending matched by an equal
increase in taxation $(\Delta G = \Delta T)$, raises national income by the
increase in government spending, i.e.

$$\Delta Y = \frac{\Delta G - a \Delta T}{1 - a} = \frac{\Delta G - a \Delta G}{1 - a} = \Delta G \tag{5.4}$$

This is an example of the so-called balanced budget multiplier
theorem, and corresponds to the original case, namely a balanced
budget multiplier of unity.

We may approach what are essentially the same results another
way. Suppose we wish to raise income from $Y$ to $Y_f$. The increase
in government spending required to do this is $(Y_f - Y)(1 - a)$. The
decrease in taxation required to do this is $(Y_f - Y)(1 - a)/a$. Thus
the same income effect requires a larger absolute tax change than
public expenditure change. (Incidentally, the two formulae we
have just given are our first examples, in static terms, of control laws
or policy rules.)

If we assume the existence of a relationship between GDP and employment or unemployment, we can infer a policy conclusion about these variables from our conclusion on output. An increase in government spending will raise employment and lower unemployment. More generally we may argue as follows:

Change in unemployment resulting from given change in government expenditure =
(change in output resulting from that change in government expenditure)
X (change in employment resulting from that change in output)
X (change in unemployment resulting from that change in employment)

In mathematical terms

$$\frac{dU}{dG} = \frac{dU}{dN} \cdot \frac{dN}{dY} \cdot \frac{dY}{dG}$$

where $U$ is unemployment and $N$ is employment.

As an arithmetic example, (a) suppose $dY/dG$, the multiplier, is 2, (b) assume $N$ is measured in thousands of people and $Y$ in millions of pounds, and that $dN/dY$ is $\frac{1}{2}$, and (c) assume for every two people who became employed one was previously employed so that $dU/dN$ is $-\frac{1}{2}$. Putting these together we conclude

$$\frac{dU}{dG} = -\frac{1}{2} \cdot \frac{1}{2} \cdot 2 = -\frac{1}{2}$$

This means that if, for example, government expenditure were raised by £1 billion, unemployment would fall by 500,000 people.

We now have a choice of a number of directions in which to proceed. The most obvious is not to assume that total taxes are fixed, but to make them a function of income:

$$T = t_1 Y + t_2; \qquad 0 < t_1 < 1 \qquad (5.5)$$

where $t_1$ is the marginal rate of tax (net of transfers). We may substitute equation (5.5) into equation (5.2) to get

$$C = a(1 - t_1)Y - at_2 \qquad (5.6)$$

From equations (5.1) and (5.6) we obtain the following

$$Y = \frac{A + G - at_2}{1 - a(1 - t_1)} \tag{5.7}$$

We now have a different formula for the multiplier. Since $t_1$ is a fraction between zero and one, $a(1 - t_1)$ is less than $a$ and $1 - a(1 - t_1)$ is greater than $1 - a$. It follows that the multiplier, $1/[1 - a(1 - t_1)]$, is less than $1/(1 - a)$, and that it diminishes as the marginal rate of taxation increases.

We may derive theorems similar to those of the more elementary case. The effects of tax changes, however, depend on whether it is $t_1$ or $t_2$ that we change, and require a slightly more difficult analysis.

If we increase $t_2$ by an amount $\Delta t_2$, national income falls by $a\Delta t_2/[1 - a(1 - t_1)]$. Because of a positive marginal tax rate, however, this income effect causes an offsetting fall in total taxes. Thus, taxes change altogether by $\Delta t_2 - \{a\Delta t_2 /[1 - a(1 - t_1)]\}t_1$. The second part of this expression is simply the change in income times the marginal rate of tax. We may simplify and rewrite the change in taxes as

$$\Delta T = \frac{\Delta t_2(1 - a)}{1 - a(1 - t_1)} \tag{5.8}$$

Note that there is a similar effect resulting from the change in government expenditure. National income changes by $\Delta G/[1 - a(1 - t_1)]$ and taxes rise by $t_1\Delta G/[1 - a(1 - t_1)]$.

Once total tax revenue is related to income (or any other variable such as consumption, for that matter), it is vital to take this into account when predicting the effects of a policy change. Simply to concentrate on the initial tax change on the assumption of constant income may be quite misleading.

To obtain the balanced budget result we express equation (5.5) in terms of changes:

$$\Delta T = t_1\Delta Y + \Delta t_2 \tag{5.9}$$

The first term is the change in taxes resulting from the change in national income.

We may also set out equation (5.7) in terms of changes:

$$\Delta Y = \frac{\Delta G - a\Delta t_2}{1 - a(1 - t_1)} \tag{5.10}$$

If we substitute for $\Delta t_2$ in equation (5.10) we obtain

$$\Delta Y = \frac{\Delta G - a(\Delta T - t_1 \Delta Y)}{1 - a(1 - t_1)} \tag{5.11}$$

If the change in government expenditure equals the change in taxes it follows that

$$\Delta Y = \frac{(1 - a)\Delta G}{1 - a(1 - t_1)} + \frac{at_1 \Delta Y}{1 - a(1 - t_1)} \tag{5.12}$$

or

$$\Delta Y \left[ 1 - \frac{at_1}{1 - a(1 - t_1)} \right] = \frac{(1 - a)\Delta G}{1 - a(1 - t_1)} \tag{5.13}$$

$$\Delta Y \left[ \frac{1 - a(1 - t_1) - at_1}{1 - a(1 - t_1)} \right] = \frac{(1 - a)\Delta G}{1 - a(1 - t_1)} \tag{5.14}$$

that is, $\Delta Y = \Delta G$.

Thus, after all the complications, the balanced budget theorem still holds.

A change in the marginal rate of tax, $t_1$, affects the value of the multiplier; the larger the marginal rate of tax, the smaller is the multiplier. A positive marginal tax rate gives rise to some *built-in flexibility* in the tax revenue in that tax receipts are responsive to income changes. In addition exogenous changes (for example, in our variable $A$) will produce smaller changes in $Y$ the larger is the marginal rate of tax. A positive marginal rate of tax produces a measure of what might be called *automatic stability* compared with our earlier case of a zero marginal rate of tax. (This is discussed at greater length in the appendix to this chapter.)

As we have remarked, the analysis of a change in $t_1$ is a little complicated. It is helped if we rewrite equation (5.7) as follows

$$[1 - a(1 - t_1)]\, Y = A + G - at_2 \tag{5.15}$$

In terms of first differences this may be expressed as

$$[1 - a(1 - t_1)]\, \Delta Y + aY\Delta t_1 = 0 \tag{5.16}$$

(Note that $A$, $G$, and $t_2$ are unchanged and do not appear in this expression.) The change in $Y$ is then equal to

$$\Delta Y = \frac{-aY\Delta t_1}{1 - a(1 - t_1)} \tag{5.17}$$

This in turn may be written as

$$\Delta Y = \frac{-a(A + G - at_2)}{[1 - a(1 - t_1)]^2} \cdot \Delta t_1 \qquad (5.18)$$

If we rewrite equation (5.5) in terms of changes we get

$$\Delta T = t_1 \Delta Y + Y \Delta t_1 \qquad (5.19)$$

Using equations (5.7) and (5.17) this simplifies to

$$\Delta T = \frac{(1 - a)}{1 - a(1 - t_1)} Y \Delta t_1 = \frac{(1 - a)}{[1 - a(1 - t_1)]^2} (A + G - at_2)\Delta t_1 \qquad (5.20)$$

If we compare equations (5.17) and (5.20) we can derive from them an expression relating the change in total taxes to the change in national income. It is, indeed, the extremely simple expression which we have already derived from equation (5.3):

$$\Delta Y = \frac{-a}{1 - a} \Delta T \qquad (5.21)$$

Do not forget in interpreting equation (5.21), however, that the change of taxes includes the effect of the change in income itself. We have already remarked on this and it is extremely important in practice not to fall into the trap of assuming that $\Delta T$ is simply the impact effect of the tax change. To make the point clearer we may examine an arithmetic example.

Suppose $t_1 = 0.2$, $t_2 = 5$, $A + G = 20$, $a = 0.7$. If we put these values into equation (5.7), we can work out that

$$Y = 37.5$$

$$T = 12.5$$

Suppose the marginal rate of income tax is raised to 0.25. We now get figures for income and total taxes of

$$Y_1 = 34.74$$

$$T_1 = 13.68$$

$$\Delta Y = Y_1 - Y_0 = -2.76$$

$$\Delta T = T_1 - T_0 = 1.18$$

$$\frac{\Delta Y}{\Delta T} = -2.3$$

This equals $-a/(1-a)$ as equation (5.21) says.

But suppose we calculate total taxes at the old level of income. This would give us a figure for total taxes of $5 + 0.25 \times 37.5 = 14.38$, and an increase of taxes of 1.88. To predict the effects of the tax change in this way would, of course, lead to erroneous conclusions, because it takes no account of the reduction in the tax base as income falls as a result of the policy change, i.e. income will not fall by $2.3 \times 1.88$.

For the sake of completeness we will derive the balanced budget theorem once more.

$$\Delta Y = \frac{\Delta G}{1 - a(1 - t_1)} - \frac{aY\Delta t_1}{1 - a(1 - t_1)} \tag{5.22}$$

Therefore

$$\Delta Y = \frac{1}{1 - a(1 - t_1)} [\Delta G - aY\Delta t_1] \tag{5.23}$$

From equation (5.19) we may substitute an expression for $-aY\Delta t_1$

$$\Delta Y = \frac{1}{[1 - a(1 - t_1)]} (\Delta G - a\Delta T + at_1\Delta Y) \tag{5.24}$$

Thus

$$\Delta Y[1 - a + at_1 - at_1] = \Delta G - a\Delta T \tag{5.25}$$

If $\Delta G = \Delta T$, we obtain

$$\Delta Y(1 - a) = \Delta G(1 - a) \tag{5.26}$$

that is,

$$\Delta Y = \Delta G$$

Let us now broaden the subject further by bringing indirect taxes into the picture. This obliges us to take note of the general level of prices. We have used the symbol $Y$ to mean real national income; we shall use $X$ to mean money national income. Assume (i) that the price of $A + G$ is unity, i.e. the relevant price index number is set equal to 1, and (ii) that the price of consumer goods at factor cost is also unity, but (iii) that market price that exceeds by the rate of indirect taxes:

$$1 = (1 - t_3)P \qquad (5.27)$$

where $P$ is the market price of consumer goods, $t_3$ is the rate of indirect taxes calculated at the market price.
Money national income is expressed as follows

$$X = PC + A + G \qquad (5.28)$$

Real personal disposable income is money national income minus income taxes deflated by the consumer price index:

$$D = \frac{(1 - t_1)Y}{P} \qquad (5.29)$$

where $D$ is real disposable income and $t_1$ is a proportionate income tax.

Using the expression for $P$ from equation (5.27) in equation (5.29), we discover that

$$D = (1 - t_1)(1 - t_3)Y \qquad (5.30)$$

Note that in this expression $t_1$ and $t_3$ appear symmetrically. Assume as before that consumption at constant prices, $C$, is proportional to real disposable income:

$$C = aD \qquad (5.31)$$

Inserting this into equation (5.1) and solving for real national income we get a typical multiplier expression

$$Y = \frac{A + G}{1 - a(1 - t_1)(1 - t_3)} \qquad (5.32)$$

From this equation using a little mathematics we can determine how real income varies as we vary tax rates:

$$\Delta Y = - \frac{a(1 - t_3)(A + G)}{[1 - a(1 - t_1)(1 - t_3)]^2} \Delta t_1 \qquad (5.33)$$

$$\Delta Y = - \frac{a(1 - t_1)(A + G)}{[1 - a(1 - t_1)(1 - t_3)]^2} \Delta t_3 \qquad (5.34)$$

Note how similar these multipliers are. They only differ in one term of their numerators. The effect of a change in income tax depends on the rate of indirect tax and vice versa. This is an extremely important point; the effect of one tax change, not only on income but also on tax revenue, depends on the level of the other tax.

We can also work out the effects of these tax changes on total direct tax revenue and total indirect tax revenue. Let these be $T_d$ and $T_i$ respectively.

$$\Delta T_d = Y \frac{1 - a(1 - t_3)}{1 - a(1 - t_1)(1 - t_3)} \cdot \Delta t_1 \qquad (5.35)$$

$$\Delta T_i = a(1 - t_1)Y \frac{1 - a(1 - t_1)}{1 - a(1 - t_1)(1 - t_3)} \cdot \Delta t_3 \qquad (5.36)$$

$$\Delta T_d = -Y \frac{t_1 a(1 - t_1)}{1 - a(1 - t_1)(1 - t_3)} \cdot \Delta t_3 \qquad (5.37)$$

$$\Delta T_i = -Y \frac{t_3 a}{1 - a(1 - t_1)(1 - t_3)} \cdot \Delta t_1 \qquad (5.38)$$

A careful examination of the first two expressions shows they are positive, i.e. an increase in a tax rate leads to an increase in the total revenue from that tax. The second two expressions are negative, indicating that if one tax rate increases it lowers the total revenue from the other tax.

Suppose we now vary the tax structure so that total tax revenue is held constant. This means that the sum of the left-hand sides of equations (5.35) − (5.38) is zero and, therefore, that the sum of the right-hand sides is zero too. We then get a relationship between the changes in the two tax rates:

$$\Delta t_3 = -\frac{\Delta t_1}{a(1 - t_1)^2} \qquad (5.39)$$

What now happens to national income as we increase, for example, the rate of income taxes, reduce the rate of indirect taxes, and hold total tax revenue constant? This situation is made up of two parts:

(a) The direct effect of a change in $t_1$ on $R$ given by equation (5.33).

(b) The indirect effect of a change in $t_1$ on $R$ via the effect of the change in $t_1$ on $t_3$ and the effect of the change in $t_3$ on $R$, given by equations (5.34) and (5.39).

Thus, we have

$$\Delta Y = -\frac{a(1-t_3)(A+G)}{[1-a(1-t_1)(1-t_3)]^2}\,\Delta t_1 + \frac{a(1-t_1)(A+G)}{[1-a(1-t_1)(1-t_3)]^2}$$

$$\cdot \frac{\Delta t_1}{a(1-t_1)^2}$$

$$= Y\left[\frac{1}{[1-a(1-t_1)(1-t_3)]\,(1-t_1)}\right.$$

$$\left.-\frac{a(1-t_3)}{1-a(1-t_1)(1-t_3)}\right]\Delta t_1$$

$$= Y\,\frac{1-a(1-t_3)(1-t_1)}{[1-a(1-t_1)(1-t_3)]\,(1-t_1)}\cdot\Delta t_1$$

$$= \frac{Y}{1-t_1}\,\Delta t_1 \tag{5.40}$$

This expression is positive and shows that if we keep total taxes constant but shift the tax structure towards income taxes, national income will rise. In other words, it is not sufficient to consider macroeconomic policy solely in terms of total taxes; the individual taxes must also be taken into account.

There is no limit to the number of models that can be examined in this way. The few we have discussed are simply meant to be illustrative and to show how careful we must be in drawing conclusions about the effect of policy instruments, in this case chiefly taxes. While they are extremely simple, models of this kind lie behind a great deal of popular and common sense discussion of macro-policy and, if their limitations are realised, can be of considerable use. They are specially useful for making rough and ready calculations of the ultimate effects of broad policy changes. As an example let us examine equation (5.33). This may be rewritten as

$$\Delta Y = \frac{-a(1-t_3)Y}{[1-a(1-t_1)(1-t_3)]}\cdot\Delta t_1 \tag{5.41}$$

This may be further rewritten as

$$\frac{\Delta Y}{Y} = -\frac{a(1-t_3)t_1}{[1-a(1-t_1)(1-t_3)]}\cdot\frac{\Delta t_1}{t_1} \tag{5.42}$$

In other words, we have an expression relating the proportional change in national income to the proportional change in income taxes. As an arithmetic example, assume the following values

$$a = 0.85$$

$$t_1 = 0.25$$

$$t_3 = 0.2$$

This then tells us that the proportional change in income is equal to approximately 0.35 of the proportional change in income tax rates. A 10 per cent cut in the latter will lead to a 3.5 per cent increase in the former. (Note that we are dealing with a multiplier in percentage terms, i.e. an elasticity. In some real problems this is a more useful form than the conventional multiplier.)

Let us now bring foreign trade into the picture. The simplest model is one in which imports are determined by national income or its components, and exports are taken as given. This would be as follows:

$$Y = A + C + G + E - M \qquad (5.43)$$

$$C = a(Y - T) \qquad (5.44)$$

$$M = m_1 C + m_2 G \qquad (5.45)$$

Note that the marginal propensity to import out of consumer expenditure, $m_1$, may be different from the marginal propensity to import out of government expenditure, $m_2$. Apart from that the model is very much of the kind we have discussed already. It may be solved in the usual way to obtain an expression for national income:

$$Y = \frac{A + E + (1 - m_2)G - a(1 - m_1)T}{1 - a(1 - m_1)} \qquad (5.46)$$

From this we may work out the effects of variations on national income of changes in government spending and total taxes.

$$\Delta Y = \frac{1 - m_2}{1 - a(1 - m_1)} \cdot \Delta G \qquad (5.47)$$

$$\Delta Y = -\frac{a(1 - m_1)}{1 - a(1 - m_1)} \cdot \Delta T. \qquad (5.48)$$

If we assume that government expenditure and taxation change simultaneously by the same absolute amount, we get the balanced budget change

$$\Delta Y = \left[ \frac{m_2}{1 - a(1 - m_1)} \right] \Delta G \qquad (5.49)$$

If $m_2 = 0$, i.e. there is no direct government effect on imports, the balanced budget multiplier is unity; otherwise it is less than unity. Note that if $1 - a(1 - m_1)$ is small relative to $m_2$ it is even possible for the balanced budget multiplier to be zero or negative, although this is hardly likely to be the situation in practice.

What is the effect on imports of an increase in government expenditure? It is made up of two parts, the direct effect plus the indirect effect via the change in $Y$ and $C$.

$$\Delta M = m_1 \Delta C + m_2 \Delta G \qquad (5.50)$$
$$= m_1 a \Delta Y + m_2 \Delta G$$
$$= \left[ \frac{m_1 a(1 - m_2)}{1 - a(1 - m_1)} + m_2 \right] \Delta G$$
$$= \frac{am_1 + (1 - a)m_2}{1 - a(1 - m_1)} \Delta G$$

This is clearly positive so that, other things being equal, an increase in government expenditure raises imports and, if exports are taken as fixed, worsens the balance of payments.

We may produce a similar analysis for the change in total taxes:

$$\Delta M = m_1 \Delta C$$
$$= am_1(\Delta Y - \Delta T)$$
$$= \left[ \frac{-a^2 m_1(1 - m_1)}{1 - a(1 - m_1)} - am_1 \right] \cdot \Delta T$$
$$= \frac{-am_1}{1 - a(1 - m_1)} \cdot \Delta T \qquad (5.51)$$

This is negative telling us that the reduction in consumer expenditure resulting from raising total taxes will cause imports to fall.

The balanced budget change in imports is given by

$$\Delta M = \frac{m_2(1-a)}{1-a(1-m_1)} \Delta G \qquad (5.52)$$

This is positive, which means that a fully taxed financial increase in government expenditure would raise imports. Curiously enough, this must happen even though, as we have already seen, it is possible that the balanced budget change could in theory lower national income.

A simpler version of our model would be one in which imports were determined by national income rather than by its individual components.

We would then have a rather different import function

$$M = mY \qquad (5.53)$$

and a simpler expression for national income

$$Y = \frac{A+G-aT}{1-a+m} \qquad (5.54)$$

In themselves these two models have little intrinsic interest. Their main function is pedagogic, and possibly as a foundation for more advanced work. In a sense they do little more than illustrate the point that the results one gets depend on the assumptions one makes. There is, however, an interesting lesson to be learned by contrasting them.

In the second model, imports are uniquely related to national income. This means that, although we have two instruments, $G$ and $T$, we are unable to set the levels of $M$ and $Y$ as separate targets. (Given exports, this means we are unable to set the balance of payments as a separate target.) Once we set either, the other is determined. While this gives us greater freedom in determining $G$ and $T$, our freedom with respect to $M$ and $Y$ is curtailed.

This is illustrated in figure 5.1 where, with exports given (and prices given), an increase in $Y$ leads to a worsening in the balance of payments, the slope of the line being equal to $-m$. We have, therefore, a typical trade-off problem. We can either set $Y$ at a desired level and be content with the resulting conditions of the balance of payments or set $M$ and be content with the resulting level of income. Thus, if income is varying (because, for example,

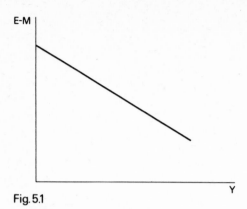

Fig. 5.1

exogenous spending represented by $A$ is varying) we can offset this
by using our policy instruments, but be left with the balance of
payments varying and out of control. Alternatively, we can control
the balance of payments and be left with income out of control.

What we have instead is some choice about government expenditure and total taxes. With $Y$ given, we can determine the
alternative possible combinations of $G$ and $T$.

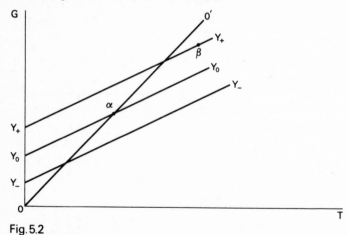

Fig. 5.2

In figure 5.2 we start by assuming that income is fixed at $Y_0$.
This may be reached by the combinations of government expenditure
and taxation given by the line $Y_0Y_0$ which has a slope of $a$. The
combinations giving a higher level of income are given by $Y_+Y_+$,

i.e. we must have higher $G$ or lower $T$ or both; the combinations giving a lower level are given by $Y$-$Y$-. Both lines are parallel to $Y_0 Y_0$. $OO'$ is a 45° line, each point of which represents a situation of budget balance. Points above the line imply a budget deficit, points below the line a budget surplus. A point such as $\alpha$ represents a policy leading to national income at the level $Y_0$ with the budget in balance while a point such as $\beta$ represents a higher level of income and a budget surplus.

Let us now revert to the first model. From the national income equation (5.46), we can determine the various combinations of $G$ and $T$ which generate some specified level of national income. We can also work out a rather complicated looking equation which relates imports to $G$ and $T$. It is as follows:

$$M = \frac{m_1 a(A + E) + [am_1 + (1 - a)m_2]G - am_1 T}{1 - a(1 - m_1)} \qquad (5.55)$$

From this we can work out the combinations of $G$ and $T$ which give rise to a specified level of imports.

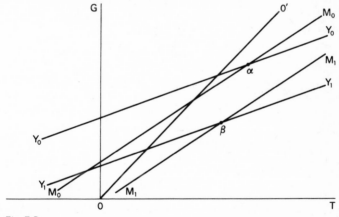

Fig. 5.3

In figure 5.3 $Y_0 Y_0$ is a line showing the alternative combinations of government spending and taxation which generate a level of national income equal to $Y_0$. It has a slope of $a(1 - m_1)/(1 - m_2)$. $M_0 M_0$ is a line showing the alternative combinations of $G$ and $T$ which produce imports equal to $M_0$. It has a slope of

$$am_1/[am_1 + (1 - a)m_2]$$

It is easy to see that if $m_1$ is greater than $m_2$ (i.e. the import content of consumption is greater than the import content of government expenditure) then the slope of $M_0M_0$ is greater than the slope of $Y_0Y_0$.

The two lines have been drawn to intersect in the positive quadrant and to the right of the $45°$ line. This means that the desired levels of government expenditure and imports are achieved at the policy point $\alpha$ with positive public expenditure and a budget surplus.

The obvious question to be asked now is how the policy instruments are to vary as exogenous spending varies, taking the objectives as given. If we examine equation (5.46), we can see that an increase in $A$ will enable us to reach any specified level of $Y$ with a lower level of $G$ or a higher level of $T$. Similarly, an examination of equation (5.55) shows that we can now reach the desired level of $M$ with a lower level of $G$ or a higher level of $T$. This means in terms of figure 5.3 that both curves shift downwards to $M_1M_1$ and $Y_1Y_1$. But note that, since $A$ has a coefficient of unity in the numerator of the income equation (5.46) and a coefficient of $am_1$ which is less than unity in the imports equation (5.55), the income curve will shift more than the imports curve.

We have drawn $M_1M_1$ and $Y_1Y_1$ in figure 5.3 so that they intersect at policy point $\beta$. In that situation both taxes and government expenditure are lower, which may be thought to accord with commonsense. We have also drawn the lines so that $\alpha$ is nearer than $\beta$ to $OO'$; i.e. the taxes have been cut less than public expenditure and the budget surplus is higher. This is based on the assumption (that may not always be true in practice) that the marginal propensity to import out of government expenditure is much less than the marginal propensity to import out of private consumption expenditure. Reductions in $G$ and $T$ sufficient to offset a rise in exogenous spending will each affect imports. The cut in $G$ will lower imports but the cut in $T$ will raise imports via an increase in $C$. If the latter effect is larger than the former, imports will rise and we will fail to meet the import target. Thus, the cut in $T$ should be smaller than the cut in $G$.

We can, of course, solve equations (5.46) and (5.55) to show explicitly how $G$ and $T$ vary as exogenous spending, $A$, varies. The formulae are as follows:

$$\Delta G = \frac{-am_1(1-am_1)[1-a(1-m_1)]}{am_1[1-m_2-am_1-(1-a)m_2]} \cdot \Delta A \qquad (5.56)$$

$$\Delta T = \frac{-m_2[1-a(1-m_1)]}{am_1[1-m_2-am_1-(1-a)m_2]} \cdot \Delta A \qquad (5.57)$$

The crucial expression in both these formulae is that in the denominator, $[1-m_2-am_1-(1-a)m_2]$. This is best looked at as $1-m_2$ minus a weighted average of $m_1$ and $m_2$. Assuming, as is reasonable, that $m_1$ and $m_2$ are both below 0.5, their weighted average will also be below 0.5 while $1-m_2$ will be above 0.5. Thus, this whole expression must be positive. This means in turn that the formulae on the right-hand side of equations (5.56) and (5.57) are negative, i.e. both government spending and taxation vary inversely with exogenous spending.

As to which varies more, a further inspection of the two equations shows that this depends on the relative magnitudes of $am_1(1-am_1)$ and $m_2$. Basically $G$ will be reduced more than $T$ if $a(1-am_1)$ is larger than $m_2/m_1$ which again, while not necessarily the case, is surely more likely than not.

Let us now consider how the instruments vary as the targets vary. An examination of equations (5.46) and (5.55) allows the following rather elaborate expressions to be derived:

$$\Delta G = \frac{-m_1(1-m_2)[am_1+(1-a)m_2]}{a(m_2-m_1)} \cdot \Delta Y \qquad (5.58)$$

$$\Delta T = \frac{-[am_1+(1-a)m_2]^2(1-m_2)}{a(m_2-m_1)} \cdot \Delta Y \qquad (5.59)$$

Both these expressions are positive if $m_2$ is less than $m_1$. This means that an increase in the target level of income will lead to an increase in both government spending and taxation:

$$\Delta G = \frac{(1-m_1)(1-m_2)[am_1+(1-a)m_2]}{a(m_2-m_1)} \cdot \Delta M \qquad (5.60)$$

$$\Delta T = \frac{(1-m_2)^2[am_1+(1-a)m_2]}{a(m_2-m_1)} \cdot \Delta M \qquad (5.61)$$

On the same assumptions these two expressions are negative, i.e. an increase in the desired level of imports leads to a decrease in government spending and taxation.

These results can also be derived diagrammatically.

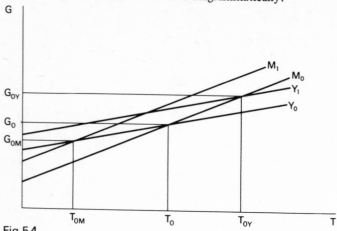

Fig. 5.4

In figure 5.4 $M_0$ and $Y_0$ are the initial levels of imports and income giving rise to levels of government spending and taxation of $G_0$ and $T_0$, respectively. Note that our assumption of the marginal propensity to import of the public sector being below that of the private sector implies that the $M_0$ line is steeper than the $Y_0$. An increase in desired income leads to a new line, $Y_1$, above the old income line. The intersection of $Y_1$ and $M_0$ leads to higher government spending, $G_{OY}$, and higher taxation, $T_{OY}$. An increase in desired imports leads to a new line, $M_1$, above the old imports line. The intersection of $M_1$ and $Y_0$ leads to lower government spending, $G_{OM}$, and lower taxation, $T_{OM}$. This is precisely the result we obtained mathematically.

Figure 5.5 can be employed to clarify policies in a useful way. Points above the import line, $M_0$, imply imports above the desired level, $M_0$, while points below the line imply imports below the desired level. Similarly, points above the line $Y_0$, imply income above the desired level, $Y_0$, while points below the line imply income below the desired level. The quadrant may then be partitioned as follows:

Region $\alpha$ — above both lines — income and imports too high.
Region $\beta$ — above $Y_0$ but below $M_0$ — income too high and imports too low.
Region $\gamma$ — below both lines — income and imports too low.

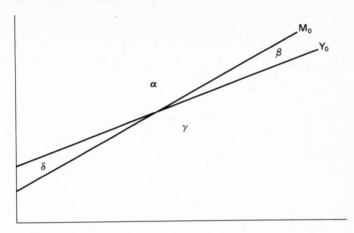

Fig. 5.5

Region $\delta$ — below $Y_0$ and above $M_0$ — income too low and imports too high.

We shall return to this classification when we discuss the dynamic adjustment in the instruments in chapter 7.

In this chapter we now turn to an entirely different subject, income distribution. Thus, we shall ignore the foreign trade sector and concentrate on the distribution of income between wages and profits. Once again many possible models can be constructed; we shall look at the simplest.

We assume that the tax rate on profits is higher than that on wages possibly because the tax system is progressive and the average incomes of profits earners is above that of pure wage earners. We also assume for the same reason that the marginal propensity to consume of profits earners is less than that of wage earners. The model is similar to all the others in this chapter and includes, apart from equation (5.1), the following equations:

$$Y = W + \Pi \tag{5.62}$$

$$C = a_1(1 - t_1)W + a_2(1 - t_2)\Pi \tag{5.63}$$

$$T = t_1 W + t_2 \Pi \tag{5.64}$$

where $t_1 < t_2, a_1 > a_2$, $W$ is total wages, $\Pi$ is total profits, $T$ is total taxes, $t_1$ is the marginal rate of tax on wages, $t_2$ is the marginal rate of tax on profits, $a_1$ is the marginal propensity to consume out of wages, and $a_2$ is the marginal propensity to consume out of profits. Using elementary algebra we obtain the following expression for national income:

$$Y = a_1(1 - t_1)W + a_2(1 - t_2)\Pi + A + G \qquad (5.65)$$

We can proceed no further, without taking a view on how $W$ and $\Pi$ are related to $Y$. One possibility is to assume that they are proportional to $Y$:

$$W = bY \qquad (5.66)$$

Therefore

$$\Pi = (1 - b)Y \qquad (5.67)$$

In this case

$$C = [a_1(1 - t_1)b + a_2(1 - t_2)(1 - b)] Y \qquad (5.68)$$

This rather complicated expression still says that consumption is proportional to income. It leads to the following multiplier expression:

$$Y = \frac{A + G}{1 - a(1 - t_1)b - a_2(1 - t_2)(1 - b)} \qquad (5.69)$$

The expression for total taxes becomes

$$T = [t_1 b + t_2(1 - b)] Y \qquad (5.70)$$

Suppose now we decide to raise more tax revenue from wages and less from profits leaving total tax revenue the same. Does this have an effect on national income? To answer this question requires even more elaborate formulae than those we have come across so far. From equation (5.69) we conclude:

$$\Delta Y = \frac{- a_1 bY}{[1 - a_1(1 - t_1)b - a_2(1 - t_2)(1 - b)]} \cdot \Delta t_1 \qquad (5.71)$$

$$\Delta Y = \frac{- a_2(1 - b)Y}{[1 - a_1(1 - t_1)b - a_2(1 - t_2)(1 - b)]} \cdot \Delta t_2 \qquad (5.72)$$

From equation (5.70) we conclude

$$\Delta T = Yb \frac{[1 - a_1 b - a_2(1-b) + (a_2 - a_1)t_2(1-b)]}{1 - a_1(1 - t_1)b - a_2(1 - t_2)(1-b)} \cdot \Delta t_1$$

(5.73)

$$\Delta T = Yb \frac{[1 - a_1 b - a_2(1-b) + (a_1 - a_2)t_1 b]}{[1 - a_1(1 - t_1)b - a_2(1 - t_2)(1-b)]} \cdot \Delta t_2 \quad (5.74)$$

The first two expressions are negative, telling us that an increase in either tax rate lowers national income. The second two expressions are positive, telling us that an increase in either tax rate raises total tax revenue. The question we are asking concerns the relative power of the two taxes measured by their deflationary effect per unit of tax revenue raised.

From these four equations we can derive the effect on national income of an increase in $t_1$, assuming $t_2$ is reduced at the same time to hold $T$ constant. The formula is as follows:

$$\Delta Y = \left. \frac{Yb(a_2 - a_1)\Delta t_1}{1 - a_1 b - a_2(1-b) + (a_1 - a_2)t_1 b} \right|_{T \text{ held constant}} \quad (5.75)$$

If the marginal propensity to consume out of profits, $a_2$, is less than the marginal propensity to consume out of wages, $a_1$, this expression is negative. In other words, an increase in the tax revenue from a tax on wages, exactly offset by a decrease in the tax revenue from a tax on profits, lowers national income. This reinforces a point made earlier, that the effect of taxes on national income depends on the nature of the taxes levied. It follows that there is no unequivocal relationship between total taxes and national income and, therefore, a fortiori no unequivocal relationship between the budget deficit or surplus and national income. In this context, the relevant point is not that the balanced budget multiplier may differ from unity, but that it is not well defined at all.

One can now go on to consider the effects of profits taxation on investment. To simplify matters we shall look at total taxes on wages and profits rather than tax rates. This leaves the multiplier as a simple expression. Assume investment varies directly with national income and inversely with profits taxes.

$$I = I(Y, T_2) = I_1 + k_1 Y + k_2 T_2 \qquad k_1 > 0; k_2 < 0 \quad (5.76)$$

where $I$ is private investment, $I_1$ is autonomous private investment, $T_2$ is total taxes on profits, $T_1$ is total taxes on wages.

The consumption function is

$$C = a_1(bY - T_1) + a_2[(1-b)Y - T_2]  \tag{5.77}$$

This leads to the following expression for national income

$$Y = \frac{A + G + I_1 - a_1T_1 + (k_2 - a_2)T_2}{1 - a_1b - a_2(1-b) - k_1}  \tag{5.78}$$

If total taxes are constant,

$$\Delta T = \Delta T_1 + \Delta T_2 = 0  \tag{5.79}$$

This means that

$$\Delta Y = \frac{-a_1 - (k_2 - a_2)}{1 - a_1b - a_2(1-b) - k_1} \cdot \Delta T_1  \tag{5.80}$$

The denominator of this expression is positive, so that the sign of
the whole expression will depend on the sign of the numerator. If
we ignore $k_2$, the value of the numerator will be negative, confirming
our previous result that an increase in a tax on wages coupled with
an equal decrease of tax on profits lower national income. But $k_2$
itself is negative. It could be larger in absolute magnitude than
$a_1 - a_2$. In this case the numerator and the whole expression will
be positive. In other words, if investment is sufficiently sensitive
to a tax on profits, a switch towards taxes on wages may actually
raise national income. Note that, on our assumption that the multiplier itself is positive, this conclusion does not depend on the effects
of national income on investment.

The purpose of this chapter has been to illustrate the connection
between various instruments and targets within a static context. All
of the instruments considered so far have been of an explicitly fiscal
kind. Before concluding it is useful to see how much the same kind
of result can be obtained using monetary instruments. Since this
whole area is fraught with controversy it is as well to emphasise
that our purpose here is solely illustrative of some kinds of models
that have appeared in the literature and have policy connotations.

We revert to our original simple model, but this time assume
that $A$, autonomous spending, is affected by the quantity of money
either directly or via the rate of interest.

$$A = A_1 + bL  \tag{5.81}$$

where $L$ is the quantity of money. In the interest rate interpretation, $b$ is the product of the effect of the quantity of money on the rate of interest and the effect of the rate of interest on autonomous spending. If we add this equation to equations (5.1) and (5.2) we finish up with the following expression for national income:

$$Y = \frac{A_1 + bL + G - aT}{1 - a} \tag{5.82}$$

We can as before compare $L$, $G$, and $T$ in terms of their effectiveness in varying $Y$. This depends in the static model on the comparative sizes of $a$, $b$, and unity, and how easy it is to vary $G$, $T$, and $L$. In a more dynamic context the stability of the relevant coefficients may also be taken into account. Since this is largely an empirical matter it is worth remarking that it is quite possible that variations in $L$ might be a more suitable way of controlling $Y$ in one economy at one time while variations in $T$ might be a more suitable way in another economy at another time.

Some part of any change in the money supply may be an independent decision of the government, i.e. 'printing more money', while another part may depend on the budget deficit or surplus. Assume that some fraction of the change in the money supply is determined by the change in the budget deficit.

$$\Delta L = h(\Delta G - \Delta T) \qquad 0 < h < 1 \tag{5.83}$$

The change in national income may then be expressed as follows:

$$\begin{aligned} \Delta Y &= \frac{bh(\Delta G - \Delta T) + \Delta G - a\Delta T}{1 - a} \\ &= \frac{(1 + bh)\Delta G - (a + bh)\Delta T}{1 - a} \end{aligned} \tag{5.84}$$

This then tells us that the expansionary effects of increased government spending or reduced taxation is accentuated by the resulting increase in the quantity of money; and the more effective that increase, the more powerful the accentuation.

To round off the discussion let us bring the transactions demand for money into the picture and assume that this is proportional to income. This means that the effective increase in the quantity of money to influence autonomous spending is not $\Delta L$ but $\Delta L - j\Delta Y$, where $j\Delta Y$ is the increase in the transactions demand for money. Assume also, as in equation (5.76), that there is some positive connection between national income and autonomous spending (e.g. high national income encourages private investment). This means that instead of equation (5.81) our equation for autonomous spending becomes

$$A = A_1 + b(L - jY) + kY \tag{5.85}$$

Our equation for national income may then be written as

$$Y = \frac{G - aT + A_1 + bL}{1 - a - k + bj} \tag{5.86}$$

Compared with equation (5.82) the value of the multiplier is changed. It may be larger or smaller depending on the size of $(bj - k)$. If the marginal transactions demand for money is large and the effectiveness of the quantity of money on autonomous spending is also large while the positive impact of income on autonomous spending is small, the multiplier will be diminished in size.

As a final elaboration let us put the last two models together, so that we have both a transactions demand for money and variations in the money supply due to variations in the budget deficit. This leads to the following expression for the change in national income.

$$\Delta Y = \frac{(1 + bh)\Delta G - (a + bh)\Delta T}{1 - a - k + bj} \tag{5.87}$$

We can also derive an expression for the change in autonomous spending

$$\Delta A = \frac{[bh(1 - a) + (k - bj)]\Delta G - [bh(1 - a) + a(k - bj)]\Delta T}{1 - a - k + bj} \tag{5.88}$$

It can be seen that if $j$ is sufficiently large the effect of an increase in government spending on autonomous investment could actually be negative. In other words, if (a) not much extra money is created, (b) most of that money is taken for transactions purposes, and (c) higher income is not very conducive to private investment, then an increase in government spending could lead to lower private investment.

### Appendix

There are a number of concepts which have arisen in the fiscal policy literature of the past few years which we have alluded to in the text and which we now take a little further.

We have mentioned built in flexibility. This derives from the fact that certain taxes are positively related to income. The effect of this, as we have seen already, is to reduce the value of the multiplier. As an example, in the main text the multiplier in equation (5.3) is larger than the multiplier in equation (5.7). A consequence is that given fluctuations in the exogenous variables, since they are multiplied by a smaller number, will give rise to smaller changes in national income. The fact that income fluctuates less is sometimes referred to as 'automatic stabilisation'.

If the average values of the exogenous variables are given, with a smaller multiplier they will generate a lower average level of national income. If the fluctuations are measured as percentage changes and not as absolute changes, this means that they will be the same no matter what is the value of the multiplier as long as it is constant. This is shown in the following arithmetic example. Let the exogenous variable have three possible values, 10, 20, and 30, its average value being 20. If the multiplier is 2, national income will have three possible values, 20, 40, and 60 with an average value of 40. It may fluctuate, therefore, by ± 20 from its mean. If the multiplier is 1.5, national income will have three different possible values, 15, 30, and 45 with an average value of 30. It may then fluctuate by ± 15 from its mean. In both cases, however, its percentage fluctuation from the mean is 50%.

Let us compare two models, one with built in flexibility and the other without:

$$Y_1 = \frac{G + A}{1 - a(1 - t)} \tag{5.89}$$

$$Y_2 = \frac{G - aT_2 + A}{1 - a} \tag{5.90}$$

where $T_2$ is total tax revenue. In the first case there is built in flexibility, and the multiplier is smaller than in the second case. This means that given fluctuations in $A$ will lead to lower fluctuations in income in case 1 than in case 2, other things being equal. The difficulty, however, is what other things are to be regarded as equal. In particular, the average level of national income may not be the same in the two cases.

The difference between the average value of national income in the two cases is given by the following expression (where a bar over a variable means average value.)

$$\bar{Y}_2 - \bar{Y}_1 = \frac{\bar{G} - a\bar{T}_2 + \bar{A}}{1 - a} - \frac{\bar{G} + \bar{A}}{1 - a(1 - t)}$$

$$= \frac{at(\bar{G} + \bar{A}) - a[1 - a(1 - t)]T_2}{(1 - a)[1 - a(1 - t)]} \qquad (5.91)$$

Now, in case 1, total tax revenue is given by

$$T_1 = tY_1 \qquad (5.92)$$

Average tax revenue is given by

$$\bar{T}_1 = \frac{t(\bar{G} + \bar{A})}{1 - a(1 - t)} \qquad (5.93)$$

If we substitute this expression into equation (5.91), we obtain

$$\bar{Y}_2 - \bar{Y}_1 = \frac{a(\bar{T}_1 - \bar{T}_2)}{1 - a} \qquad (5.94)$$

In other words, if average tax revenue is the same in the two cases, average income will be the same. It will then be reasonable to compare the fluctuations in income since these will be related to the same base. Suppose, however, $\bar{T}_1$ is greater than $\bar{T}_2$, and $\bar{Y}_2$ is greater than $\bar{Y}_1$. It might then be possible that the percentage fluctuations in $Y_1$ are less than the percentage fluctuations in $Y_2$. In other words, if built in flexibility also involved a higher tax revenue on average, while it might give rise to more stability, it would have done so partly as a result of reducing the average level of income. This would not be desirable, and additional steps (such as raising the average level of government expenditure) would have to be taken to rectify matters. More generally, of course, what one is saying is that stability as such may not be desirable if it involved a depressed state of the economy. A perpetual slump may be an extremely stable state of affairs economically but is scarcely an attractive one.

Let us examine built in flexibility in a little more detail. We drop the subscripts since we shall no longer refer to case 2. If the marginal tax rate $t$ increases, the multiplier will be reduced. Thus, the lower will be the variance of national income given the variance of the random shocks which cause the economy to fluctuate. At the same time, in order to maintain the same average level of national income the higher must be the level of government expenditure. In sum, built in flexibility as a means of automatic stabilisation requires higher marginal tax rates and higher levels of public expenditure, at least as viewed within a static context. If taxes are proportional to national income, another requirement is a higher total tax revenue. It can also be shown that the average budget surplus is higher (or the average budget deficit is lower) the greater the degree of built in flexibility.

From equation (5.93), the mean level of $Y$ is related to the mean level of $A$,

$$\bar{Y} = \frac{\bar{A} + G}{1 - a(1 - t)} \tag{5.95}$$

where $\bar{Y}$ is the mean level of $Y$ and $\bar{A}$ is the mean level of $A$. Given $\bar{Y}$ and $\bar{A}$, $G$ is related to $t$ in the following way

$$G = (1 - a)\bar{Y} - \bar{A} + a\bar{Y}t \tag{5.96}$$

This tells us how to vary government spending to maintain the same average national income, i.e.

$$\Delta G = a\bar{Y}\,\Delta t \tag{5.97}$$

The variance of national income is given by

$$(Y - \bar{Y})^2 = \frac{E(A - \bar{A})^2}{[1 - a(1 - t)]^2} \tag{5.98}$$

As $t$ increases from zero to unity the variance of national income falls.

Total taxes, $T$, depend on $t$ and $Y$:

$$T = tY \qquad (5.99)$$

The mean level of taxes is given by

$$\overline{T} = t\overline{Y} \qquad (5.100)$$

$$\Delta\overline{T} = \overline{Y}\Delta t \qquad (5.101)$$

Comparing equations (5.97) and (5.101), a given increase in tax rates leads to a larger increase in total taxes than in government expenditure. These two equations are plotted in figure 5.6 to show how the difference between mean total tax revenue and government spending grows as $t$ grows.

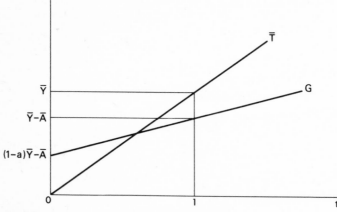

Fig. 5.6

An examination of equation (5.98) shows how the variance of national income decreases as the marginal tax rate increases, but at a decreasing rate. This is illustrated in figure 5.7 (where we write $\sigma_Y^2$ for the variance of $Y$.)

The curve $V_1$ shows the relationship between the variance of national income and $t$ given the variance of $A$. On the assumption that the government has preferences concerning the variability of income and the level of the tax rate, being antipathetic to each over the relevant range, we have also drawn some indifference curves in figure 5.7. Utility increases towards the origin and the optimum policy is given by the tangency point a. If the variance of uncontrolled spending increases, the constraint shifts to $V_2$, and the new optimum policy at b involves a higher variance of national income and a higher marginal rate of tax.

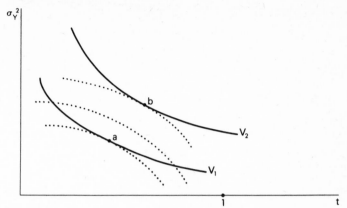

Fig. 5.7

Much of our analysis in the main text leads to the conclusion that there is not a simple relationship between total taxes (or total expenditure, for that matter) and national income, and that it is necessary to pay some attention to fiscal structure in devising appropriate macroeconomic policy. Nonetheless, given various tax rates and expenditure rates it is possible to show how the budget surplus varies with national income (assuming this variation is due to some other forces).

In figure 5.8 as national income is increased (as a result, for example, of increasing private investment expenditure) total taxes will rise and so will the budget surplus. This is indicated by the line $B_0$. This means that with income at a low level (say) $Y_1$ there can be a budget deficit but, with no tax changes, in principle, if income can be got to a higher level (say) $Y_f$, which is full employment, there will be a budget surplus.

With lower tax rates the relevant relationship shifts to $B_1$. If nothing else happened, the budget deficit would increase by the difference between $B_0$ and $B_1$. But, as we have shown earlier, there will be an expansion of national income and an increase in total tax revenue so that the budget deficit will increase by a smaller amount. It is even possible to produce a series of changes such that the slope of the line relating the budget surplus to national income changes, increasing the deficit at low levels of income and increasing the surplus of higher levels of income. Such a line is $B_2$.

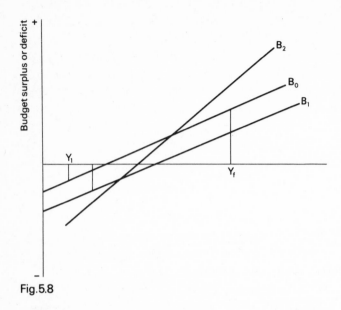

Fig.5.8

Although the budget surplus or deficit does not have a major role to play in the economics of fiscal policy, it may be important in politics especially in the USA. In that country, therefore, economists have been at pains to emphasise that the deficit must be placed in the context of the level of national income relative to full employment, and have argued that comparisons should correctly be made of deficits or surpluses at full employment. References are, therefore, frequently found in the literature to the *full employment surplus or deficit*.

Related to all these concepts are two others called 'fiscal drag' and 'fiscal leverage'. The first of these is sometimes defined in much the same way as built in flexibility, namely the increase in total taxes as income rises. It can, however, be extended somewhat, as can built in flexibility, to refer to a more than proportionate increase in total taxes. This may be due to people entering the tax system for the first time or, more generally, to the existence of progressivity in the tax system, namely increasing marginal rates of tax. It may be of special importance in inflationary situations since tax rates are related to money incomes which rise faster than real incomes and, thus, exacerbate the fiscal drag. The effect of fiscal drag is to reduce the value of the multiplier as income rises and, therefore, again to dampen down the fluctuations in national income (assuming again that national income is determined in a simple multiplicative way by autonomous spending). It too, therefore, may be seen as giving rise to some automatic stability.

In recent discussions fiscal drag has also been related to the growth of national income and not simply to its stability. With given but progressive tax rates, as spending rises national income will rise more slowly because of the drag. This means that with no other changes there will be a tendency for excess capacity and unemployment to appear. It is then suggested that, if the margin of spare capacity is not to increase, either public expenditure must be expanded more rapidly or there must be overall tax cuts to offset the fiscal drag.

The concept of fiscal leverage has been introduced to answer the question: What is the overall effect on national income of all the government's budgetary activity? This may be answered by comparing the actual level of national income with that which would be obtained if all public expenditure and taxation were put equal to zero. Fiscal leverage may be illustrated by means of the following model.

$$Y = A + G + C + E - M \qquad\qquad (5.102)$$

$$C = a(1 - t_1)(1 - t_3)Y + (1 - t_3)T_r \qquad\qquad (5.103)$$

$$M = m_1 C + m_2 G \qquad\qquad (5.104)$$

All the symbols are as appear in the main text except for $T_r$ which represents total transfer payments. We assume that the propensity to consume out of these is unity. The level of national income will then be given by

$$Y = \frac{A + (1 - m_2)G + (1 - t_3)(1 - m_1)T_r + E}{1 - a(1 - m_1)(1 - t_1)(1 - t_3)} \qquad (5.105)$$

If $t_1$, $t_3$, $G$ and $T_r$ were equal to zero, national income would be given by the following expression

$$Y_0 = \frac{A + E}{1 - a(1 - m_1)} \qquad (5.106)$$

Fiscal leverage is then given by

$$Y - Y_0 = \frac{1}{1 - a(1 - m_1)(1 - t_1)(1 - t_3)} \times$$
$$\left[ (1 - m_2)G + (1 - t_3)(1 - m_1)T_r \right.$$
$$\left. - \frac{(A + E)a(1 - m_1)[1 - (1 - t_1)(1 - t_3)]}{1 - a(1 - m_1)} \right] \qquad (5.107)$$

This amounts to little more than saying that fiscal leverage depends on the level of government spending on goods and services and on transfers, on various tax rates, and on the government's marginal propensity to import.

Built in flexibility and fiscal drag have both been about the responsiveness of total tax revenue to changes in national income. The remaining changes in total tax revenue may then be defined as discretionary.

If $T = tY$, the changes in taxes may be expressed as $\Delta T = t\Delta Y + Y \Delta t$. The *discretionary* part of the change, which depends on changes in the tax rates, may be defined as $Y\Delta t$.

While this distinction may turn out to be useful for some purposes, it is important to emphasise certain difficulties that arise in connection with it. Firstly, it refers solely to tax revenue and is not, therefore, about discretionary and non-discretionary policy as a whole. Changes in public expenditure, the quantity of money, etc., may all have an influence on national income and on total tax revenue which may then be called discretionary. We return to this point below. Secondly, in any empirical studies $\Delta t$ could be measured as the change in total tax revenue between two dates which may be far apart. If they are far apart, tax rates may change several times in the period, but only the change from the beginning to the end of the period will be taken into account. Thus, to take an extreme case, if the tax rate at the beginning of the period is the same as that at the end, all the change in tax revenue will appear to be non-discretionary even though considerable changes may have occurred within the period. It is important, therefore, to choose a time period which neither exaggerates nor underestimates the discretionary part of the total tax change. Thirdly, and perhaps more important than the previous points, is the fact that the true tax system is non-linear, different incomes and different goods being taxed at different rates. Thus, if there is a progressive tax system, average and marginal tax rates actually paid will increase as income increases without any discretionary action on the part of the government. If we assume that total taxes are proportional to income, it will appear that tax rates have gone up when they have not. Similarly, if consumer expenditure shifts to goods with a higher tax content, average tax rates will rise without any positive action on the part of the government.

The point may be made more clearly as follows. The average tax paid in any period is $T/Y$. Suppose this is defined as the tax rate so that

$$t_0 \equiv \frac{T_0}{Y_0} \qquad (5.108)$$

where the subscript 0 refers to the initial period. In the subsequent period we have

$$t_1 \equiv \frac{T_1}{Y_1} \qquad (5.109)$$

Without any change in rates of tax set by the government we may have $t_0$ differing from $t_1$ simply because of tax rate progressivity or heterogeneity. In other words, the change in the average rate of tax actually paid, $t_1 - t_0$, is not a perfect measure of discretionary tax policy.

The final point that needs to be made concerns the definition of total tax revenue. To consider this narrowly as the gross proceeds of the tax departments may be to miss certain essential matters. The surpluses of the nationalised industries, for example, are akin to indirect tax revenue, and varying the financial targets of those industries may be just as much a tax change as variations in purchase tax or VAT. Transfer payments are negative taxes which suggests that we ought to concentrate on tax revenue net of transfers if we are not to miss discretionary changes on that side. The trouble with that, however, is that we are then led to consider other parts of public expenditure and to enquire which of those are discretionary and which not. Since such expenditure is not normally set as a function of income, it is hard to distinguish that part which corresponds to a change in the functional relationship and is called discretionary from the remainder which depends on income fluctuations and is non-discretionary. The temptation, therefore, is to treat all public expenditure change as discretionary even though much of it is in accord with set principles and programmes and is no more discretionary than $t\Delta Y$.

An interesting problem in this connection concerns the total wage bill paid by the government. Write this as

$$W = wN \tag{5.110}$$

where $W$ is the government's wage bill, $w$ is the average wage rate paid by the government, $N$ is the number of people employed by the government.

$$\Delta W = \Delta wN + w\Delta N \tag{5.111}$$

If wages are regarded as set in the market, the discretionary part of $\Delta W$ may be interpreted as $w\Delta N$, i.e. as due to employment decisions. If the government has an incomes policy, it may vary $\Delta w$, so that $\Delta wN$ becomes the discretionary part. It may even also ration its employment so as to take on less people than it could at the going rate, the result being that the whole of the variation in its wage bill is discretionary.

Let us now consider how the distinction between discretionary and non-discretionary changes relate to fiscal drag and fiscal leverage.

We use the model from the main text described in equations (5.5), (5.6) and (5.7). We interpret $t_2$ as transfer payments for this purpose, i.e. $t_2$ is negative and diminishes as transfer payments increase. If now autonomous spending, government spending, transfer payments, and the marginal tax rate all change, the change in national income will be as follows:

$$\Delta Y = \frac{\Delta G + \Delta A - a\Delta t_2}{1 - a(1 - t_1)} - \frac{aY\Delta t_1}{1 - a(1 - t_1)} \tag{5.112}$$

If we regard $\Delta G$, $\Delta t_2$ and $\Delta t_1$ as discretionary, the effect on income due to discretionary policy will be

$$\Delta Y_D = \frac{\Delta G - a\Delta t_2 - aY\Delta t_1}{1 - a(1 - t_1)} \tag{5.113}$$

where $\Delta Y_D$ is the discretionary effect.

We can rearrange the terms in equation (5.112) as follows:

$$\Delta Y = \Delta Y_D + \frac{\Delta A}{1 - a(1 - t_1)} \tag{5.114}$$

This in turn can be rewritten as

$$\Delta Y = \Delta Y_D + \frac{\Delta A}{1 - a} - \frac{at_1 \Delta A}{[1 - a(1 - t_1)] \, (1 - a)} \tag{5.115}$$

The second term on the right-hand side is the effect of an increase in exogenous expenditure on national income assuming all marginal tax rates are zero. The third term is the difference between the actual effect of an increase in exogenous expenditure and $\Delta A/(1 - a)$.

If we rewrite equation (5.115) we have

$$\Delta Y - \frac{\Delta A}{1 - a} = \Delta Y_D - \frac{at_1 \Delta A}{[1 - a(1 - t_1)](1 - a)} \tag{5.116}$$

The left-hand side of this equation may be interpreted as the change in national income due to government policy and may be thought of as a sort of marginal fiscal leverage. It is then partitioned into $\Delta Y_D$, the part due to discretionary policy, and a second term which is the part due to non-discretionary or automatic policy.

The ratio of the shares due to automatic policy and to discretionary policy is, ignoring the sign,

$$R = \frac{at_1 \Delta A}{(\Delta G - a\Delta t_2 - aY\Delta t_1)} (1 - a) \tag{5.117}$$

It can be seen immediately that there are dangers in interpreting a ratio such as this as measuring the extent of discretionary policy.

The reason is that government expenditure and tax rates may change a great deal, but in the same direction so that their total impact on national income will be small. While for some purposes it may be right to measure the significance of these instruments by their effects, for other purposes interest may focus on the extent to which they are used.

It is also worth recalling our discussion in chapter 1 on the meaning of discretionary policy. Suppose transfers are related to national income by the following formula

$$\Delta t_2 = b\Delta Y \qquad\qquad (5.118)$$

Equation (5.28) would become

$$\Delta Y - \frac{\Delta A}{1-a} = \frac{\Delta G - aY\Delta t_1}{1 - a(1 - t_1 - b)} - \frac{a(t_1 + b)\Delta A}{(1-a)[1 - a(1 - t_1 - b)]} \qquad (5.119)$$

The share due to automatic policy then becomes

$$R^* = \frac{a(t_1 + b)\Delta A}{(\Delta G - aY\Delta t_1)(1-a)} \qquad\qquad (5.120)$$

If $b$ is positive, the numerator and denominator of this expression will be larger than in the analogous expression for $R$. It is easy to see that $R^*$ will be greater than $R$ if the following condition holds:

$$\Delta G - aY\Delta t_1 > \frac{a(t_1 + b)\Delta A}{1-a} \qquad\qquad (5.121)$$

In other words, if marginal fiscal leverage is positive the share due to automatic policy will appear to rise; equally, if marginal fiscal leverage is negative the share due to automatic policy will fall. We have argued in chapter 1 that whether or not a tax change is regarded as discretionary can be somewhat arbitrary, especially as we can rarely know whether, say, $\Delta t_2$ was decided on *ad hoc* by the government or according to a prepared decision rule such as equation (5.118). Separate from that, the conclusion emerges that even if the tax change is regarded as automatic, this does not always show up clearly in a formula for determining the automatic share of income change.

# 6
# A first approach to risk and uncertainty

In our earlier discussions we took the values of certain variables as given. These were exogenous variables or lagged endogenous variables, both of which were out of the control of policy makers in the present or future. Policy itself was then contingent on the assumed values of these variables. In the simple model of chapter 1 we explained what should be the level of government expenditure for various possible levels of exogenously given investment. In the rather more elaborate model of chapter 2 the analysis of policy was contingent on given values of world economic activity, the foreign price level, and certain parts of domestic spending notably that of the government.

We have also been at great pains to emphasise the effects of risk and uncertainty on public policy, but so far have not really investigated them in any detail. In this chapter we shall begin to see how the lack of certain knowledge of the economic environment in one form or another may influence policy making.

Assume, for example, that we do not know for certain the value of investment. We may know the range within which it must lie or the set of values one of which it must take, but we do not know which one for certain. We have at our disposal a policy variable, government expenditure, which, if we knew exactly what investment was going to be, could be adjusted exactly to ensure full employment but, if it has to be used in conditions of uncertainty, may sometimes be too low causing unemployment and sometimes too high causing inflation.

(In the technical literature the possible values for the exogenous variable are referred to in general as 'the set of possible states of nature', the possible values for the policy variable as 'the set of possible acts', and the resulting conditions of the economy as 'the set of outcomes'.)

Let us consider the simplest possible case, namely two possible values for investment, $I_0$ and $I_1$, and two possible values for government expenditure, $G_0$ and $G_1$. Suppose $G_0$ is perfectly adjusted to $I_0$, and $G_1$ to $I_1$ in the sense of achieving full employment in both cases. Suppose also $I_0$ is greater than $I_1$. We have four possible combinations, $G_0I_0$, $G_0I_1$, $G_1I_0$, and $G_1I_1$. These are set out in table 6.1.

Table 6.1

|       | $I_0$           | $I_1$           |
|-------|-----------------|-----------------|
| $G_0$ | Full employment | Unemployment    |
| $G_1$ | Inflation       | Full employment |

In table 6.1 each box describes the outcome for the economy given the state of investment above it and the economic policy to its left. Thus, the second box in the top row refers to the combination $G_0I_1$. $I_1$ is the lower level of investment and it is coupled with the lower level of public expenditure; therefore, effective demand is too low and unemployment results.

Table 6.1 characterises the decision situation, but it does not go far enough. In order to solve any economic problem of choice it is not sufficient merely to know what the choices are and what the consequences of different actions will be in different circumstances. It is also necessary to place a value or utility on the outcomes. In place of the outcomes in the boxes of table 6.1 we want to have the utility or value of the outcomes.

It is not our purpose in this chapter to discuss again where the government gets its preferences from. We assume that it does have preferences that can be applied to the outcomes. Let it give a weight to full employment of 100. If unemployment occurs let this be given the lower weight of 80, while if inflation occurs let this be given the lower weight of 90. In place of table 6.1 we now have table 6.2.

Table 6.2

|       | $I_0$ | $I_1$ |
|-------|-------|-------|
| $G_0$ | 100   | 80    |
| $G_1$ | 90    | 100   |

The elements in the box give the relative evaluations of the outcomes. (The 80 for unemployment does not mean that the government likes unemployment, but rather that it regards the unemployment resulting from the combination $G_0 I_1$ as costing us 20% of the welfare obtainable at exactly full employment.) These evaluations are often called payoffs and tables such as table 6.2 payoff matrices.

What now can be said about decision making in this situation? Several criteria have been put forward. We shall examine a few of them.

The first is to focus attention on the worst outcome for each of our actions. If we put government expenditure at a level of $G_0$, the worst that can happen is that $I_1$ will occur. This we value at 80. If we put government expenditure at a level of $G_1$, the worst that can happen is that $I_0$ will occur. This we value at 90. The criterion is then proposed that we should follow that course of action the worst outcome of which is better than the worst outcome of any other course of action. The worst that can happen in each case is the minimum outcome, i.e. the minimum value of each row in table 6.2. The largest of these minima may also be referred to as the maximum among them. This approach of avoiding the worst is, therefore, frequently called the maximin criterion. In our example, the minimum outcome for $G_0$ is 80, and for $G_1$ is 90. Thus, the pure maximin is $G_1$ yielding a worst outcome of 90.

The other extreme from maximin is to make the optimistic assumption that the best is sure to happen and, therefore, we ought to focus on the maximum outcome of each action. It is then proposed that our decision criterion should be to choose that action the maximum outcome of which is larger than that of any other action. Such a criterion is for obvious reasons called maximax. In our example the maximax outcome is the same for each level of expenditure so that on that basis we would be indifferent between the two.

A third criterion concentrates on the notion of regret. The

argument is as follows. Suppose a level of investment $I_0$ occurs and we had adopted a policy of $G_0$. We would then be quite satisfied because we had done the right thing. If, however, we had chosen $G_1$, we would regret this action because it is less satisfactory than $G_0$. Our measure of this regret is the difference between the value of the outcome if we had done exactly the right thing and the value of the outcome given what we did do. Thus, the combination $G_0 I_0$ gives us zero regret while $G_1 I_0$ gives us 10 units of regret.

Table 6.3

|        | $I_0$ | $I_1$ |
|--------|-------|-------|
| $G_0$  | 0     | 20    |
| $G_1$  | 10    | 0     |

Table 6.3 indicates the regret corresponding to each outcome. Since we do not like regret, it is now suggested that for each policy we focus on its maximum regret. This is 20 for $G_0$ and 10 for $G_1$. The best decision is then the policy whose maximum regret is less than that of any other policy. It would be called the criterion of *minimax regret*. In this example the policy yielding minimax regret is $G_1$. Note that in our example $G_1$ is both the minimax regret and the maximin policy; this equality does not necessarily hold for all problems as a second example will show.

Before doing that we shall examine a fourth criterion. Suppose as a result of research we knew that the probability of $I_0$ occurring is $p$, and of $I_1$ occurring is $1 - p$. The average or expected payoff to $G_0$ is $100p + 80(1 - p)$ or $80 + 20p$. The average or expected payoff to $G_1$ is $90p + 100(1 - p)$ or $100 - 10p$. The decision criterion is now to choose that course of action which has the largest expected payoff. In our case if $p = 0.9$ the expected payoff to $G_0$ is 98 and to $G_1$ 91 so that $G_0$ is selected; but if $p = 0.4$, the expected payoff to $G_0$ is 88 and to $G_1$ 96 so that $G_1$ is chosen.

There exists a whole subject called 'statistical decision theory' devoted to an analysis of these and other criteria, and the question of whether and in what sense any criterion is better than any other. So far no criterion has been established as superior to all others, yet it is hard to accept the view that decision making under uncertainty is arbitrary.

In the main body of this chapter we shall consider some more substantive matters. In our previous example we discovered that the maximin criterion and the minimax regret criterion led to the same action. Suppose in a new example that the government prefers the combination $G_0I_0$ to $G_1I_1$, i.e. it prefers a lower level of public expenditure to a higher, given the level of employment. Let its preferences between inflation and unemployment also change so that the payoff matrix is as in table 6.4 and the regret matrix as in table 6.5

Table 6.4                    Table 6.5

|       | $I_0$ | $I_1$ |
|-------|-------|-------|
| $G_0$ | 100   | 88    |
| $G_1$ | 90    | 95    |

|       | $I_0$ | $I_1$ |
|-------|-------|-------|
| $G_0$ | 0     | 7     |
| $G_1$ | 10    | 0     |

In table 6.4 the minimum payoff to $G_0$ is 88 and to $G_1$ 90 so that $G_1$ is the maximin policy. In table 6.5 the maximum regret for $G_0$ is 7 and for $G_1$ 10 so that $G_0$ is the minimax regret policy.

Several important conclusions follow from the discussion so far despite its elementary nature. Firstly, given the existence of risk and uncertainty the government not only needs to predict the possible outcomes of its actions, it also needs to evaluate them. It then needs to characterise the risk in terms of the probabilities of various exogenous events and approach the uncertainty by means of a decision criterion. Secondly, since the risk and uncertainty are not fiction but fact, they are unavoidable. They derive from shortage of data and of theory, from variables outside the policy makers' control, and from the general unpredictability of the economy, society, the natural universe, or what have you. For this reason it is foolish to think in terms of the perfect policy which always comes out all right. As far as outcomes are concerned such a policy is not available, certainly in fact, almost certainly in principle; as far as payoffs are concerned such a policy could be available and is likely to be sub-optimal.

Consider, for example, a level of public expenditure, $G_2$, so much above $G_0$ and $G_1$ that it produces a raging inflation no matter what the level of investment. This may lead to the following payoff matrix:

Table 6.6

|  | $I_0$ | $I_1$ |
|---|---|---|
| $G_0$ | 100 | 80 |
| $G_1$ | 90 | 100 |
| $G_2$ | 50 | 50 |

There is no uncertainty about the payoff to $G_2$, but it is hard to see it as other than inferior to $G_1$ and $G_0$. As a general rule the pursuit of certainty in the area of economic policy making will lead to results much inferior to those resulting from a reasonable acceptance of and response to uncertainty.

This leads inevitably to the third conclusion that not only will the best policies *ex post facto* seem to go wrong, so also will the best forecasts *ex post facto* appear to be erroneous. What then is the role of *ex post* study of public sector decision making? If the task is praise or blame for the decision itself, the initial decision situation must be recreated and within that the decision justified. The justification could be of the form 'we knew this decision could have an unsatisfactory outcome but that was not as bad as the worst outcomes of the alternative choices', or the justification could be in the form 'this decision if things went wrong would cause us less regret than any other'. Blame could then be attached because the decision situation itself was incorrectly formulated, e.g. no account was taken of a possible level of $I$ or a possible policy $G$, or because the outcomes or evaluations were not estimated correctly, or because the decision criterion was applied incorrectly. It is also reasonable for the government to be criticised for the decision criterion it uses, e.g. maximin rather than minimax regret, although as we have already remarked it is not easy to justify one against the other. A more valid criticism would be that the government applied no consistent criterion at all or an obviously absurd criterion such as maximax, i.e. hoping for the best all the time.

The policy of governments has been so faulty in all these respects that there need be no shortage of work for the critics. Certainly there is no need for them to concentrate on the one invalid criticism that mistakes must always be avoided, as if risk and uncertainty did not exist.

Apart from the *ex post* evaluation of policy there is also the

process of learning through time as new information is acquired.
Assume that either $I_0$ or $I_1$ will happen. We are then confronted with
the question, given the event that occurs, how will that influence
the decision situation and the decision next time round? The easiest
way to think of this is in terms of the probability of $I_0$ or $I_1$. If $I_0$ occurs,
do we now raise our estimate of the probability of occurrence of $I_0$
and, if so, by how much? (To keep the example simple we abstract
from the consideration of new levels of investment $I_2, I_3$, etc. The
essential point remains the same.)

Suppose that our uncertainty in the initial situation was about
the probability of $I_0$ occurring. We assumed that this could be $p_0$ or
$p_1$. Applying these to our first example we can now rewrite our
payoff matrix as follows:

Table 6.7

|       | $p_0$ | $p_1$ |
|-------|-------|-------|
| $G_0$ | $80 + 20p_0$ | $80 + 20p_1$ |
| $G_1$ | $100 - 10p_0$ | $100 - 10p_1$ |

Note that the uncertain states of the world are now probabilities.
We calculate the average or expected payoff to each policy given
these probabilities, but a decision problem remains because we do
not know which probability is the correct one.

Applying again the numbers of our earlier example, and
assuming $p_0 = 0.9, p_1 = 0.4$, we have a payoff matrix as in table
6.8.

Table 6.8

|       | $p_0 = 0.9$ | $p_1 = 0.4$ |
|-------|-------|-------|
| $G_0$ | 98 | 88 |
| $G_1$ | 91 | 96 |

Given this payoff matrix we would choose $G_1$ for both the
maximin and minimax regret criteria. Having set government expenditure at $G_1$ either $I_0$ or $I_1$ occurs. Suppose $I_0$ occurs. This may

cause us to say that the probability of $I_0$ occurring cannot be as low as 0.4; the lowest it can be is 0.6. In table 6.9 we show the new payoff matrix under this assumption.

Table 6.9

|  | $p_0 = 0.9$ | $p_1 = 0.6$ |
|---|---|---|
| $G_0$ | 98 | 92 |
| $G_1$ | 91 | 94 |

This now causes us to switch policies since $G_0$ is now best under both minimax regret and maximin. In the next period again either $I_0$ or $I_1$ occurs and we reconsider their probabilities of occurrence. This can go on from period to period sometimes causing us to switch policies and sometimes not. If we are lucky and the determination of investment is subject to a statistical law which has appropriate stability properties the range of possible probabilities (in our case $p_0 - p_1$) will diminish, and may eventually converge on a specific value. In our case this might be $p_0 = p_1 = 0.8$. There is then a single expected payoff to each policy, 96 to $G_0$ and 92 to $G_1$, so that from that point on we will always pursue $G_0$ on the grounds that its payoff is highest on average and we have no more information.

What has happened in this example is that the uncertainty which was attributable to lack of knowledge of the probabilities of the different levels of investment has disappeared through the acquisition of new information. This does not mean that we then enter a world of certainty, because investment is still subject to random fluctu-ations and $G_0$ will turn out to be the wrong policy *ex post facto* twenty per cent of the time. That, however, is the best we can do. Although $G_1$ would be the correct policy twenty per cent of the time, by assumption we can never know when those times are, and if occasionally we try $G_1$, the only effect of this is to worsen our performance on average. In sum, in our example the existence of uncertainty may cause us to change policies as we acquire new information, but if the statistical situation is stable we shall con-verge on a single policy which we stick to even though the exogenous variable is still subject to random fluctuations. Ultimately we reach a situation where calculations of expected payoffs lead to a specific choice of policy and there is no room for decision left.

Our example is extremely simple so as to illustrate some very important points. In particular, exogenous investment was subject to no dynamics causing $I_0$ and $I_1$ to be replaced by different values $I_2, I_3$ next period, and $I_4, I_5$ the following period, etc. In addition, a real-world problem would have many more exogenous variables and many more possible policies all able to take many more possible values. All the sources of risk and uncertainty which we have mentioned several times above might pertain. Convergence to stable probability distributions may, therefore, be a much longer process and may never even occur for practical purposes. This means that it is unlikely that public policy will settle down to a single level or even change in a simple systematic way over time. The policy situation will contain sufficient novel elements so that a major role for decision making under uncertainty always remains.

Let us now complicate our example by assuming that various levels of government expenditure can be chosen and not simply $G_0$ and $G_1$. We retain the assumption that only $I_0$ and $I_1$ are possible levels of investment.

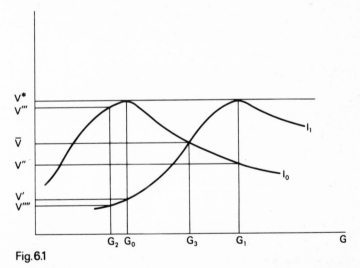

Fig. 6.1

In figure 6.1 the curve $I_0$ is intended to show the way the decision maker evaluates the consequences of various levels of government expenditure given that investment is at a level $I_0$. If government expenditure is put at a level $G_0$, full employment is achieved which is assumed to be the best outcome. At higher levels of government expenditure there is excess demand leading to inflation; at lower levels of government expenditure there is excess supply leading to unemployment. The curve $I_0$ shows what value, $V$, is placed on these things on the assumption that the further away one is from full employment in either direction the worse one regards the resulting state of affairs. The curve is not symmetrical so that an excess expenditure of £10m. is not automatically taken to be as bad as a deficient expenditure of £10m.

The curve $I_1$ indicates the same sort of thing but this time based on a lower level of investment, $I_1$, which for full employment requires a higher level of government expenditure, $G_1$.

Since the government is assumed not to know whether investment will be at $I_0$ or $I_1$, the problem is to decide at which level to place its expenditure in this situation of uncertainty. If expenditure is equal to $G_0$ and $I_0$ occurs, the outcome will be at $V^*$, i.e. as good as possible. But, if $I_1$ occurs, there will be unemployment and the outcome is valued at the lower level of $V'$. Similarly, if expenditure is $G_1$ and $I_1$ occurs, the outcome will again be $V^*$, but if $I_0$ occurs, there will be inflation which is valued at $V''$.

Consider now levels of government expenditure below $G_0$. An example would be $G_2$. If a level of investment $I_0$ occurred, the payoff would be $V'''$ which is less than $V^*$, while if $I_1$ occurred the payoff would be $V''''$ which is less than $V'$. Thus, whatever happens to investment, the policy $G_2$ yields a poorer outcome than $G_0$. This is true not only for $G_2$ but for all levels of expenditure below $G_0$. A similar argument applies to levels of expenditure above $G_1$. They are worse than $G_1$ in all circumstances. (We sometimes use the expression, 'They are *dominated* by $G_1$.')

Our argument so far leads to the conclusion that the best policy for government expenditure lies in the range $G_0 - G_1$. What can be said about policies in that range?

To start with attention may be focussed on the level of expenditure, $G_3$, defined by the point where the two curves intersect. This policy has the characteristic that the values of its outcomes are the same whether $I_0$ or $I_1$ pertains. In other words, it gives a certain payoff of $\bar{V}$. Other policies have a chance of a better payoff but also a chance of a worse one. We are back, therefore, to the problem we discussed in our first example, but with many more available strategies. We examine these in figure 6.2.

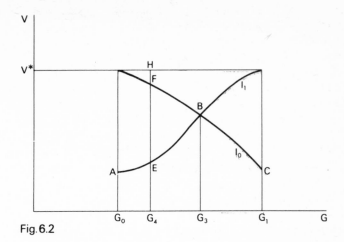

Fig. 6.2

Figure 6.2 is derived from figure 6.1 by omitting all policies outside the range $G_0 - G_1$. Each policy has a best and a worst outcome. The line ABC specifies for each policy what its worst outcome is. It is easy to see that the highest point of ABC is B, corresponding to a level of public expenditure $G_3$ which is, indeed, the level where the payoff is a certain one. This, therefore, is the maximin strategy.

Let us now tackle the same problem assuming we have probabilities for $I_0$ and $I_1$.

The slope of each $I$-curve is the change in the payoff as $G$ varies, given $I$. It is the marginal payoff to $G$. Let this be $M_0$ for the $I_0$ curve, and $M_1$ for the $I_1$ curve. We can see from figure 6.2 that the $I_0$ curve is falling and $I_1$ rising as government expenditure is increased beyond $G_0$. (We have drawn the curves so that $I_0$ is getting steeper as we go from left to right and $I_1$ flatter.)

If the probability of $I_0$ occurring is $p$, the probability of $I_1$ occurring is $1 - p$. If we increase the level of government expenditure by one unit above $G$, we will get a marginal benefit of $M_1$, assuming $I_1$ occurs. Since this happens on average $1 - p$ of the time, the average or expected marginal benefit is $(1 - p)M_1$. Similarly, there will be a marginal fall in benefit (i.e. a marginal cost) if $I_0$ occurs. Since this happens on average $p$ of the time the expected marginal disbenefit will be $pM_0$. The effect of this marginal variation in $G$ will amount altogether to $(1 - p)M_1 + pM_0$. Note $M_0$, being a cost, is negative. It pays to go on increasing government expenditure as long as expected marginal benefit exceeds expected marginal disbenefit. The best policy would be when the two were equal, i.e.

$$(1-p)M_1 + pM_0 = 0 \qquad (6.1)$$

$$(1-p)M_1 = -pM_0 \qquad (6.2)$$

[In mathematical terms, assume the expected payoff is

$$pf(G, I_0) + (1-p)f(G, I_1)$$

where $f$ is the actual payoff as a function of $G$ and $I$. This is at a maximum when

$$-p\frac{\partial f(G, I_0)}{\partial G} = (1-p)\frac{\partial f(G, I_1)}{\partial G} \qquad (6.3)$$

This is the same as the previous expression with $M_0$ equal to $\partial f(G, I_0)/\partial G$ and $M_1$ equal to $\partial f(G, I_1)/\partial G$.]

Our condition may be rewritten as

$$\frac{p}{1-p} = -\frac{M_1}{M_0} \qquad (6.4)$$

In figure 6.3 we illustrate this argument. The line $V$ shows the

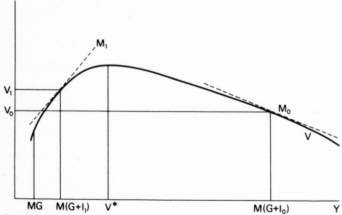

Fig. 6.3

government's preferences as a function of national income. If $G$ is given, national income will be $M(G + I_1)$ if $I_1$ occurs, and this will be valued at $V_1$. If $I_0$ occurs, national income will be $M(G + I_0)$ and this will be valued at $V_0$. In the former case the marginal benefit due to variations in $G$ is $M_1$; in the latter case the marginal benefit is $M_0$. $G$ is determined so that the ratio of the two slopes is $p/(1-p)$.

Suppose now that $p$ rises. It follows that $p/(1-p)$ rises. This means that $M_1/M_0$ must rise; which in turn means that $M_1$ must rise and $M_0$ must fall in absolute value. Since $M_1$ has been assumed to fall as government expenditure increases and $M_0$ has been assumed to rise, government expenditure must fall. In other words, as the probability of $I_0$ rises, policy shifts to a level of government expenditure nearer to that which would be appropriate if $I_0$ were to happen for certain. This is, presumably, an answer which is intuitively reasonable.

There is a particular variation of the probability approach which has had considerable impact on a great deal of the theory of economic control during the past few years.

Let $Y^*$ be full employment income. It follows that $Y^* - M(I + G)$ is the deviation of actual income from full employment income. Suppose that the government views positive deviations from full employment as possessing equal disutility to negative deviations of the same magnitude. This is not what we have assumed in figure 6.1, and it implies that the $I$-curves are symmetrical about their maximum points. Let us go further and say that disutility is measured by the square of the deviations from full employment. This may be written as

$$D = [Y^* - M(I + G)]^2 \tag{6.5}$$

Average or expected disutility is then obtained from this by multiplying it by the appropriate probabilities. Write this as

$$E(D) = p[Y^* - M(I_0 + G)]^2 + (1-p)[Y^* - M(I_1 + G)]^2 \tag{6.6}$$

If $D$ is disutility it is easy to work out that marginal disutility is

$$D' = -2M[Y^* - M(I + G)] \tag{6.7}$$

that is

$$M_0 = 2M[Y^* - M(I_0 + G)] \tag{6.8}$$

$$M_1 = 2M[Y^* - M(I_1 + G)]$$

Now, because we are discussing the problem in terms of disutility, we want this to be as small as possible. This is the same as making utility as large as possible since disutility is the negative of utility.

Our maximisation condition may then be expressed as

$$(1-p)M[Y^* - M(I_1 + G)] + pM[Y^* - M(I_0 + G)] = 0$$

(6.9)

This may be simplified to

$$Y^* - M[(1-p)I_1 + pI_0] = MG$$

(6.10)

If we examine the expression in square brackets we find it is equal to the average or expected value of investment. Write this as $\bar{I}$. Our equation is then

$$\frac{Y^*}{M} - \bar{I} = G.$$

(6.11)

This is exactly the same as the simple model discussed in chapter 1 except that average or expected investment has been substituted for actual investment. In other words, to solve the decision problem in these circumstances the rule is to find the expected value of investment and to adjust government expenditure to that as if it were the actual value. This is sometimes referred to as the *certainty equivalence principle*. [These results hold more generally for exogenous variables treated statistically. It will certainly hold if the disutility function is quadratic and symmetric as is $D$. In the quadratic case, expected disutility is given by

$$E(D) = \int_{-\infty}^{\infty} f(I)[M(I + G) - Y^*]^2 \, dI$$

(6.12)

where $f(I)$ is the probability distribution of $I$.

If we differentiate with respect to $G$ under the integral sign, this is a minimum when

$$\int_{-\infty}^{\infty} f(I)2M[M(I + G) - Y^*] \, dI = 0$$

(6.13)

$$\int_{-\infty}^{\infty} Mf(I) \, I dI + MG - Y^* = 0$$

(6.14)

$$G = \frac{Y^*}{M} - \bar{I}$$

(6.15)

where $\bar{I} = \int_{-\infty}^{\infty} f(I) \, I dI$, or the expected value of $I$.]

Although the *certainty equivalence principle* is of some importance in the theory of macroeconomic policy, it should not be taken for granted that its range of applicability is extremely large. In a great many cases it would not be correct to assume even as a first approximation that the government's preferences are symmetric about some ideal level so that, for example, excess demand is regarded as equally injurious as excess supply or that an excessive balance of payments surplus is as bad as a shortfall of the same absolute magnitude.

Where the symmetry assumption does not hold, policy must be adjusted accordingly. If, for example, excessive demand is not regarded with as much concern as deficient demand, government expenditure will be higher than would be given by the certainty equivalence principle. The government would be more worried about investment being too low and would over-compensate for that. Since the average level of national income would be determined by the average level of investment and government expenditure, this would be larger than the desired level of national income. The greater fear of unemployment as opposed to inflation will lead to a policy which produces more inflation on average. The economy will not fluctuate about full employment but about over-full employment. This is a perfectly correct consequence of the government's preferences.

In our original example, assume that the utility function up to full employment is $aY$, but that, if we overshoot, utility falls by $b$ times the overshoot. This may be written as

$$U = aY \quad \text{if} \quad Y \leqslant Y^* \tag{6.16}$$

$$U = aY + b(Y^* - Y) \quad \text{if} \quad Y \geqslant Y^* \tag{6.17}$$

where $Y^*$ is the desired or full employment level of income.

It will be recalled that investment could take two values, $I_0$ or $I_1$, the former with probability $p_0$, and the latter with probability $1 - p_0$. Assume $I_0$ is greater than $I_1$.

If we fix government expenditure so that exactly full employment were ensured when $I_0$ occurred, there would be unemployment at the lower level of investment, $I_1$, should that occur. National income would equal $M(G + I_0)$ a fraction, $p_0$, of the time and $M(G + I_1)$ a fraction, $1 - p_0$, of the time. Neither of these is above full employment so that the expected level of national income will be $M(G + I)$. Since we have fixed $G$ to ensure full employment when $I_0$ occurs, this means;

$$G = \frac{Y^*}{M} - I_0 \tag{6.18}$$

The expected utility can, therefore, be written as

$$E(U) = aY^* + aM(\bar{I} - I_0).\tag{6.19}$$

Suppose now we increase $G$ by one unit. When $I_0$ occurs there will now be excess demand and utility will fall by an amount $b$. When $I_1$ occurs there will now be less unemployment and utility will rise by an amount $a$. The former event occurs $p_0$ of the time, the latter $1 - p_0$. Thus, if we increase $G$ by one unit, our expected gain will be $a(1 - p_0) - bp_0$. If this is positive it pays to increase $G$ to its largest level, which is that which ensures full employment when $I_1$ occurs and inflation when $I_0$ occurs. If the expression is negative it pays to leave $G$ at its smallest level, which ensures full employment when $I_0$ occurs and unemployment when $I_1$ occurs. The decision depends on the probabilities of $I_0$ and $I_1$ and the relative marginal valuation of unemployment and inflation. It cannot, however, be reduced to a formula where $G$ is dependent on the average value of $I$. Since our utility function is a first approximation to any asymmetric utility function it can be seen that more generally asymmetry does not lead to the principle of certainty equivalence.

Another question to be answered is: 'What happens if one of the possible levels of investment falls? Suppose instead of $I_1$ we now consider that the two possible occurrences are $I_0$ and $I_2$, the latter being less than $I_1$. The $I_0$-curve stays where it is but the $I_2$-curve must lie to the right of $I_1$. For full employment given $I_2$ we require a higher level of $G$, say $G_2$. This is equally true for any other level of employment so that to every level of government expenditure given $I_1$ we require a higher level given $I_2$ if the same payoff is to be achieved.

In figure 6.4 we show a curve $I_2$ which is exactly the same as $I_1$ but shifted a given constant distance to the right. The minimum payoff curve becomes $A' B' C'$, and the maximin policy becomes $G_3'$. This is an increase compared with $G_3$ and results from the reduction in the possible level of investment. In other words, if the level to which investment may fall itself falls, the maximin policy for government expenditure rises. Another conclusion that we can reach concerns the maximin payoff. In the first case this is point B, and in the second case B'. The widening of the possible outcomes, if we use the maximin strategy, is not costless but does cause us to be worse off.

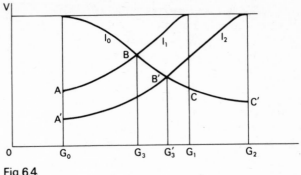

Fig. 6.4

Turning back to the probability approach, let us examine the consequences of a lower level of investment being possible. Because of our assumptions the slope of the $I_2$ curve is less than the slope of the $I_1$ curve at every level of government expenditure between $G_0$ and $G_1$. (This is easily seen in figure 6.4.) This means that at the level which maximised the expected payoff previously $M_2$, the new marginal benefit, is less than $M_1$ and, therefore, $M_2/M_0$ must be less than $p/(1-p)$. To find the new maximum position we must increase government expenditure to increase $M_2$ and reduce $M_0$ until the maximisation condition holds again. Thus, with this approach too, the effect of a reduction in the possible lower level of investment is to increase government expenditure.

In our first example we also discussed the minimax regret decision criterion. We can apply that here too. The best possible outcome is when policy is perfectly adjusted to investment so as to achieve full employment. We have assigned this a payoff of $V^*$. The regrets are $V^*$ minus the actual payoffs that occur, given $I_0$ or $I_1$. In figure 6.2 these are the vertical distances of the $I_0$ and $I_1$ arrows from the line $V^*V^*$. Consider, for example, the level of government expenditure $G_4$. If $I_0$ occurs, the payoff will be at point F which deducted from $V^*$ gives a regret of H F. If $I_1$ occurs, the payoff will be E giving a regret of H E. It is easy to see that the regret curves are just the same as the payoff curves except that they are measured downwards from $V^*V^*$ rather than upwards from the horizontal axis. The maximum regret is then the curve A B C, but again viewed from the line $V^*V^*$, e.g. the maximum regret for public expenditure of $G_4$ is H E. The policy of minimax regret is then clearly to reach point B and to set public expenditure at the same level as for the maximin strategy, $G_3$. It follows immediately, of course, that if $I_2$ replaces $I_1$ as in figure 6.4 the minimax regret policy shifts to the right and the level of minimax regret increases.

### Appendix

In this section we take the discussion of the certainty equivalence principle further than we were able to do in the main text.

Assume the government's preference function is symmetric about the desired level $Y^*$ as illustrated in figure 6.5.

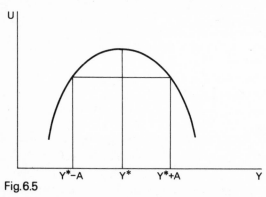

Fig. 6.5

This means (a) that the disutility of income being too high by a given amount is equal to the disutility of income being too low by the same amount and (b) that marginal utility at any income a given amount below the desired level is equal to marginal disutility of income at the same given amount above the desired level, i.e.

$$U(Y^* - Y) = U(Y - Y^*) \tag{6.20}$$

and

$$U'(Y^* - Y) = U'(Y - Y^*) \tag{6.21}$$

Suppose also the probability distribution of investment is symmetrical about the mean value of $I$ so that $f(\bar{I} + B) = f(\bar{I} - B)$.

If $Y = M(I + G)$, the utility of choosing a policy $G$ will be $U(MI + MG)$ and the expected utility will be $E(U) = \int_{-\infty}^{\infty} f(I)U(MI + MG)\mathrm{d}I$. This is at a maximum with respect to $G$ when

$$\frac{\partial E(U)}{\partial G} = \int_{-\infty}^{\infty} f(I)U'(MI + MG)\mathrm{d}I = 0 \tag{6.22}$$

(There are also second-order conditions of importance to take into account to make sure that this is a maximum and not a minimum. We forgo discussion of them because they raise matters of a more advanced nature. Suffice it to say that if the utility function is as illustrated in figure 6.5 and the frequency distribution for $I$ also is bell shaped, the appropriate second-order conditions will hold.)

Suppose we put $MG = Y^* - M\bar{I}$, i.e. determine policy according to the deviation of desired income from that given by the multiplier times expected investment. It follows that

$$\int_{-\infty}^{\infty} f(I)U'(MI + MG)\mathrm{d}I = \int_{-\infty}^{\infty} f(I)U'(Y^* + MI - M\bar{I})\mathrm{d}I \tag{6.23}$$

When $I = \bar{I}$, $U'$ is zero. Consider any positive deviation, $B$, of investment above $\bar{I}$ with marginal utility $U'(Y^* + B)$. Corresponding to it is a negative deviation with marginal utility $U'(Y^* - B)$ equal to $- U'(Y^* + B)$. Since $\bar{I} + B$ and $\bar{I} - B$ are equally probable, i.e. $f(\bar{I} + B) = f(\bar{I} - B)$ they cancel out in the expression for $\partial E(U)/\partial G$. It follows that $\partial E(U)/\partial G = 0$ when $MG = Y^* - M\bar{I}$.

What this tells us is that optimal policy (in this case for government expenditure) is determined by desired income, expected investment and the multiplier. What is more, the formula or *decision rule* for policy is a linear function of the objective and gives the expected value of the exogenous variable. Such formulae, therefore, are usually referred to as *linear decision rules*. If through time desired income grows by a given percentage, and expected investment grows by the same percentage, optimal expenditure will also grow by that percentage if the multiplier is constant.

In the main text we considered a quadratic utility (or disutility) function which was symmetric about the desired level of income. Suppose the government's preferences do not show this symmetry and that positive deviations from $Y^*$ are not treated as involving the same loss as equal negative deviations. An example would be a utility function of the form

$$U = aY^3 + bY^2 + C \tag{6.24}$$

This is at a maximum when $a < 0; b > 0$

$$3aY^2 + 2bY = 0 \quad \text{and} \quad Y + 2b < 0 \tag{6.25}$$

When $Y = 0$, our assumptions imply $U$ is a local minimum. When $Y = -2b/3a$, our assumptions imply $U$ is a maximum.

Given this utility function the formula for expected utility becomes

$$E(U) = \int_{-\infty}^{\infty} f(I)[a(MI + MG)^3 + b(MI + MG)^2 + C] \, dI \quad (6.26)$$

This is at a maximum when

$$\frac{\partial E(U)}{\partial G} = \int_{-\infty}^{\infty} f(I)[3a(MI + MG)^2 + 2b(MI + MG)] \, dI = 0$$

$$(6.27)$$

Quite clearly $G$ in this case depends not simply on the expected values of $I$ but also on its second moment $\int_{-\infty}^{\infty} f(I)I^2 \, dI$.

We have already said that the quadratic utility function must be used with caution, and that it is easy to construct examples where some other, asymmetric, utility function would be appropriate. Let us now backtrack a little and also stress the merits of the quadratic utility function, for it is a good deal more flexible than might appear at first sight.

Our earlier argument was that income being a given amount too high might not be thought as bad as income being the same amount too low. The reason for this was that the government might not be as averse to inflation as it is to unemployment. Is this argument as compelling as it seems, namely does an asymmetry in attitudes to unemployment and inflation necessarily lead to an asymmetric utility of income function? The answer is no. It is quite possible to construct a case where greater weight is given to deviations of unemployment from its desired level than to deviation of income, and yet the result is still a symmetric utility of income function. Let $U$ be actual unemployment, $U^*$ be desired unemployment, $\dot{P}$ be actual rate of change of prices, and $\dot{P}^*$ be desired rate of change of prices. Assume the government's valuation of these is

$$V = C_1(U - U^*)^2 + C_2(\dot{P} - \dot{P}^*)^2 \quad (6.28)$$

$C_1$ and $C_2$ measure the relative significance of deviations of each variable from its desired level.

Suppose our economic model relates both unemployment and price inflation to national income. We express this as a linear model which may be interpreted as an approximation in the relevant range of income.

$$U = A - aY \tag{6.29}$$

$$\dot{P} = B + bY \tag{6.30}$$

Assume also that the usual multiplier equation holds for $Y$

$$Y = M(I + G) \tag{6.31}$$

$I$ is a random variable with probability distribution $f(I)$.

Note immediately that, since $U$ and $\dot{P}$ are linear functions of $Y$, $V$ may be expressed as a function of $Y$. What is more, it is a quadratic function of $Y$. Despite this, by the way it has been constructed it does not treat unemployment and inflation symmetrically. The explanation is, of course, a simple one; $V$ treated as a function of $Y$ depends on the coefficients $C_1$, $C_2$, $a$ and $b$. A given change in $Y$ does not have the same effect on $U$ as on $\dot{P}$, and its effect on $V$ works via $C_1$ and $C_2$. The value of $Y$ for which $V$ is a minimum and about which $V$ is symmetrical is itself determined by these coefficients. The symmetry then takes into account the effectiveness of $Y$ on $U$ and $\dot{P}$ and the relative significance of that effectiveness. Thus, 1% extra unemployed may be worse than 1% added to the increase in prices, but it may be regarded as equivalent (in badness) to 2 % added to the increase in prices. If £$X$ m. excess demand causes a 2 % addition to price inflation and £$X$ m. excess supply causes a 1 % addition to unemployment, the two excesses generate equal disutility and the utility of income function is symmetric.

We can now analyse our little model further. Expected payoff to public policy is

$$E(V) = \int_{-\infty}^{\infty} f(I)[C_1(U - U^*)^2 + C_2(\dot{P} - \dot{P}^*)^2]\,dI \tag{6.32}$$

The derivative of this with respect to $G$ is

$$\frac{\partial E(V)}{\partial G} = 2M[(C_1 a^2 + C_2 b^2)M(G + \bar{I}) + C_2 b(B - \dot{P}^*)$$

$$- C_1 a(A - U^*)] \tag{6.33}$$

$E(V)$ is a minimum when $\partial E(V)/\partial G$ is zero, that is

$$G + \bar{I} = \frac{C_1 a(A - U^*) + C_2 b(\dot{P}^* - B)}{(C_1 a^2 + C_2 b^2)M} \tag{6.34}$$

$G$ is equal to a constant minus $\bar{I}$ and will vary as $\bar{I}$ varies.

Going back to our earlier equations we may ask what is the correct level of $Y$ if $U = U^*$ or if $\dot{P} = \dot{P}^*$. The ideal level for $Y$ is determined from equation (6.29) by replacing $U$ by $U^*$, and from equation (6.30) by replacing $\dot{P}$ by $\dot{P}^*$. Write these respectively as $Y_U$ and $Y_{\dot{P}}$.

$$Y_U = \frac{A - U^*}{a} \tag{6.35}$$

$$Y_{\dot{P}} = \frac{\dot{P} - B}{b} \tag{6.36}$$

Given our earlier expression for $G + \bar{I}$, we multiply this by $M$ to get the expected value of $Y$, $\bar{Y}$.

$$\bar{Y} = M(G + F) = \frac{C_1 a(A - U^*) + C_2 b(\dot{P}^* - B)}{C_1 a^2 + C_2 b^2} \tag{6.37}$$

This may be manipulated a little to get it into the following form

$$\bar{Y} = \frac{C_1 a^2 \dfrac{(A - U^*)}{a} + C_2 b^2 \dfrac{(\dot{P}^* - B)}{b}}{C_1 a^2 + C_2 b^2} \tag{6.38}$$

$$= \frac{C_1 a^2 Y_U + C_2 b^2 Y_{\dot{P}}}{C_1 a^2 + C_2 b^2} \tag{6.39}$$

In other words, public policy works to set income at a weighted average of its two desired levels. The weights depend on the relative importance of the two objectives, $C_1$ and $C_2$, and the efficiency of possible attempts to control income to reach these objectives, $a$ and $b$.

# 7
# The elements of the dynamic problem

It is apparent that a correct characterisation of the economic system must be in dynamic terms. External forces to which the system is subject are changing through time. The interactions of endogenous variables take time to work themselves out. Above all, the effects of targets on instruments and instruments on targets do not occur instantaneously, but are processes involving time lags of all kinds.

The purpose of this chapter is to illustrate certain problems and to clarify some concepts which are important in the study of dynamic economic policy. Many problems are, however, rather difficult mathematically, and cannot be dealt with satisfactorily in an elementary exposition. Reference to appropriate literature is, therefore, given at the end of the book.

Let us start with an examination of time lags. The policy maker is assumed as usual to be employing a battery of instruments to control a variety of targets. We may think of him monitoring the behaviour of the targets, adjusting the instruments, noting the effect of the instruments on the targets, readjusting the instruments, etc. The monitoring process may be continuous and he may feel free to act at any time; alternatively, observation and action may occur at predetermined points of time. Practical policy making in the UK seems to be a mixture of the two. While some data are collected at predetermined intervals, the data collection process as a whole may be thought to be a continuous one. Again, while the Treasury and others make regular quarterly assessments and forecasts of the state of the economy, attempts are made to note any major changes in the intervening time. Fiscal policy, at least on the tax side, has a favoured date of use, namely the annual budget, but can be and is used at other arbitrary times of the year. Monetary policy whether it be in the form of interest rate or quantity of money variations may be brought into play at any time.

The time lag in macroeconomic policy making may be thought of as comprising three parts, an inside lag, an intermediate lag, and an outside lag. (This curious terminology derives from the writings of such US economists as Kareken and Solow and Ando and Brown.) An understanding of these lags also requires a distinction to be made between the actual instruments at the disposal of policy makers and the nominal instruments. The former are the instruments that the government actually uses. Examples would be particular rates of tax or transfer payments, purchases or sale of bonds in the open market, criteria for public investment decisions. The latter, the nominal instruments, are those that directly affect the targets. Examples would be total tax revenues, total transfer payments, total public expenditure on current account, total public investment. A moment's reflection shows that the distinction between nominal and actual instruments is partly a matter of definition and partly a matter of aggregation, namely how much concern one has with the detailed linkage between policy and its ultimate effects. Clearly, this depends on the problem in hand and what questions one wishes to answer. Suffice it to say that it is not always necessary to examine every link in the chain between action and its effects, but there is also the danger of placing too much in a 'black box' and ignoring a vital connection.

Given the distinction between actual and nominal instruments, the definitions of the three sorts of time lag are as follows:

(a) The *inside lag* is that between the observation of the target and the use of the actual instruments.

(b) The *intermediate lag* is that between the use of the actual instruments and their effects on the nominal instrument.

(c) The *outside lag* is that between the nominal instruments and the targets.

This is set out in figure 7.1. Note also the feedback between targets and instruments.

As an explicit example consider the use of monetary policy to control national income. The inside lag will comprise the delay

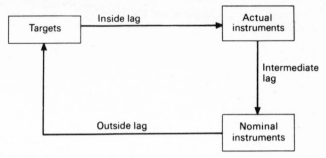

Fig. 7.1

between the actual behaviour of the level of economic activity
and its appearing in a recognisable form in statistics and other
indicators. In addition, there will be delays while decisions are
taken on the basis of the available information and further delays
in implementing the decisions. The length of this lag will not be
constant, but will vary with the length of data collection intervals,
with the accuracy of data required for decision, administrative
arrangements within government, and a host of other factors. At
a guess its average length in the United Kingdom for normal
variations in income is somewhere in the region of two months.

Turning to the intermediate lag, assume that the actual
instrument at the government's disposal is the credit base and
that policy consists of open market operations to vary the money
supply. The intermediate lag, therefore, concerns the delay
between the purchase or sale of securities in the open market and
the subsequent adjustments of the banking system leading to
changes in the quantity of money. All of this depends on the
speed with which banks can reduce overdrafts or persuade firms
and households to borrow, and on what other methods are
allowed to them to vary their asset structure. This may also turn
on the state of the economy, whether it is in boom or depression;
and the length of the intermediate lag may not be the same for
an increase in the money supply as for a decrease, or for a large
change as for a small change. It is almost impossible to guess the
average length of this intermediate lag in the UK but again in
normal conditions something like two weeks would be about right.

Finally, there is the outside lag. This depends on variations
in the quantity of money in the hands of firms and households

and what they do with it. Since we are discussing open market operations, there is initially no net wealth effect, simply a variation in liquidity. This may affect propensities to spend directly, especially if it involves a tightening or loosening of credit rationing. Alternatively, the effect may be indirect via changes in interest rates on private investment spending or purchases of consumer durable goods. Whatever happens there will again be recognition, decision, and implementation lags before consumption and investment expenditures change, and further lags before these work through into national income. Here again there will be all sorts of complications depending on the state of the economy and the length of the lag must be regarded as a random variable; but, to make a further foolhardy guess, it could well be that the average outside lag is about six months in duration.

(In this connection reference may be made to another classification of lags which economists have found useful. This is a sort of partition of the outside lag and is as follows:

    (a) the Robertsonian lag between income and expenditure;
    (b) the Lundbergian lag between expenditure and production;
    (c) the 'unnamed' lag between production, sales, receipts, and the payment of factor incomes.)

If we add all these up, we find that the average lag in monetary policy is about nine months. In fact, there have been economists who have suggested it is longer than that. Indeed, if the target variable is unemployment rather than income, the total lag is certainly longer since the former lags behind the latter by anything up to six months. This would be the case if we could only control unemployment by controlling income but always based our actions on observations of unemployment.

There is one additional remark that must be made about the nature of time lags. Although we have talked about the lags between targets and instruments and instruments and targets as if these were well-defined fixed intervals, a more nearly correct statement would be about a time lag structure. The effect of a unit change in the level of an instrument is not simply a fixed quantity occurring with a delay, but a whole array of quantities occurring with a range of delays. Some examples are illustrated in figures 7.2 to 7.5. In each case we are showing what happens to the target over time as the instrument is varied by one unit in period zero, and then returned to its initial level.

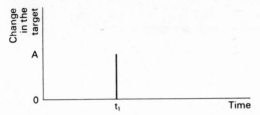

Fig. 7.2. The target is increased by an amount OA after a lag of $t_1$ periods.

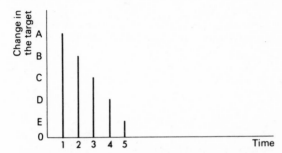

Fig. 7.3. There is an effect after one period, a smaller effect after two periods, a yet smaller effect after three, etc., the whole eventually damping out to zero.

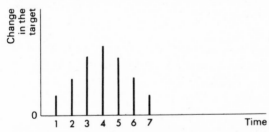

Fig. 7.4. There is a small effect after one period, a larger effect after two periods, the maximum effect is reached after four periods and then the effects die away as in the previous example.

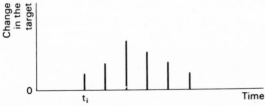

Fig. 7.5. A combination of the dynamic effects of figure 7.2 and figure 7.4. There is an initial delay of $t_1$ periods before anything happens, followed by a growth then decline in effects.

The cases shown in figures 7.2 to 7.5 are examples of what
are called *impulse responses*. They show how the target responds
to the additional use of the instrument for one period. We may also
be interested in what happens if we vary the instrument by one
unit and keep it there permanently. This is called a step response
and is equal to the sum of a whole series of impulse responses
through time. To take the example of figure 7.3:

(a) in period 1 the target changes by the impulse response
of the first period;

(b) in period 2 the effect of the first period is maintained
because the instrument is kept at its new level but there is
also the effect due to the instrument being at that level in
the previous period, i.e. the impulse response of period 2
is added on;

(c) in period 3 the whole effect of period 2 is maintained
together with the impulse response of period 3.

This may be extended for any number of periods until the
complete set of impulse responses have been added up to give the
step response, illustrated in figure 7.6. In period 1 the target
changes by OA, which is the first impulse response in figure 7.3.
In period 2 the target has changed by an *additional* AB which is
equal to O B in figure 7.3. In period 3 the target has changed by
an additional B C, which is equal to O C in figure 7.3. It should be
clear now that the impulse response is equal to the change in the

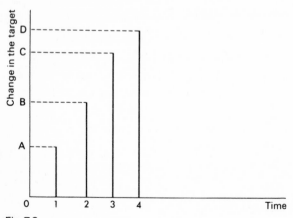

Fig. 7.6

step response. (For the mathematicians, the former is the time derivative of the latter, the latter is the time integral of the former.)

In the examples we have shown the impulse response eventually dies away to zero, which means the step response eventually converges to a definite value. In the use of policy instruments this is a desirable thing to happen, the alternative being that the use of the instruments causes the targets to diverge explosively from where we would like them to be. We may also be interested in whether the response involves a smooth path always heading for the desired target level or a cyclical path which may temporarily diverge although ultimately converging. In essence this will depend on the direct dynamic relationship between the instrument and the target, and also on the dynamic behaviour of the target itself. Figures 7.7 and 7.8 illustrate (as continuous curves) a cyclical and a divergent impulse response.

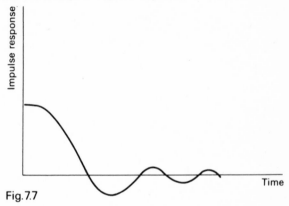

Fig. 7.7

We now turn from these time lags to examine the possible effects of the instrument on the target. Suppose, for example, that national income is changing cyclically about its trend as shown in figure 7.9. Also shown in this figure are various possible additional effects of the instrument.

If the effect $E_1$ is combined with $\Delta Y$, this will lead to a completely stable situation. If the effect $E_2$ is combined with $\Delta Y$, this will lead to an intensification of the cycle. If the effect $E_3$ is combined with $\Delta Y$ the cycle is intensified, but not as much as in the previous case, and it is also distorted somewhat. This shows

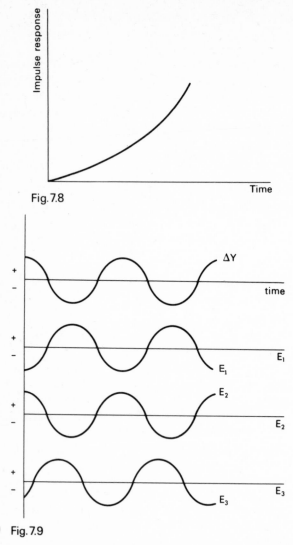

Fig. 7.8

Fig. 7.9

that the effect of the instrument may be perfectly right in scale, but can worsen the behaviour of the budget because of an error in timing. $E_1$ represents the perfect effect of the instrument if it is desired to achieve complete stability. There may still be improvements in stability if the effect of the instrument is delayed by up to a further one-twelfth of a cycle; but, if it is delayed by anything up to an additional three-quarters of the cycle, the behaviour of the target will become more unstable.

What this amounts to is that for complete stability the effects of policy must lag half a cycle behind the target. If the objective is simply to increase stability, the condition is a little eased. It is that the effects must be delayed by at least a third of a cycle, but no more than seven-twelfths of a cycle. Note that this means that destabilization can result because of effects occurring too early as well as too late.

These lags in the effects of policy are not the same as lags in the instruments of policy and it would be erroneous to make inferences about the latter simply from observations of the former. Suppose in our example that national income followed a regular four-year variation around its trend. Complete stability would require the effects of policy to lag two years behind national income. Improved stability would require the lag to be no greater than two and a third years and no less than one and a third years. This tells us neither what the lag between instrument and target actually is, nor what it should be.

This leads us to ask more generally what the significance of the length of the time lags between instrument and target is. Broadly speaking, the more rapidly the policy takes effect, the more reliable and less subject to error will that policy be. To invert this proposition, we can say that the longer the delay, the more likely it is that a mistake in policy will lead to instability. A failure to act quickly will mean that the period in which the target variables differ from their desired values will be prolonged which is itself a bad thing. Moreover, having failed to act quickly there are great dangers to the stability of the system if we then act strongly. Stronger action later is not a substitute for weaker action earlier.

One way of throwing a light on this is to examine an elementary example. Suppose national income is determined partly by some forces outside the government's control and partly by a policy instrument, e.g. government spending. This is represented as follows:

$$Y_t = aY_{t-1} + G_t + A \qquad (7.1)$$

where $G_t$ is government spending, $A$ is the effect of the external forces, and $0 < a < 1$. Note that the lagged value of $Y_t$ implies some dynamic reaction in the system anyway, e.g. a lagged propensity to consume.

Actually, government spending will be the outcome of past decisions and past observations of national income. We may replace $G_t$ by $bY_{t-1}$ if the delay is one period, by $bY_{t-2}$ if it is two periods, etc.

We may generally assume that $b$ is negative, i.e. policy will be used to reverse undesirable movements in national income. It is also reasonable to assume that $b$ is greater than $-1$, i.e. we will not want to over-compensate for undesirable changes in $Y$.

If the delay is one period, for the model to remain stable and also not oscillate towards its desired equilibrium, the absolute value of $b$ must be less than that of $a$. The reason is that the dynamic behaviour of this first-order difference equation is determined by $a + b$, and we want this to remain positive but less than unity.

If the delay is equal to two periods, the dynamic behaviour of national income is determined by the following equation:

$$Y_t = aY_{t-1} + bY_{t-2} \tag{7.2}$$

The condition for this equation not to behave cyclically is that

$$a^2 + 4b > 0$$

For given values of $a$, this confines us to a smaller (and lower) range of values of $b$. (As a matter of interest in this case, if the system shows no cycles with our assumptions it will also have no tendency to explode. In the modern jargon, it will be both 'stable' and 'hyperstable'.)

If the delay is equal to three periods, the dynamic behaviour of the system is determined by the following equation:

$$Y_t = aY_{t-1} + bY_{t-3} \tag{7.3}$$

The condition for this equation not to behave cyclically is that

$$\frac{4a^3}{27} + b > 0.$$

This confines us to an even smaller and lower range of values for $b$. (We examine this further in the appendix and show that, in this simple model, if the delay is greater than three periods the effect of government action must be to introduce some instability into the system.)

Let us now approach the problem of stability in a slightly different way. In the model set out in equation (7.1), if there is a change in the effect of the external forces equal to $\Delta B$, the change in national income will be given by:

$$\Delta Y = a^t \Delta B \qquad (7.4)$$

where $t$ is the time that has elapsed since the change. We can show this in figure 7.10.

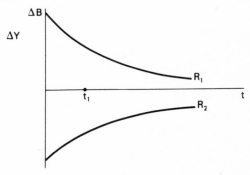

Fig. 7.10

$R_1$ shows $\Delta Y$ on the assumption that $\Delta B$ is positive, while $R_2$ shows the effect of a negative $\Delta B$. If the initial situation was satisfactory, the result of variations in the external forces is excess demand and inflation, or deficient demand and unemployment. The government may wish to vary its own level of spending to offset this.

Assume the government acts with a delay of $t_1$ periods. Let the scale of government action be $\Delta G$. The deviation of national income from its desired value from period $t_1$ onwards is given by

$$\Delta Y = a^t \Delta B + a^{t-t_1} \Delta G \qquad (7.5)$$

For this to represent an improvement the absolute value of the deviations of $Y$ from its desired value must be reduced when the government acts, i.e.

$$|a^t \Delta B + a^{t-t_1} \Delta G| < |a^t \Delta B| \tag{7.6}$$

Let us concentrate on the case when $\Delta B$ is positive. We then have

$$\left| 1 + a^{-t_1} \frac{\Delta G}{\Delta B} \right| < 1 \tag{7.7}$$

If $\Delta G$ is also positive, this condition cannot hold. In other words, to improve matters the effects of government policy must obviously reverse the effects of the external forces. Given that $\Delta G$ is negative, the condition then becomes

$$-2 < a^{-t_1} \frac{\Delta G}{\Delta B} \tag{7.8}$$

or

$$-2a^{t_1} \Delta B < \Delta G < 0 \tag{7.9}$$

A similar result with the inequality signs reversed holds when $\Delta B$ is negative, i.e.

$$-2a^{t_1} \Delta B > \Delta G > 0 \tag{7.10}$$

What this tells us essentially is that the longer the delay in government action the greater the cost due to national income being away from its desired level. Of course, there is an advantage to be set against this, namely that the likelihood of the government assessing the situation correctly (in this case estimating $\Delta B$ with more accuracy) will increase. Up to a point, at least, the government may find itself in a situation where it is comparing at the margin the costs of delay against the benefits of more accurate policy.

This leads to a brief consideration of the variable (or variables) which the government is able to observe. Policy is designed to offset the effects of exogenous forces and it would be nice if these could be anticipated, by examining and predicting the behaviour of the exogenous forces themselves. In practice this is not easily done and it is the target variable itself (e.g. national income) on which policy must be based.

The way in which policy may be related to the target is frequently classified as follows:

(a) *Proportional policy*. In this case the policy variable is related to the level of the target variable, i.e.

$$G_t = b_1 Y_{t-1}$$

(b) *Derivative policy*. In this case the policy variable is related to the change in the target variable, i.e.

$$G_t = b_2(Y_{t-1} - Y_{t-2})$$

(c) *Integral policy*. In this case the policy variable is related to the sum (or integral) of the past levels of the target variable, i.e.

$$G_t = b_3 \sum_{i=1}^{\infty} Y_{t-i}$$

Another way of looking at integral policy is that the change in the policy variable is related to the level of the target variable, i.e.

$$G_t - G_{t-1} = b_3 Y_{t-1}$$

It is not easy to explain the importance of these lags non-mathematically. The first two can, however, be related to the concepts of outside and inside lags. Once the nominal instrument is actually working, we would like it to be related to the state of the target at that time. This is essentially the point of the examples already discussed in this chapter. Earlier on, however, when decisions are being taken about the actual instruments, we will be aware that the state of the target then is not what matters and we must attempt to forecast its future state when the effects of the instrument are being felt. It is here that the rate of change, or derivative, of the target, becomes significant. An attempt to offset changes in uncontrolled expenditure by a proportional policy alone is in danger of inducing cyclical fluctuations in the economy. These may be offset to a considerable extent by adding a derivative policy.

The role of integral policy arises from another of our objectives. The concern of the policy maker is not simply to stabilise the economy. It is also to keep it as close as possible to some desired level. Stability at too low a level may be more undesirable than instability at a higher level. What integral policy does is to take account of the cumulative movement away from the desired level and reverse that.

In sum, if we wish to control the economy at a desired level, we must offset the effects of variations in forces outside our direct control. To do this fully and without inducing unstable oscillations requires a mixture of proportional, derivative, and integral policies.

One of the themes of our approach to economic policy making is that the use of the instruments should not be regarded as costless. The designer of optimal policy should attach some weight to the cost of using particular instruments. This point may be illustrated by an extremely simple example which pays explicit attention to dynamics.

Assume as before that real national income has fallen below its desired level. This may be offset by a step increase of government expenditure to a new level. The effect of raising government spending by an amount $\Delta G$ is to raise the time path of national income by an amount

$$\Delta Y = \frac{\Delta G}{1-a}(1 - a^{t+1}) \tag{7.11}$$

We now assume that the government has a time horizon of $T$ periods, but that it does not discount the future. The total gain in real income accumulated from the time policy takes effect is

$$V = \frac{\Delta G}{1-a} \sum_{t=0}^{T} (1 - a^{t+1}) \tag{7.12}$$

The marginal gain from a unit increase in government expenditure is

$$\frac{1}{1-a} \sum_{t=0}^{T} (1 - a^{t+1}).$$

This has to be compared with the marginal cost of increasing government expenditure, i.e. a measure of the disutility that results from such action.

In figure 7.11 the horizontal line measures the increase in income resulting from increasing government expenditure. (We assume that $\Delta G$ cannot exceed that level, $\Delta G^*$, which would ultimately bring about full employment.) The curve marked $f'(\Delta G)$ measures the marginal cost of increasing government expenditure. Where the curves intersect determines the optimum level of increase in government expenditure which in turn determines the amount of spare capacity that is taken up.

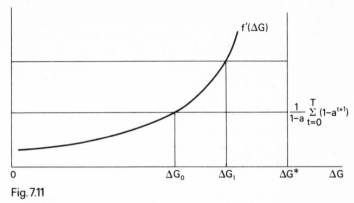

Fig. 7.11

An examination of the expression for the marginal gain shows that it increases when the time horizon increases or when the marginal propensity to spend increases. (The marginal gain may be rewritten as $\sum_{t=0}^{T} \sum_{r=0}^{t} a^r$. This is clearly an increasing function of $a$ and $T$. (Thus, the longer is the time horizon that the government takes into account or the larger is the marginal propensity to spend, the larger will be the increase in government expenditure. The higher horizontal line in figure 7.11 corresponds to one or other of these changes and leads to a larger increase in government expenditure.

What we have shown in a rather primitive way is how the government might respond to the existence of excess capacity. The more real output a given increase in expenditure will generate and the longer the period of time for which it generates it, the larger will the increase in expenditure be. In addition, the less costly it is to change the policy instrument, the more closely government expenditure will be adapted to that level which generates full employment.

If the government also dislikes decreases in public expenditure (because, for example, the expenditure is to meet long range objectives which it does not want to deviate from in either direction), a similar result will apply to situations of excess demand. The government will remove that up to the point where the marginal benefit equals the marginal cost of reducing public expenditure. Again, the more effective public expenditure is in reducing excess demand and the longer the period for which the effect holds, the larger will be the cut in public expenditure and the more excess demand will be removed.

In sum, the average level of government expenditure may be set so that on average the economy is in a state of full employment. If there are costs in varying government expenditure from this level, external shocks to the system will be only partially offset by economic policy. The extent of the offsets will be determined by the benefits and costs of policy changes. The higher the former and the lower the latter, the more will policy be used to diminish the variance of national income.

This kind of analysis can be taken a good deal further, and a more mathematical but still elementary example is given in Appendix 2. The last part of this chapter is devoted to a discussion of the two target/two instrument problem which was considered in static terms in chapter 4. The two targets may be regarded as the balance of payments and national income; the two instruments are government expenditure and taxation. The model may be set out simply as follows:

$$Y = a_1 G - a_2 T + a_3 \tag{7.13}$$

$$B = -b_1 G + b_2 T + b_3 \tag{7.14}$$

The combinations of $G$ and $T$ which cause $Y$ to be at a given level lie on a straight line with a slope of $a_2/a_1$. The combinations of $G$ and $T$ which cause $B$ to be at a given level lie on a straight line with a slope of $b_2/b_1$. In chapter 4 we assumed that the marginal import content of private consumer spending was higher than the marginal import content of government spending. This implied that $a_2/a_1$ was less than $b_2/b_1$. In figure 7.12 the lines $M_0 M_0$ and $Y_0 Y_0$ are drawn appropriately. The equilibrium position is where the two lines intersect at $\alpha$.

Let us consider what meaning can be attached to the slopes of the two lines. The fraction $a_2/a_1$ measures the effect of $T$ on $Y$ relative to the effect of $G$ on $Y$. The fraction $b_2/b_1$ measures the effect of $T$ on $B$ relative to the effect of $G$ on $B$. It is possible that both these fractions are greater than unity, implying that $T$ is the more effective instrument with respect to both targets, or they may

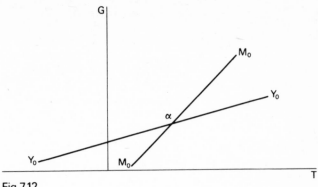

Fig. 7.12

both be less than unity implying that $G$ is the more effective instrument, or one may be greater than unity and the other less than unity, implying $T$ is absolutely the more effective instrument for one target and $G$ for the other. The fact that $a_2/a_1$ is less than $b_2/b_1$ tells us nothing about which instrument is absolutely the most effective since this depends on the value of these fractions relative to unity. What we can infer, however, is something about the *comparative* advantage of each instrument. This is that $T$ has a comparatively larger effect on $B$, and that $G$ has a comparatively larger effect on $Y$. This analogy between the theory of economic policy and the pure theory of international trade is due to Mundell, and is of some considerable interest. It leads to the suggestion that just as it may pay countries to specialise in the production of those commodities in which they have a comparative advantage, so policy instruments may be specialised to the control of those targets in which they have a comparative advantage. In other words, taxation would be used to correct deviations in the balance of payments from its desired value, and government spending to correct deviations in national income from its desired value.

In figure 7.13 we start from an initial position, $\alpha_1$, in which the balance of payments is excessively in surplus, and there is unemployment. Taxes are cut and government expenditure is increased until $\alpha_2$ is reached where we have full employment, but still too large a balance of payments surplus. The suggested rule is then to introduce a tax cut to control the balance of payments. This would move us to $\alpha_3$ where the balance of payments is

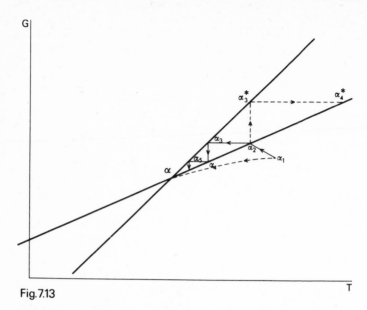

Fig. 7.13

satisfactory, but we have over-full employment. The suggested rule
is now to leave taxes alone and cut government expenditure. This
moves us to $\alpha_4$, etc. It can be seen that successive applications of the
rule give rise to a dynamic process converging on the equilibrium, $\alpha$.
Indeed, it is easy to see that starting anywhere in the diagram, and
applying the rule generates an equilibrating process, albeit one which
oscillates.

Suppose instead of following this rule, we reverse it and use
government spending to deal with the balance of payments and
taxation to deal with the home economy. At $\alpha_2$ the balance of
payments is in surplus and we can attempt to remove this by increasing government spending. We will then get to $\alpha_3^*$ where the balance
of payments is satisfactory, but there is over-full employment.
If we attempt to remove this by tax increases, we get to $\alpha_4^*$. It is
easy to see that what is now happening is an explosive dynamic
process which moves further and further away from equilibrium.

It seems, therefore, that the Mundell rule does make sense
and helps to avoid the danger of an explosive departure from equilibrium. It is by no means perfect, of course, because of the possibility
that it generates oscillations. But in situations where the decision

maker lacks the information on which to base a more subtle rule, or the capacity to determine it and put it into practice, the simple rule may be the best available.

The optimal path itself is represented by the dotted line in the diagram. It differs from the Mundell path in that it converges to equilibrium without cycles. The reason for this is twofold: (a) optimum policy will take into account the relative deviations of the target variables from their desired values, and (b) optimal policy will not specialise the instruments completely to the targets, but only partially. In other words, $G$ will be used largely to control $Y$, but not entirely, and $T$ will be used largely to control $B$, but not entirely.

We can set out the analysis in the form of a simple mathematical model by adding time subscripts to equations (7.13) and (7.14).

$$Y_t = a_1 G_t - a_2 T_t + a_3 \tag{7.15}$$

$$B_t = -b_1 G_t + b_2 T_t + b_3 \tag{7.16}$$

Assume now $G_t$ and $T_t$ are used to control $Y_t$ and $B_t$, respectively, according to the following rules

$$G_t = G_{t-1} + k_1(Y^* - Y_{t-1}); \qquad 0 < k_1 < 1 \tag{7.17}$$

$$T_t = T_{t-1} + k_2(B^* - B_{t-1}); \qquad 0 < k_2 < 1 \tag{7.18}$$

where $Y^*$ and $B^*$ are the desired values of $Y$ and $B$. Note that the effect of these rules is to change the instruments when the target variables differ from their desired values, and that the rules themselves do not include the coefficients, $a_i$ and $b_i$, i.e. they do not appear to depend on knowledge of the structure of the model.

We may now solve to get the following expressions

$$Y_t = a_1 G_{t-1} - a_2 T_{t-1} - a_1 k_1 Y_{t-1} + a_2 k_2 B_{t-1} + a_1 k_1 Y^*$$
$$\quad - a_2 k_2 B^* + a_3 \tag{7.19}$$

$$B_t = -b_1 G_{t-1} + b_2 T_{t-1} + b_1 k_1 Y_{t-1} - b_2 k_2 B_{t-1}$$
$$\quad - b_1 k_1 Y^* + b_2 k_2 B^* + b_3 \tag{7.20}$$

The dynamics of this model depend on the characteristic equation of the homogeneous part:

$$\lambda^2 + (k_1 a_1 + k_2 b_2)\lambda + k_1 k_2 (a_1 b_2 - b_1 a_2) = 0 \tag{7.21}$$

We have assumed that the coefficient of $\lambda$ and the constant term are both positive. This means that the roots, if they are real, are both negative. The discriminant is

$$(k_1a_1 + k_2b_2)^2 - 4k_1k_2(a_1b_2 - b_1a_2)$$

$$= (k_1a_1 - k_2b_2)^2 + 4k_1k_2b_1a > 0 \tag{7.22}$$

This means that both roots are real.

We can make $k_1$ and $k_2$ sufficiently small so that the following conditions hold

$$k_1a_1 + k_2b_2 < 1 \tag{7.23}$$

$$k_1k_2(a_1b_2 - b_1a_2) < 1 \tag{7.24}$$

It then follows that each root is negative but less than unity in absolute value.

What we have shown is that, if instruments are assigned to targets following the principles of comparative advantage, the system will be stable in the sense of converging to an equilibrium. It will not do this smoothly, however, but will fluctuate. Note also that for the policy to work it is also necessary that the instruments do not over-respond to the targets.

### Appendix 1

The problem we wish to discuss concerns the effects of the delay in government action on the stability of the economic system. We assume that except for the government the behaviour of the economy can be represented by a first-order difference equation:

$$Y_t = -aY_{t-1} + G_t + A, \qquad 0 > a > -1 \tag{7.25}$$

Government expenditure is related to income at time $t - n$, and we assume that it is lagged at least two periods:

$$G_t = -bY_{t-n}, \qquad b > 0; n \geqslant 2 \tag{7.26}$$

We have, therefore,

$$Y_t = -aY_{t-1} - bY_{t-n} + A \tag{7.27}$$

We wish to know what is the effect on the stability of the system of increasing $n$.

The dynamic behaviour of the system depends on the roots of the polynomial

$$f(X) = X^n + aX^{n-1} + b \qquad (7.28)$$

When we wish to consider explicitly the variation of $n$, we may write the function as $f(X, n)$.

Let us note the following characteristics of $f(X)$.

$$f(0) = f(-a) = b > 0 \qquad (7.29)$$

$$f(1) = 1 + a + b > 0 \qquad (7.30)$$

$$\begin{rcases} f(-1) = 1 - a + b > 0, & \text{for } n \text{ even} \\ \qquad = -1 + a + b \gtrless 0, \text{for } n \text{ odd} \end{rcases} \qquad (7.31)$$

$$f'(X) = nX^{n-1} + a(n-1)X^{n-2} = X^{n-2}[nX + a(n-1)] \qquad (7.32)$$

$$f'\left(-\frac{a(n-1)}{n}\right) = 0 \qquad (7.33)$$

$$f'(0) = 0, \qquad \text{for } t > 2 \qquad (7.34)$$

$$f'(1) = n + a(n-1) > 0 \qquad (7.35)$$

$$\begin{rcases} f'(-1) = -n + a(n-1) < 0, & \text{for } n \text{ even} \\ \qquad = n - a(n-1) > 0, & \text{for } n \text{ odd} \end{rcases} \qquad (7.36)$$

$$f'(X) < 0, \qquad \text{for } 0 < X < \frac{-a(n-1)}{n} \qquad (7.37)$$

NB: $X^{n-2} > 0$, and $nX + a(n-1) < 0$

$$f'(X) > 0, \qquad \text{for } X > \frac{-a(n-1)}{n} \qquad (7.38)$$

Since $f(X)$ has a turning point at $-a(n-1)/n$, either it has two zeros for positive real $X$ or no positive real roots at all. This is true for all $n \geq 2$.

Examining $f'(X)$ further, it is easy to see that $nX + a(n-1)$ is negative if $X$ is negative; thus, the sign of $f'(X)$ for $X$ negative is determined by the sign of $X^{n-2}$.

$$f'(X) < 0, \qquad \text{for } X < 0 \text{ and } n \text{ even} \bigg\}$$
$$> 0, \qquad \text{for } X < 0 \text{ and } n \text{ odd} \bigg\} \qquad (7.39)$$

This means that $f'(0)$ gives a maximum for $n$ odd and a point of inflexion for $n$ even and greater than 2. It follows that for $n$ even there are no negative real roots. Since $f(X) \to X^n \to -\infty$, there will be only one negative real root if $n$ is odd.

An immediate conclusion, therefore, is that with $n$ even $f(X)$ has at most two real roots, and with $n$ odd at most three real roots. Since $f(X)$ has $n$ roots altogether, it must have some complex roots for $n \geqslant 4$. In other words, lagged government expenditure must induce cyclical behaviour into national income if the lag is at least four periods.

From equation (7.30), $f(1)$ is positive and $f'(X)$ is positive for $X > -a(n-1)/n$, which is less than unity. This means that any positive real root is less than unity.

Note also from equation (7.35) that $f'(1)$ increases with $n$, i.e. $\partial f'(1)/\partial n = 1 + a > 0$. Thus $f(1, n)$ does not vary with $n$, but $f'(1, n)$ increases as $n$ increases, i.e. $f(1, n_1)$ cuts $f(1, n_2)$ from below if $n_1$ is greater than $n_2$.

Consider also from equation (7.32) $f'(-a)$. This is equal to $(-a)^{n-2}(-a)$, i.e. $(-a)^{n-1}$. This decreases with $n$. Since from equation (7.29) $f(-a, n)$ does not vary with $n$, this means that $f(-a, n_1)$ cuts $f(-a, n_2)$ from above if $n_1$ is greater than $n_2$. This means that the largest positive real root is less than $-a$ and decreases as $n$ increases. It is also easy to see that $f[-a(n-1)/n]$ increases as $n$ increases, so that for $n$ sufficiently large there are no positive real roots at all.

Let us now examine the negative real root when $n$ is odd. As we increase $n$ (by 2 to keep it odd) we have

$$f(X, n+2) - f(X, n) = (X^2 - 1)(X + a)X^{n-1} \qquad (7.40)$$

Since $n - 1$ is even, $X^{n-1}$ is positive. The second term, $X + a$, is negative since we are considering only negative values of $X$.

Thus, we have

$$f(X, n+2) > f(X, n) \qquad -1 < X < 0 \bigg\}$$
$$f(x, n+2) < f(X, n) \qquad X < -1 \bigg\} \qquad (7.41)$$

Thus, $f(X, n + 2)$ lies above $f(X, n)$ between zero and minus one, and below it beyond minus one. Moving from right to left it cuts $f(X, n)$ from above.

Note from equation (7.31) that $f(-1, n + 2) = f(-1, n)$.

Suppose now that $-1 + a + b > 0$. Since $f'(X)$ is positive by equation (7.36), its negative real root will be greater than unity in absolute value. If, however, $-1 + a + b < 0$, its negative real root will be less than unity in absolute value.

If we consider the former case, because $f(X, n + 2)$ cuts $f(X, n)$ from above, it must intersect the abscissa to the right of the point where $f(x, n)$ is zero. In other words, its negative real root will remain above unity in absolute value, but will be less than the negative real root of $f(X, n)$.

In the latter case the reverse happens. The negative real root of $f(X, n + 2)$ is larger in absolute value than that of $f(X, n)$ but remains less than unity.

All of this leads to the rather curious conclusion that increasing the delay to which the government's action is subject is likely to introduce cycles into the economy but, as far as the real roots are concerned, cannot give rise to a root of absolute value greater than unity where one did not exist before.

Turning now to consider variations in $b$, as this increases two sorts of results follow. The effect of increasing $b$ is to shift $f(X)$ vertically by the increase in $b$. This means that given $n$, for a sufficiently large increase in $b$, $f(X)$ will not intersect the abscissa for positive $X$ at all, i.e. there will be no positive real roots. For $n$ even this then implies that there will be no real roots at all. For $n$ odd, for a sufficiently large increase in $b$ the negative real root will be greater than unity in absolute value.

### Appendix 2

A simple control problem concerns the optimum response of the instrument, in this case government spending, to a fall in exogenous expenditure. The dynamic model is as follows, where the symbols have their usual meaning.

$$\dot{Y} = aY + A + G; \qquad a < 0 \tag{7.42}$$

It is assumed that the government's preference function is

related to deviations of $Y$ and $G$ from their respective desired values, $Y^*$ and $G^*$. The government is also assumed to have a time horizon, but does not discount the future. Its preference function is as follows

$$W = \int_0^\tau [b_1(Y - Y^*)^2 + b_2(G - G^*)^2]\,dt \qquad (7.43)$$

The problem is to maximise $W$ subject to equation (7.42).

One method of solving this problem is based on the consideration of the following expression

$$J = \int_0^\tau [b_1(Y - Y^*)^2 + b_2(G - G^*)^2] + \lambda[aY + A + G - \dot{Y}]\,dt \qquad (7.44)$$

This may be rewritten as

$$J = \int_0^\tau (H - \lambda\dot{Y})\,dt \qquad (7.45)$$

where

$$H = b_1(Y - Y^*)^2 + b_2(G - G^*)^2 + \lambda[aY + A + G] \qquad (7.46)$$

$H$ is referred to as the *Hamiltonian.*

Let us now consider the integration of $\lambda\dot{Y}$. This may be done by parts to yield

$$\int_0^\tau \lambda\,\dot{Y}dt = \lambda(\tau)\,Y(\tau) \quad -\lambda(0)\,Y(0) - \int_0^\tau\dot{\lambda}\,Y\,dt \qquad (7.47)$$

This may be inserted in (7.45) to obtain

$$J = \int_0^\tau (H + \dot{\lambda}\,Y)dt - \lambda(\tau)\,Y(\tau) \quad + \lambda(0)\,Y(0) \qquad (7.48)$$

In our problem $Y(0)$, the initial level of natural income, is given. We have not added any special term to $W$ to constrain $Y(\infty)$.

Given the time horizon, i.e. the terminal date, consider how $J$ varies as we vary the instrument, $G$, through time.

$$\Delta J = -\lambda(\tau)\Delta Y(\tau) + \int_0^\tau \left[\left(\frac{\partial H}{\partial Y} + \dot{\lambda}\right)\Delta Y + \frac{\partial H}{\partial G}\Delta G\right]dt \qquad (7.49)$$

We could in principle now consider how $\Delta Y$ relates to $\Delta G$, but an easier procedure is available. The $\lambda$ are a set of undetermined multipliers the values of which we are free to choose. Let us choose them, therefore, so that the coefficient of $\Delta Y$ is zero, i.e.

$$\frac{\partial H}{\partial Y} + \dot{\lambda} = 0 \tag{7.50}$$

from equation (7.46). This means that

$$2b_1 (Y - Y^*) + \lambda a + \dot{\lambda} = 0 \tag{7.51}$$

We are now left with

$$\int_0^\tau \frac{\partial H}{\partial G} \Delta G \, dt$$

If $J$ is to be a maximum this means that $\Delta J$ must be zero for all $\Delta G$; thus, $\partial H/\partial G$ must be zero.

$$\frac{\partial H}{\partial G} = 0 \qquad 0 \leqslant t \leqslant \tau \tag{7.52}$$

from equation (7.46); this implies

$$2b_2(G - G^*) + \lambda = 0 \tag{7.53}$$

To find the optimum time path for the instrument $b$ we have to solve equations (7.42), (7.51) and (7.53).

By taking time derivatives in equation (7.53) we obtain an expression for $\dot{G}$

$$\dot{\lambda} = -2b_2\dot{G} \tag{7.54}$$

We may use (7.53) and (7.54) to substitute $G$ for $\dot{\lambda}$ in (7.51) to obtain

$$\dot{G} = \frac{b_1}{b_2} Y - aG - \frac{b_1}{b_2} Y^* + aG^* \tag{7.55}$$

Equations (7.42) and (7.55) are a dynamic system in $Y$ and $G$ which may be written in matrix terms as follows

$$\begin{bmatrix} \dot{Y} \\ \dot{G} \end{bmatrix} = \begin{bmatrix} a & 1 \\ b_1/b_2 & -a \end{bmatrix} \begin{bmatrix} Y \\ G \end{bmatrix} + \begin{bmatrix} A \\ aG^* - (Y^*b_1/b_2) \end{bmatrix} \tag{7.56}$$

A particular solution is obtained when $\dot{Y} = \dot{G} = 0$

$$\begin{bmatrix} Y \\ G \end{bmatrix} = -\begin{bmatrix} a & 1 \\ b_1/b_2 & -a \end{bmatrix}^{-1} \begin{bmatrix} A \\ aG* - (Y*b_1/b_2) \end{bmatrix} \tag{7.57}$$

$$= \frac{1}{a^2 + (b_1/b_2)} \begin{bmatrix} -a & -1 \\ -b_1/b_2 & a \end{bmatrix} \begin{bmatrix} A \\ aG* - (Y*b_1/b_2) \end{bmatrix}$$

An examination of the homogeneous part of (7.56) leads to a characteristic equation as follows:

$$-(a-r)(a+r) - \frac{b_1}{b_2} = 0 \tag{7.58}$$

$$(a^2 - r^2) + \frac{b_1}{b_2} = 0$$

$$r = \pm \left( \frac{b_1}{b_2} + a^2 \right)^{1/2}$$

Assuming $b_1$ and $b_2$ have the same sign the expression inside the brackets is positive. The homogeneous part of the solution for $Y$ will then be of the form:

$$c \exp -\left( \frac{b_1}{b_2} + a^2 \right)^{1/2} t + g \exp \left( \frac{b_1}{b_2} + a^2 \right)^{1/2} t$$

$c$ and $g$ are constrained by the initial value of $Y$. For the system to converge to an equilibrium value we must put $g$ equal to zero, and determine $c$ accordingly. Thus, we have

$$Y = c \exp -\left( \frac{b_1}{b_2} + a^2 \right)^{1/2} t - \left\{ \left[ a(A+G) - \frac{b_1}{b_2} Y* \right] \middle| \left( \frac{b_1}{b_2} + a^2 \right) \right\} \tag{7.59}$$

This means that

$$Y(0) = c - \left\{ \left[ a(A+G*) - \frac{b_1}{b_2} Y* \right] \middle| \left( \frac{b_1}{b_2} + a^2 \right) \right\} \tag{7.60}$$

$$Y = \left[ Y(0) + \left\{ \left[ a(A+G*) - \frac{b_1}{b_2} Y* \right] \middle| \left( \frac{b_1}{b_2} + a^2 \right) \right\} \right]$$

$$\times \left[ \exp -\left( \frac{b_1}{b_2} + a^2 \right)^{1/2} t - \left\{ \left[ a(A+G*) - \frac{b_1}{b_2} Y* \right] \middle| \left( \frac{b_1}{b_2} + a^2 \right) \right\} \right]$$

$$\tag{7.61}$$

Let us now define $Y'$ as $-(A + G^*)/a$. $Y'$ is the equilibrium level of income, given exogenous spending, when government expenditure is at its most desirable level. Equation (7.61) may now be rewritten as

$$Y = \left[ \left( \frac{b_1}{b_2} Y^* + a^2 Y' \right) \bigg/ \left( a^2 + \frac{b_1}{b_2} \right) \right]$$
$$+ \left[ \left( \frac{b_1}{b_2} [Y(0) - Y^*] + a^2 [Y(0) - Y'] \right) \bigg/ \left( a^2 + \frac{b_1}{b_2} \right) \right]$$
$$\exp - \left( a^2 + \frac{b_1}{b_2} \right)^{1/2} t \qquad (7.62)$$

Thus, national income tends to a weighted average of its own most desired value and the value determined by the most desired level of government expenditure. If its initial value is above this level, it falls smoothly towards it; if its initial value is below this level, it rises smoothly towards it. The speed with which this happens depends on $[a^2 + (b_1/b_2)]$. It can be seen that the larger is the absolute value of $a$, i.e. the faster the system adjusts automatically, the larger is the speed of controlled adjustment. Similarly, the larger is $b_1$ relative to $b_2$, the larger is the speed of controlled adjustment, i.e. the more significant are deviations of $Y$ from its desired value compared with deviations of $G$ from its desired value, the faster will the former be corrected by means of the latter. Note also that the system when not controlled adjusts at the rate $a$ which is less than the controlled speed of adjustment $[a^2 + (b_1/b_2)]^{1/2}$.

We now turn to a solution for the time path for $G$. This is as follows:

$$G = h \cdot \exp - \left( \frac{b_1}{b_2} + a^2 \right)^{1/2} t + \left[ \left( a^2 G^* - a \frac{b_1}{b_2} Y^* - \frac{b_1}{b_2} A \right) \bigg/ \left( a^2 + \frac{b_1}{b_2} \right) \right] \qquad (7.63)$$

The expression $(-aY^* - A)$ may be defined as the level to set $G$ at to achieve the desired level of $Y$, given the level of exogenous spending. Write this as $G'$. Equation (7.62) may be rewritten as

$$G = h \cdot \exp - \left( \frac{b_1}{b_2} + a^2 \right)^{1/2} t + \left[ \left( a^2 G^* + \frac{b_1}{b_2} G' \right) \bigg/ \left( a^2 + \frac{b_1}{b_2} \right) \right] \qquad (7.64)$$

Thus, government spending also tends to a weighted average of its own most desired value and the value determined by the most desired value of national income.

How do we determine $h$? We can do this by assuming $G$ satisfies equation (7.42). This lends to the following equation

$$G = -\left[a + \left(a^2 + \frac{b_1}{b_2}\right)^{1/2}\right]$$

$$\left[\left(\frac{b_1}{b_2}\left[Y(0) - Y^*\right] + a^2\left[Y(0) - Y'\right]\right) \middle/ \left(a^2 + \frac{b_1}{b_2}\right)\right] \cdot$$

$$\exp - \left(a + \frac{b_1}{b_2}\right)^{1/2} t + \left[\left(a^2 G^* + \frac{b_1}{b_2} G'\right) \middle/ \left(a^2 + \frac{b_1}{b_2}\right)\right]$$

This in turn may be rewritten                                    (7.65)

$$G = -a\left[a + \left(a^2 + \frac{b_1}{b_2}\right)^{1/2}\right]\left[\left(\frac{b_1}{b_2}\left[G(0) - G'\right] + a^2\left[G(0) - G^*\right]\right) \middle/ \right.$$

$$\left(a^2 + \frac{b_1}{b_2}\right)\right] \exp - \left(a + \frac{b_1}{b_2}\right)^{1/2} t + \left[\left(a^2 G^* + \frac{b_1}{b_2} G'\right) \middle/ \left(a^2 + \frac{b_1}{b_2}\right)\right]$$

$$(7.66)$$

What this means essentially is that $Y$ and $G$ are varying inversely through time. If one is rising to its ultimate value, the other is falling. Note that we can express $G$ as a function of $Y$:

$$G = -\left[a + \left(a^2 + \frac{b_1}{b_2}\right)^{1/2}\right] Y + B \qquad\qquad (7.67)$$

where $B$ is a constant.

In other words, we have derived two sorts of control law. We can express the behaviour of the instrument as a path through time. This we have done, for example, in equation (7.66). Such a law is sometimes called an *open-loop control law*. Alternatively, we can express the behaviour of the instrument as a function of the behaviour of the target. This we have done in equation (7.67). Such a law is sometimes called a *closed-loop control law*.

# 8
# Economic forecasting and economic prediction

In this chapter we consider those aspects of economic policy making connected with taking a view of the future course of events. Not all policy making involves this. Some of it may be determined within a static framework. In other cases the future may be unforecastable, but nonetheless rational action is possible. This kind of situation has been discussed in chapter 6, on risk and uncertainty.

In this chapter we discuss two matters: firstly, we give an elementary exposition of the way forecasting is done in practice; secondly, we consider the theory of prediction. Although the two look as if they ought to be related, usually they are not. Indeed, the very terminology differs; forecasting refers to practice, prediction to theory, and it sometimes looks as if never the twain shall meet.

One is tempted to distinguish the two by suggesting that practical forecasting is subjective and involves judgement while prediction is objective. This is surely not true because forecasting must contain objective elements (e.g. the data and some kind of economic model), and prediction cannot ignore the problems of model formulation and estimation which are in themselves an art.

A more useful point is that much forecasting is non-objective in the sense that its method is not specified in such a way that someone else can follow it and reproduce the forecast. It is also true that the criterion determining what is or is not a good forecast is left vague as is the method of testing and evaluating the forecast. This can hardly be regarded as a satisfactory state of affairs.

What is true, however, is that economic theory and econometrics

177

are in a primitive state so that no one model of the economy is universally accepted, and no model is able to incorporate all the available information. Any researcher must have grave doubts about the equations he has estimated and is aware of information (usually of a qualitative kind) that he has been obliged to neglect. In making a forecast, therefore, account must be taken of all this, an approach which can be encompassed under the general heading of judgement. It seems reasonable to suggest, however, that such judgements should be explicit, systematic, and capable of evaluation.

As an example, the forecaster may be basing his work on a particular estimate of the marginal propensity to consume. Although he is aware that other variables are important in the determination of consumer spending, he may have failed to incorporate them satisfactorily in his estimation. He may, therefore, be obliged to take account of them in an *ad hoc* manner. Thus, it may become clear that everybody expects an increase in the rate of VAT in the budget. For the first quarter of the year it would then make sense to add something to the forecast of consumer spending to allow for this anticipations phenomenon.

Such adjustments are quite proper provided that they fulfil the criteria mentioned in the previous paragraph. In particular, emphasis must be laid on evaluation; there must be a continual backward look to see whether judgements of this kind have really improved forecasting performance.

Let us now look at the subject in practice (suitably simplified, of course).

In order to see more clearly the problem of economic forecasting we set out national income and its components in the form of a tableau:

| $t$ | $Y$ | $C$ | $G$ | $I_1$ | $I_2$ | $E$ | $M$ |
|------|------|------|------|------|------|------|------|
| 1968 | 35.7 | 22.7 | 5.9 | 3.9 | 3.2 | 7.7 | 7.7 |
| 1969 | 36.5 | 22.8 | 5.8 | 4.2 | 3.0 | 8.6 | 7.9 |
| 1970 | 37.2 | 23.4 | 5.9 | 4.3 | 3.0 | 9.0 | 8.4 |
| 1971 | 37.8 | 24.0 | 6.1 | 4.0 | 3.0 | 9.4 | 8.7 |

(where $I_1$ is capital formation in the private sector and $I_2$ capital formation in the public sector).

These are at 1963 market prices and appear in *National Income and Expenditure 1972*, which was published in the autumn of 1973, but much of the information of which was available to the government in the spring of 1972. What the forecaster has at his disposal, therefore, is a history of the variables he is interested in forecasting and a blank sheet corresponding to the same variables in the period to be forecast. It is the blank sheet that has to be filled out. In practice, of course, the tableau will be broader because he has many other variables which he is interested in forecasting. It may also be finer in that he may wish to forecast the variables in quarterly rather than annual terms. But our example contains enough to convey the essence of his task.

He also has at his disposal a great deal of other information. Apart from more detailed knowledge of these variables (e.g. division of consumer expenditure between durables and non-durables, or division of exports between the markets they are destined for), he may also have so-called anticipations data derived from asking samples of businessmen and households what they intend to do, or what their expectations are. Typical of this information would be the results of an investment survey which asked businessmen whether and to what extent they proposed to raise their investment next year compared with this. The forecaster will also have available all sorts of casual information made up of statements by leading businessmen of their view of the economy, reflections of opinions in newspapers and, of course, forecasts made by many other people of varying degrees of technicality and objectivity.

Separate from that there is economic theory which postulates certain relationships between the variables to be forecast and applied econometrics which will have endeavoured to estimate and test these relationships: one between consumer non-durable spending once and for all. Indeed, economics is noteworthy for the instability, especially in the short term, of some of its crucial relationships. It is also the case that the science is developing, and over time we get a better understanding of what causes what. Thus, at one time, a simple relationship between consumer spending and household disposable income may have been postulated, but later on this may be replaced by two relationships: one between consumer non-durable spending and income and the other between consumer durable spending, the stock of durables, and wealth and income.

One other piece of information at the forecaster's disposal, especially if he is in Whitehall, concerns the plans of the public authorities. Government spending and public sector capital formation will be decided up to a pretty high degree of accuracy by the government so that the forecaster may treat these planned values as his forecast values. It should be borne in mind, however, that government policies can change, because circumstances and preferences change (and sometimes because governments change) and, in addition, not even governments are in full control of the business in which they are engaged. Thus, a decision to lower public expenditure (or its rate of growth) may not be capable of being realised in practice, or may be reversed if otherwise national income will fall too far below capacity.

Turning to the past history of the variables to be forecast, it is important to remember that this is not known for certain. Consider, for example, national income for 1968. This is reported as follows:

| Blue Book for | 1969 | £35.4 th.m. |
|---|---|---|
| | 1970 | £35.5 |
| | 1971 | £35.6 |
| | 1972 | £35.7 |
| | 1973 | £35.7 |

In other words, the estimate for gross national product at 1963 market prices for 1968 has been changed in four successive Blue Books, the total change being £300m. Now this is, of course, only a small fraction of the total, being of the general order of 1 per cent. It should be realised, however, that the average annual change in gross national product is about 3 per cent so that the variation in the measurement relative to this is quite large.

Another way of looking at this is to see how the change in income between 1967 and 1968 is reported in various Blue Books. This is as follows:

| | Per cent change in GNP 1967–1968 |
|---|---|
| Blue Book for 1969 | 2.96 |
| 1970 | 3.06 |
| 1971 | 3.10 |
| 1972 | 3.24 |
| 1973 | 3.29 |

Since these are all measurements of the same thing, it is apparent that great caution must be exercised before any meaning is attached to small variations in the rate of change of GNP.

Two last examples are given just to emphasise that the changes are not always in the upwards direction. The following table shows the revision in the figures for exports of goods and services at 1968 prices:

|                      | Per cent change in exports of goods and services 1967–1968 |
|----------------------|-----------------|
| Blue Book for 1969   | 11.53           |
| 1970                 | 12.29           |
| 1971                 | 12.47           |
| 1972                 | 12.23           |

The following table shows the balance of payments on current account for 1968:

|                      | Balance of Payments 1968 |
|----------------------|--------------------------|
| Blue Book for 1969   | −£265 m.                 |
| 1970                 | −£319 m.                 |
| 1971                 | −£288 m.                 |
| 1972                 | −£271 m.                 |
| 1973                 | −£284 m.                 |

Here it looks rather like a cyclical revision where the ultimate figure will be the same as the first estimate!

This leads to an important distinction between the value of a variable as it first appears in a statistical publication and the value it may ultimately settle down at in the same publication many years later. In assessing any forecast, in particular, it is important to distinguish two criteria: (a) error relative to the first measurement of the variable being forecast, (b) error relative to the ultimate measurement of the variable being forecast. In addition, we may distinguish the forecast made at a point of time on the basis of data actually available then from a national forecast made later on the basis of new measurements. Thus, we may consider a forecasting method used in 1972 to forecast national income in 1974 on the basis of the data actually available in 1972. This forecast may be compared with national income of 1974 as it is recorded in 1975, 1976, 1977, etc. The same method may be employed in 1975 to 'forecast' national income in 1974 on the basis of the latest estimates for all sorts of variables up to 1971, i.e. we would then have the 1975 estimate for national income in 1971 rather than the 1972 estimate. These forecasts may then be compared with the actual national income for 1974 as it is estimated in 1975, 1976, 1977, etc. It is possible that a forecasting method which works badly when applied to highly imperfect data, works quite well when applied to much better data. In other words, it may be highly sensitive to errors in the data. Another method may work rather well when applied to imperfect data. but not improve very much when applied to better data. It may be less sensitive to data imperfections which will be an advantage when data are poor but will cause us to forgo some benefit when data are good.

As far as economic policy is concerned we are interested in the accuracy of forecasting before the event so that we can do something about it, if necessary. We are also, presumably, concerned with the actual economic experiences which people have, assuming, of course, that they are reflected in the variables, the measurements of which we have at our disposal. This seems to suggest that what we should chiefly be devoting our energies to is the forecasting of the final estimates of economic variables. Thus, in 1972 we should try to forecast actual national income in 1974, by which is meant the value it will ultimately settle down to in the Blue Books of the future. There are two difficulties with this, however. One is that reported national income is also part of people's experience, namely the experience of economists, economic journalists, business men, officials, etc. Their behaviour will be affected by the earlier published figures and may cause changes in the behaviour of others. For this reason it may be important to forecast earlier estimates of variables as well as the ultimate estimates. To take an example which may appear rather cynical but is not far from recent experience, the state of the balance of payments as first estimated and published can have a major political impact. The government may be anxious, therefore, to forecast that early estimate and influence it by economic policy, and not simply concentrate on the 'true' balance of payments.

This leads on to a second complication, namely that the events that actually occur will be a function of public policy which in turn will be a function of the forecasts that are made, notably the official forecasts. Clearly, if a forecast causes an adjustment in policy, there is no point in comparing the resulting out-turn with the forecast in order to assess its accuracy. If the forecast is to be assessed fairly, some allowance must be made for the effects of the change in policy. This involves the twofold difficulty of identifying the policy changes and estimating their effects. There is also the theoretical difficulty which we have discussed before, namely what do we mean by un-changed policies? Do we mean given total tax revenue, or given tax rates, or given decision rules for adjusting tax rates to circumstances? The forecaster has to specify what he takes as given and proceed from there. Unfortunately, many forecasters do not do that, which makes interpretation and assessment of their efforts rather hard to carry out.

Some forecasters of the national economy have no connection with the government or with the making of public policy. They may forecast national income in order to operate on the stock exchange, or take major investment decisions, or put in a pay claim. Their forecast may then be based not on an assumption of no policy changes, but may try to allow for the policy which they think the government will pursue in the relevant period. In principle, their forecast will consist of two parts: a forecast with unchanged policy and a forecast of policy and its effects. The latter objective may cause these outside forecasters to try and forecast what they think the government forecasts will be, i.e. they are involved in making a forecast of a forecast. (This distinction is not a trivial one. It is quite likely that an outside agency could forecast the economy better than officials can. They may also wish, however, to have as accurate a forecast as possible of what the official forecast is likely to be. If they publish their own 'pure' forecast, they may also be interested in the effect of that on the official forecast!)

To summarise, forecasting in economics is not simply about the question: what is the value of this variable going to be in a particular year? It involves at the very least a correct specification of the vari-able, a whole set of assumptions about what is taken as given, and a description of the forecasting situation. Only then can forecasting be correctly interpreted and eventually satisfactorily assessed.

All of this is rather complicated, but it does serve to emphasise that even the simplest questions concerning what is being forecast are not as simple as all that. More to the point, a method that recognises the imperfections of the data and takes account of the fact that they may be reconstituted is likely to be more satisfactory than one that assumes the data are perfect. It is also true that a method that recognises the imperfections of economic theory and the econometric estimates of economic relationships will be superior to one that assumes that in these areas at least we have full knowledge.

Let us now go on to look more closely at how we would actually set about doing some forecasting. We shall simplify matters considerably, but hopefully this will allow the main points to be made more clearly.

We start from the initial position of the figures for 1971 given at the beginning of the chapter. We make the following assumptions:

(a) The change in consumption is equal to 0.9 times the change in personal disposable income.

(b) The change in personal disposable income equals 0.7 times the change in national income.

(c) The initial excess of exports over imports equal to £0.7 th.m. will disappear in the coming year, i.e. the change in exports minus the change in imports is taken to be equal to £0.7 th.m.

These assumptions give rise to a value of the multiplier of 2.7 and the following formula:

$$\Delta Y^* = 2.7 \, (\Delta G^* + \Delta I_1^* + \Delta I_2^* - 0.7) \tag{8.1}$$

The * beside a variable refers to its forecast value. (Note that the value of the multiplier is rather on the high side. This arises from our desire to keep the analysis as simple as possible).

To make any more progress we are next obliged to assume something about $\Delta G^*$, $\Delta I_1^*$, and $\Delta I_2^*$. Suppose as forecasters independent of the government we come across a document announcing the government's plans to allow public spending to rise by 5 per cent in the coming year. Since $G + I_2$ in 1971 equals 9.1, this means that $\Delta G^* + \Delta I_2$ will equal 0.05 of 9.1, i.e. £0.5th.m. (of course, we may not believe the government, or expect it to be unable to fulfill its plans, or to change its mind, but let us set aside such niceties for the moment.)

Our equation may now be rewritten as

$$\Delta Y^* = 2.7 \, (\Delta I_1^* - 0.2) \tag{8.2}$$

We now need a forecast for $\Delta I_1$, capital formation in the private sector. Let us pretend that we have recently read a survey of business-men's intentions and that this suggests that they are moderately opti-mistic about the coming year. We may have other information as well and this leads us to the view that $I_1$ will rise by 10 per cent, i.e. $\Delta I_1^*$ equals £0.4 th.m.

Our forecast for $\Delta Y^*$ then turns out to be

$$\Delta Y^* = 2.7 \times 0.2 = £0.54 \text{ th.m.} \tag{8.3}$$

This implies a percentage increase of 1.4 per cent.

Now, it is obvious that this forecast depends on the assumptions that have been made. If, for example, a more pessimistic view were taken about private investment or the balance of payments, a lower increase in GDP would have resulted. Equally, a more optimistic view would have led to a higher increase in GDP. Simply by varying the components of exogenous spending any number of different fore-casts can be obtained.

Let us assume, however, that the forecast is regarded as the best possible. It amounts to an increase in gross domestic product less than that usually taken to be the growth in productive capacity of the UK. The result, therefore, would be an increase in unemploy-ment and spare capacity. It is possible that the government would wish to avoid this and might cut the rate of direct taxes. The effect of such a tax cut would be to raise the value of the multiplier.

Let us now go on to make a second forecast based on a rise in the multiplier from, say, 2.7 to 2.8. The relevant formula is

$$\Delta Y^* = \text{(The change in the multiplier} \times \text{the level of} \\ \text{exogenous spending)} + \text{(the original multi-} \\ \text{plier} \times \text{the change in exogenous spending)} \tag{8.4}$$

The second part we have worked out already. The change in the multiplier equals 0.1, and the initial level of exogenous spending is $6.1 + 4.0 + 3.0 + 0.7 = 13.8$. Given this we would expect national income to rise by a further £1.38 th.m. making a total rise of £1.92 th.m. or 5.1 per cent. This would be our forecast conditional on the policy change, i.e. a tax cut leading to a multiplier of 2.8.

Having made a forecast, let us assume time has gone by and we are in a position to compare the forecast with the actual percen-tage change in national income. The position may be as follows:

Percentage change:

| | Forecast | Actual |
|---|---|---|
| $I_1$ | 10 | 5 |
| $G + I_2$ | 5 | 1.5 |
| $E - M$ | -100 | -74 |
| $Y_1$ | 1.4 ⎫ | |
| $Y_2$ | 5.1 ⎭ | 2.1 |

The forecast errors are large. This is true of the components of national income as well as of national income itself. Note, however, that some of the errors are self-cancelling in that, while $I_1$, $I_2$ and $G$ have risen less than expected, $E - M$ has fallen less than expected.

How much of the error in forecasting $Y$ is attributable to errors in forecasting $I_1 + I_2 + G + E - M$? Look again at equation (8.4). It may be written as

$$\Delta Y^* = \Delta m^* A + m \Delta A^* \tag{8.5}$$

where $m$ is the multiplier (we now use $m$ because $M$ designates imports), $A$ is $I_1 + I_2 + G + E - M$, and * refers to forecast values.

A similar expression may also be written for the actual change in national income:

$$\Delta Y = \Delta m A + m \Delta A \tag{8.6}$$

Combining the two we get an expression for the forecast error:

$$\Delta Y - \Delta Y^* = (\Delta m - \Delta m^*)A + (\Delta A - \Delta A^*)m \tag{8.7}$$

that is

Forecast error =
(Part due to errors in forecasting the multiplier)
+ (Part due to errors in forecasting exogenous spending)

In our first forecast $\Delta Y^*$ is £0.54 th.m. and $\Delta Y$ is £0.8 th.m. (i.e. 2.1 per cent of £37.8 th.m.). The actual change in exogenous spending in this period was −£0.15 th.m. Thus, $(\Delta A - \Delta A^*)m$ equals $(-0.15 - 0.2) \, 2.7$, which equals −£.95 th.m. Therefore

$$\Delta Y - \Delta Y^* = 0.8 - 0.54 = 0.26 = (\Delta m - \Delta m^*)A - 0.95 \tag{8.8}$$

Since $A$ equals 13.8, we have

$$\frac{1.21}{13.8} = \Delta m - \Delta m^* = 0.09 \tag{8.9}$$

Since we took the multiplier as constant, $\Delta m^*$ is zero making

$$\Delta m = 0.09$$

In sum, of an error in forecasting the change in $Y$ equal to £0.26 th.m., part is due to an error in forecasting the change in exogenous spending of $-$ £0.95 th.m., and part is due to an error in forecasting the multiplier of £1.21 th.m. The two errors in this case partially compensated each other.

In our second forecast we assumed the multiplier would change by 0.1 from 2.7 to 2.8. In fact it rose by only 0.09. Thus, there is a multiplier error equal to $-0.01 \times 13.8$, or $-0.14$. Our forecast of the change in national income is £1.9 th.m. (i.e. 5.1 per cent of £37.8 th.m.). The error is therefore £0.8 th.m. $-$ £1.9 th.m., i.e. $-$ £1.1 th.m. This is made up of the same error in forecasting exogenous spending, i.e. $-$ £0.95 th.m., and an additional error of $-$ £0.14 th.m. In this case the two errors are in the same direction.

We have, therefore, the rather paradoxical situation that what is an improvement in part of our forecasting worsens the overall forecast. In our second case we very nearly got the changed value of the multiplier right, but in doing so we added to the error in forecasting national income. In the example under discussion this was purely a matter of luck. It could just as well have gone the other way, the error due to mis-forecasting the multiplier being added on to that due to the exogenous variables. Indeed, as a general rule our overall forecast will improve on average as we improve the individual parts that comprise it.

Let us now look more formally and theoretically at the problem of forecasting. At any point of time we have a quantity of available information and a theory of the way the economy or some part of it works. In order to proceed we must also say what constitutes a good or bad forecast. The obvious answer to this is to say that a good forecast is one which comes closest to the actual value of the variable being forecast. This requires us to specify what we mean by closest. In addition, since we are forecasting in conditions of risk and uncertainty, we must recognise that the outcome is subject to random shocks. This suggests that we should modify the criterion to 'closest on average to the actual value'.

The variable to be forecast refers to an event some time in the future. Our theory may tell us that its value will be determined by the values of variables up to the present, and by the values of variables in the future. It seems reasonable to assume that the forecast will be determined by the observed values of the variables up to the present and the predicted values of variables in the future.

As an example, consider the following consumption function.

$$C_{t+2} = a_1 Y_{t+1} + a_3 Y_t + W_{t+2} \qquad (8.10)$$

where $W_{t+2}$ is a random shock. At time $t$ we correctly observe $Y_t$, and in forecasting $C_{t+2}$ it is surely right to use this value in the right-hand side of equation (8.10). But what about $Y_{t+2}$ and $Y_{t+1}$? These too need to be forecast. In order to forecast $C_{t+2}$ we replace $Y_{t+2}$ and $Y_{t+1}$ by their optimum forecasts at time $t$. This also applies to $W_{t+2}$ in so far as it can be forecast. In other words, our forecast becomes

$$\hat{C}_{t+2} = a_1 \hat{Y}_{t+2} + a_2 \hat{Y}_{t+1} + a_3 Y_t + \hat{W}_{t+2} \qquad (8.11)$$

where $\wedge$ refers to the forecast value. Note that $Y_t$ does not have $\wedge$ over it because there we use an actual value.

We have made a little progress but we have still to say what we mean by an optimum forecast for $Y$. To do this let us simplify further and consider the forecast of a variable from its own past values. Let $Y_{t+\tau}$ be the actual value of the variable and $\hat{Y}_{t+\tau}$ be the forecast value. The criterion function in choosing the forecast will be $U(Y_{t+\tau} - \hat{Y}_{t+\tau})$ where $U$ varies inversely with $Y_{t+\tau} - \hat{Y}_{t+\tau}$. This simply reflects the proposition that the closer the forecast is to the true value the happier we are. We wish to maximise $U$ on average, i.e. we wish to make the expected value of $U$ as large as possible.

If now $Y_{t+\tau}$ is determined by its own past values, this may be written as

$$Y_{t+\tau} = f(Y_{t+\tau-1}, \ Y_{t+\tau-2}, \ldots, \ W_{t+\tau}, \ldots) \qquad (8.12)$$

We may think of forecasting as a typical maximisation problem in economics, that is choose $\hat{Y}_{t+\tau}$ so that the expected value of

$U$ is maximised subject to the constraint specified by equation (8.12).

It is not easy to go much further than this without the use of a great deal of mathematics. We can, however, state the main result that can be proved. It is that in a wide variety of circumstances, the optimal forecast for $Y_{t+\tau}$ is its conditional expected value. In other words, the optimal forecast of a variable is the value it would take on average, given the available observations of its past values.

We shall now be more explicit still in order to make the general principles clearer. This involves us in the use of some elementary mathematics and statistics. It is, indeed, a useful example of the application of simple quantitative methods to a problem of general economic policy.

The variable we are hoping to predict is assumed to be linearly related to its own past value and to be affected by an autocorrelated disturbance. (It might, for example, be the percentage change in the general level of world economic activity which we need in analysing the behaviour of the balance of payments.)

$$Y_t = aY_{t-1} + ce_{t-1} + e_t \qquad (8.13)$$

$$E(e_t) = 0$$

where $E$ is the expected value operator.

$$\left.\begin{array}{ll} E(e_t e_{t-\theta}) = 0 & \theta \neq 0 \\ \qquad\quad = \sigma^2 & \theta = 0 \end{array}\right\} \quad |c| < 1; |a| < 1$$

We also have

$$E(Y_t) = aE(Y_{t-1}) = 0$$

In practice, of course, we may interpret the $Y$'s as deviations from a fixed mean, or percentage deviations from a trend line.

Suppose we wish to predict $Y_{t+1}$ at time $t$, i.e. we wish to predict one step ahead. We assume that we know equation (8.1) and have observations on $Y$; $Y_t$, $Y_{t-1}$, $Y_{t-2}$ ... ; as we have already remarked, these act as restraints on our prediction. We do not have observations on $e_t$, $e_{t-1}$ ...; what we do is infer something about $e_t + ce_{t-1}$, by observing the $Y$'s and using this to predict subsequent $Y$'s. Note that in order to do this we are claiming to know something about the $e$'s, usually that they are normal random variables and have a mean of zero. (We also assume that $c$ is less than unity so that $e_t + ce_{t-1}$ is a stationary, stochastic process.) In order to choose the best prediction we must also have a preference (or utility or criterion) function. Again, we assume that utility varies inversely with the square of the prediction error, i.e. large errors are proportionately worse than small errors.

We write $\hat{Y}(t + \theta/t)$ to mean the value of $Y$ at time $t + \theta$ predicted at time $t$. Note as usual the two dates: the date when the prediction is made and the date to which the prediction refers. The prediction error is given by $Y_{t+\theta} - \hat{Y}(t + \theta/t)$, the difference between the realised value and the predicted value.

Our prediction of $Y_{t+1}$ at time $t$ is given by $\hat{Y}(t + 1/t)$. The prediction error is $Y_{t+1} - Y(t + 1/t)$.

The criterion function is given by:

$$E[Y_{t+1} - \hat{Y}(t + 1/t)]^2 = E[aY_t + ce_t + e_{t+1} - \hat{Y}(t + 1/t)]^2$$
(8.14)

$$E[Y_{t+1} - \hat{Y}(t + 1/t)]^2 = \sigma^2 + E[aY_t + ce_t - \hat{Y}(t + 1/t)]^2$$
(8.15)

(Note that $e_{t+1}$ is by definition independent of all previous events.)

It follows that the optimum prediction is given by the following expression which makes the second term on the r.h.s. of (8.15) zero:

$$Y(t + 1/t) = aY_t + ce_t$$
(8.16)

This is pretty well what would be expected on commonsense grounds.

The trouble with this expression is that it depends on $e_t$ which is not observable.

Let us, however, interpret (8.13) as a first-order difference equation in $e_t$. Rewrite it as

$$(e_t - Y_t) + c(e_{t-1} - Y_{t-1}) = -(a + c)Y_{t-1}$$
(8.17)

The solution of this equation is

$$e_t = [e_{t(0)} - Y_{t(0)}](-c)^{t-t(0)} - (a+c)\sum_{r=t(0)}^{t=1}(-c)^{t-1-r}Y_r + Y_t$$
(8.18)

As $t(0) \to -\infty$ the first term on the r.h.s. tends to zero because $c < 1$.

We may then rewrite (8.18) as follows

$$e_t = Y_t - (a + c) \sum_{r=-\infty}^{t-1} (-c)^{t-1-r} Y_r \qquad (8.19)$$

Using this expression for $e_t$ we obtain

$$ce_t + aY_t = (a+c)Y_t - c(a+c) \sum_{r=-\infty}^{t-1} (-c)^{t-1-r} Y_r \qquad (8.20)$$

$$= (a+c)Y_t + (a+c) \sum_{r=-\infty}^{t-1} (-c)^{t-r} Y_r$$

$$= (a+c) \sum_{r=-\infty}^{t} (-c)^{t-r} Y_r$$

Inserting this into (8.16) gives the following expression for the optimal prediction

$$\hat{Y}(t+1/t) = (a+c) \sum_{r=-\infty}^{t} (-c)^{t-r} Y_r \qquad (8.21)$$

The optimum prediction depends on all the past values of the variable to be predicted, but the weight given to any value diminishes the further away it is. In a sense, the policy maker's expectation of the future value of this variable is a distributed lag function of its past values.

Consider now the one-step prediction to be made in the next period:

$$\hat{Y}(t+2/t+1) = (a+c) \sum_{r=-\infty}^{t} (-c)^{t+1-r} Y_r \qquad (8.22)$$

This may be rewritten as

$$\hat{Y}(t+2/t+1) = (a+c)Y_{t+1} + (a+c) \sum_{r=-\infty}^{t} (-c)^{t+1-r} Y_r$$

$$= (a+c)Y_{t+1} - c(a+c) \sum_{r=-\infty}^{t} (-c)^{t-r} Y_r$$

$$= (a+c)Y_{t+1} - c\hat{Y}(t+1/t) \qquad (8.23)$$

Therefore

$$\hat{Y}(t+2/t+1) + c\hat{Y}(t+1/t) = (a+c)Y_{t+1} \qquad (8.24)$$

We have, therefore, a simple difference equation in $\hat{Y}$ which enables us to update the one-step prediction as a new observation appears. Note that, if at time $t$ we predicted $Y_{t+1}$ correctly so that $\hat{Y}(t+1/t) = Y_{t+1}$, our prediction $\hat{Y}(t+2/t+1)$ becomes $aY_{t+1}$. It is not $aY_{t+1}$ in other circumstances as a casual examination of equation (8.13) might lead one to believe.

Our analysis of equation (8.19) and subsequent formulae involve observations on the $Y$'s back to $-\infty$. In fact, we never have such a long list of observations. Assuming that we have enough observations to estimate equation (8.13), we must treat equation (8.19) as holding approximately and use as our basic formula:

$$e_t = -(a+c) \sum_{r=t(0)}^{t} (-c)^{t-1-r} Y_r + Y_t \tag{8.19}$$

Our formula for prediction then becomes

$$\hat{Y}(t+1/t) = (a+c) \sum_{r=t(0)}^{t} (-c)^{t-r} Y_r \tag{8.21}$$

(In fact, assuming $e_{t(0)} = Y_{t(0)}$ for some $t$, this relationship is not approximate but exact.)

We should now relate our prediction of $Y_t$ to our economic policy or control of $Y_t$. We delay this until the next chapter.

Instead we take this discussion a little further by considering the two-step prediction, i.e. predicting $Y_{t+2}$ at time $t$. To ease the exposition we introduce the backward shift operator, $B$. $BX_{t+1} = X_t$ for any variable $X$.

We may rewrite equation (8.13) as

$$Y_t = aBY_t + cBe_t + e_t \tag{8.13*}$$

or

$$Y_t(1-aB) = (1+cB)e_t$$

or

$$Y_t = \frac{1+cB}{1-aB} e_t$$

Since we are considering two steps ahead we should bear in mind the following

$$Y_{t+2} = \frac{1+cB}{1-aB} e_{t+2} \tag{8.25}$$

We may rewrite this as

$$Y_{t+2} = \frac{1 - aB + cB + aB}{1 - aB} e_{t+2} \tag{8.26}$$

$$= e_{t+2} + \frac{(c + a)}{1 - aB} B e_{t+2}$$

$$= e_{t+2} + \frac{c + a}{1 - aB} e_{t+1}$$

We may rewrite this further as

$$Y_{t+2} = e_{t+2} + \frac{(c+ a)(1 - aB + aB)}{1 - aB} e_{t+1} \tag{8.27}$$

$$= e_{t+2} + (c + a)e_{t+1} + \frac{a(c + a)B}{1 - aB} e_{t+1}$$

$$= e_{t+2} + (a + c) e_{t+1} + \frac{a(a + c)}{1 - aB} e_t$$

For the third term on the r.h.s. we may substitute an expression in $Y$ to get

$$Y_{t+2} = e_{t+2} + (a + c)e_{t+1} + \frac{a(a + c)}{1 + cB} Y_t \tag{8.28}$$

Thus, we have separated the unpredictable elements of $Y_{t+2}$ from the predictable past.

If we now proceed as before, the expected value of the squared prediction error is given by

$$E[Y_{t+2} - \hat{Y}(t + 2/t)]^2 = [1 + (a + c)^2]\sigma^2$$
$$+ \left[ E \frac{a(a + c)}{1 + cB} Y_t - \hat{Y}(t + 2/t) \right]^2 \tag{8.29}$$

This is at a minimum when

$$Y(t + 2/t) = \frac{a(a + c)}{1 + cB} Y_t \tag{8.30}$$

It is as well to mention here that the introduction of the operator $B$ has not removed the infinite series problem, but merely converted it into a notionally more manageable form.

$$\frac{Y_t}{1 + cB} = Y_t[1 - (c)B + (-c)^2B^2 + (-c^3)B^3 \ldots]$$

$$= \sum_{r=0}^{\infty} (-cB)^r Y_{t-r} \tag{8.31}$$

In practice, of course, we must again make do with a finite series as a basis for prediction and control.

Note that we may rewrite our prediction formula as

$$\hat{Y}(t + 2/t) = \frac{a(a + c)(1 + cB - cB)}{1 + cB} Y_t \tag{8.32}$$

$$= a(a + c)Y_t - \frac{ca(a + c)}{1 + cB} BY_t$$

$$= a(a + c)Y_t - c\hat{Y}(t + 1/t - 1).$$

Thus, we may update the previous two-step prediction by the current observation to get the new two-step prediction.

The two-step prediction error is given by

$$Y_{t+2} - \hat{Y}(t + 2/t)$$

From (8.27) and (8.22) we may rewrite $\hat{Y}(t + 2/t)$ as

$$\hat{Y}(t + 2/t) = \frac{a(a + c)}{1 - aB}e_t \tag{8.33}$$

It follows from (8.24) that the prediction error is given by

$$Y_{t+2} - \hat{Y}(t + 2/t) = e_{t+2} + (a + c)e_{t+1} \tag{8.34}$$

In other words, it is a second-order moving average of the random shocks determining $Y_{t+2}$.

In the one-step ahead case the prediction error was equal to $e_t$ so that its variance is $\sigma^2$. In this case the variance of the prediction error is $[1 + (a + c)^2]\sigma^2$. As may be expected, the variance of the prediction error increases as the distance ahead to be predicted increases. This conclusion can be generalised to state that the variance of the prediction error increases the further ahead we try to predict. This is essentially because of the growing number of unpredictable forces that are at work.

# 9
# Elementary optimal stochastic control of the economy

The purpose of this chapter is to look briefly at the theory of optimal stochastic control as applied to a simple macroeconomic model. Despite the high flown language, what we have to say is elementary both in economics and mathematics terms. It is possible, however, even at this level to clarify a number of important matters and to indicate the direction in which more advanced work lies.

We assume we have a dynamic model of the economy or that part of it which we wish to control. We also, as usual, have at our disposal one or more policy instruments which may be used to control the economy. Now, in addition, we assume that the economy is subject to random shocks from forces outside our control. These represent the stochastic element, so to speak, and are the distinctive element of the present analysis.

This is illustrated by the following macro-model:

$$Y_t = C_t + G_t + A_t \tag{9.1}$$

where $Y_t$ is national income, $C_t$ is consumer spending, $G_t$ is government spending, $A_t$ is all other spending.

$$C_t = aY_{t-1} \tag{9.2}$$

that is, we ignore taxes and assume consumption is a lagged function of income.

$$G_t = U_{t-1} \tag{9.3}$$

We assume the level of government spending in the current period is fixed in the previous period, $U_{t-1}$ being the actual instrument and $G_t$ being the nominal instrument.

$$A_t = A + ce_{t-1} + e_t \qquad (9.4)$$

where $e_t$ is a random shock.

We do not have an economic explanation of the behaviour of all other spending. It is taken to equal a constant, $A$, plus a random amount $e_t + e_{t-1}$. We assume that $e_t$ is an independent variable with zero mean and constant variance, i.e.

$$E(e_t) = 0 \qquad (9.5)$$

$$E(e_t e_{t-\tau}) = \sigma^2 \quad (\tau = 0)$$

$$= 0 \quad (\tau \neq 0)$$

The marginal propensity to consume, $a$, is positive and less than unity. In addition, we assume that the absolute value of $c$ is less than unity. (In technical terms this means that we are dealing with a stationary stochastic process.) Our model then becomes

$$Y_t = aY_{t-1} + U_{t-1} + A + ce_{t-1} + e_t \qquad (9.6)$$

In order to decide optimum policy we now need to postulate the government's objectives. As in previous chapters, we assume there is a desired level of national income, $Y^*$. The objective of policy is to get as close to this as possible on average, or to minimise the average deviations from $Y^*$. We again postulate a utility function which is quadratic in deviations from $Y^*$, i.e.

$$Z_t = (Y^* - Y_t)^2 \qquad (9.7)$$

where $Z$ represents the government's utility or preference level.

We wish to make these deviations as small as possible, i.e. to minimise $Z$. Since $Y_t$ has a random element so will $Z_t$. It makes sense, therefore, to concentrate on the average value of $Z_t$. The decision problem may then be expressed formally as the minimisation of the average or expected value of $Z_t$, $E(Z_t)$, given by equation (9.7) subject to the constraint relating national income to the control instrument given by equation (9.6).

Maximisation subject to constraints is, of course, the typical economic problem. We referred to its applicability to macro-economic policy in chapter 2. There the reference was to a static model, but there is obviously no reason why it should not be applied to a dynamic one with stochastic elements as well.

To see how to solve the problem let us obtain an explicit expression for $E(Z_t)$. This is done by replacing $Y_t$ in equation (9.7) by its value given in (9.6).

$$E(Z_t) = E[Y^* - aY_{t-1} - U_{t-1} - A - ce_{t-1} - e_t]^2 \qquad (9.8)$$

Again, for simplicity, assume that the length of the time periods are such that $U_{t-1}$, the policy instrument, can be fixed later than the time that $Y_{t-1}$ and $e_{t-1}$ have occurred. In other words, in principle $Y_{t-1}$ and $e_{t-1}$ can be allowed to influence $U_{t-1}$. (Of these two, it must be emphasised that, while $Y_{t-1}$ can be directly observed $e_{t-1}$ cannot. Instead, its value must be inferred where necessary from that of other observations.)

Since by assumption $e_t$ is an independent random variable, we may rewrite equation (9.8) as

$$E(Z_t) = E[Y^* - aY_{t-1} - U_{t-1} - A - ce_{t-1}]^2 + E(e_t)^2 \qquad (9.9)$$

that is, $e_t$ is not dependent on any of the other variables.

Since we wish to make $E(Z_t)$ as small as possible, this means making $E[Y^* - aY_{t-1} - U_{t-1} - A - ce_{t-1}]^2$ as small as possible, for there is nothing we can do about $e_t$.

If we examine $E[Y^* - aY_{t-1} - U_{t-1} - A - ce_{t-1}]^2$, we can see that the smallest value it can possibly have is zero. This will happen when the expression in square brackets is zero. (Suppose the expression in square brackets were not zero. We then go on to square it before taking its expected value. The square of any number is positive and, therefore, its average or expected value will be positive.)

If the expression in square brackets is zero, then

$$Y^* - aY_{t-1} - U_{t-1} - A - ce_{t-1} = 0 \qquad (9.10)$$

We can rearrange this to give us an expression for $U_{t-1}$:

$$U_{t-1} = Y^* - aY_{t-1} - A - ce_{t-1} \qquad (9.11)$$

This is a policy rule for $U_{t-1}$, but it is not a very useful one in its present form because it depends on $e_{t-1}$, which has occurred, but cannot be observed. But suppose we were able to use this rule, what would be the value of $Y_t$? Substitute the expression for $U_{t-1}$ from equation (9.11) into equation (9.6). We then have

$$Y_t = Y^* + e_t \qquad (9.12)$$

In other words, income would deviate from its desired value by that part of the random shock which is uncontrollable. Moreover, since the average value of the random shock is zero, income would equal its desired value on average.

Let us now play a little trick. We may rewrite equation (9.12) with $e_t$ as the dependent variable.

$$e_t = Y_t - Y^* \tag{9.13}$$

This equation holds for every time period and, therefore, it holds for $t - 1$. Thus, we may use it to obtain an expression for $e_{t-1}$ in terms of variables which can be observed. Let us place this expression in equation (9.11)

$$
\begin{aligned}
U_{t-1} &= Y^* - aY_{t-1} - A - c(Y_{t-1} - Y^*) \\
&= (1 + c)Y^* - (a + c)Y_{t-1} - A \tag{9.14}
\end{aligned}
$$

We now have a control rule in terms of the desired value of income and its observed value. It seems as if we have eliminated the unobservable random shocks by magic! In fact, however, correctly interpreted there is no trick at all. What we are saying is that, if we always use the optimal control rule defined by equation (9.14), national income will behave according to equation (9.12) which then means that the control rule is equivalent to that of equation (9.11).

In practice, of course, we will not have always used the optimal control rule. Let us, however, insert the expression for $U_{t-1}$ given by equation (9.14) into equation (9.6):

$$
\begin{aligned}
Y_t &= aY_{t-1} + (1 + c)Y^* - (a + c)Y_{t-1} - A + A + ce_{t-1} + e_t \\
&= Y^* + e_t + c(Y^* - Y_{t-1} + e_{t-1}) \tag{9.15}
\end{aligned}
$$

This may be interpreted as a first-order difference equation in $Y_t - Y^* - e_t$. Its solution is

$$Y_t - Y^* - e_t = -c^{t-1}(Y_1 - Y^* - e_1) \tag{9.16}$$

Since $c$ is less than unity in absolute value, as $t$ tends to infinity $Y_t - Y^* - e_t$ tends to zero. In other words, with sufficient time we can get as close as we like to the optimal rule based on being able to observe the random shocks.

There is also another way of looking at this which throws some light on the problem. From equation (9.6) we have

$$Y_1 = aY_0 + U_0 + A + ce_0 + e_1 \tag{9.17}$$

Put this expression in equation (9.16):

$$Y_{t+1} - Y^* - e_{t+1} = -c^{t-1}(aY_0 + U_0 + A + ce_0 - Y^*) \tag{9.18}$$

Now, $Y^* - aY_0 - A - ce_0$ is the optimum value for $U$ in period zero according to equation (9.11). Write this as $U_0^*$. We then have

$$Y_{t+1} - Y^* - e_{t+1} = -c^{t-1}(U_0 - U_0^*) \tag{9.19}$$

Thus, we can see explicitly how the closeness of the economy to its optimally controlled state depends on how far away from that state we were initially.

In the real world, apart from the economic models themselves being immensely more complicated, we may not know either $a$ or $c$, the relevant coefficients, for certain. We may know enough, however, to pursue a control rule of the general form given by equation (9.14). In other words, if we assume $a$ to have a value $\hat{a}$ and $c$ to have a value $\hat{c}$ we may fix government spending according to the rule

$$U_{t-1} = (1 + \hat{c})Y^* - (\hat{a} + \hat{c})Y_{t-1} - A. \tag{9.20}$$

Clearly, if the values of $a$ and $c$ are a long way from the true values our policy will be far from optimal. It may even give rise to a path for national income worse than that resulting from no policy. Some economists have suggested that that is precisely the situation in which governments find themselves, which is why they have been rather sceptical of the merits of this kind of short-term stabilisation policy.

Let us examine a simplified version of this problem by assuming that the government knows the coefficient, $a$, but is mistaken about the coefficient, $c$. What this means is that the structure of the system represented by the marginal propensity to consume is known, but an attempt to obtain a quantitative representation of the behaviour of the other forces affecting the economy has not been fully successful.

The control rule will then be

$$U_{t-1} = (1 + c)Y^* - (a + \hat{c})Y_{t-1} - A. \tag{9.21}$$

If this is substituted into equation (9.6) we have

$$Y_t = Y^* + e_t + ce_{t-1} - \hat{c}(Y_{t-1} - Y^*) \tag{9.22}$$

If this expression is itself substituted into the government's utility function [equation (9.7)]. after a certain amount of mathematical manipulation we arrive at

$$E(Y^* - Y_t)^2 = \frac{(1 + c^2 - 2c\hat{c})}{1 - \hat{c}^2} \cdot \sigma^2 \tag{9.23}$$

If $c$ equals $\hat{c}$, i.e. if the government were not mistaken, this is equal to $\sigma^2$. As $\hat{c}$ diverges from $c$, this expression gets larger. Recall that it is a measure of disutility, i.e. the government wishes to minimise the expected value of $Z_t$; thus, what we are saying is that policy deteriorates according to this measure as the government's assumption about the system differs from its true nature.

The point may be made explicitly by taking the partial derivative of $E(Y^* - Y_t)^2$ with respect to $\hat{c}$:

$$\frac{\partial E(Y^* - Y_t)^2}{\partial \hat{c}} = \frac{2\partial^2(\hat{c} - c)(1 - c\hat{c})}{(1 - \hat{c}^2)^2} \tag{9.24}$$

This expression is zero when $\hat{c}$ equals $c$, it is positive when $\hat{c}$ is greater than $c$, and negative when $\hat{c}$ is less than $c$. (Recall that we

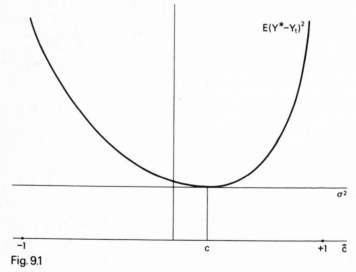

Fig. 9.1

have assumed that $c$ is less than unity in absolute value, and are only considering possible values for $\hat{c}$ in this range.) This is illustrated in figure 9.1 which shows how $E(Y^* - Y_t)^2$ varies with $c$. It is at a minimum when $\hat{c}$ equals $c$ and is then equal to $\sigma^2$. As $\hat{c}$ diverges from $c$ in either direction performance deteriorates. Moreover, the performance deteriorates proportionately more strongly the further we diverge.

We must now see what happens if we refrain from this sort of policy making. Suppose, for example, government expenditure is fixed at a constant level, $U$. According to equation (9.6) the economy is then represented by

$$Y_t = aY_{t-1} + U + A + ce_{t-1} + e_t. \tag{9.25}$$

By a certain amount of mathematical manipulation we can show that in this case

$$E(Y^* - Y_t)^2 = \frac{[U + A - (1-a)Y^*]^2}{(1-a)^2} + \frac{1 + c^2 + 2ac}{(1-a^2)}\sigma^2 \tag{9.26}$$

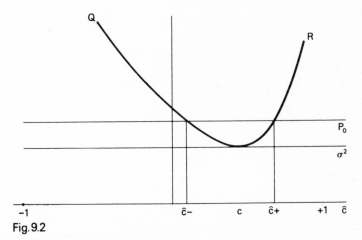

Fig. 9.2

Figure 9.2 is essentially the same as figure 9.1 with a line, $P_0$, added equal to $E(Y^* - Y_t)^2$ as given by equation (9.26). That line intersects the active policy performance curve QR at $\hat{c}-$ and $\hat{c}+$. This gives us the range of values within which active policy yields better results than passive policy. The higher is $P_0$ and the flatter is QR, the broader is this range. In other words, the greater is the potential benefit from active policy (represented by the level of $P_0$) and the lower is the possible cost (represented by the slope of QR), the less the danger from mistakes in policy.

A special case of equation (9.26) may be noted *en passant*. The first expression in square brackets is $U + A - (1 - A)Y^*$. If we look back at equation (9.6), the average value of income for given $U$ is

$$E(Y) = aE(Y) + U + A \qquad (9.27)$$

$$= \frac{U + A}{1 - a}$$

One rule of passive policy might be to fix government spending so that the average value of income equals its most desired value, $Y^*$. In this case $U + A - (1 - A)Y^*$ will equal zero, and the performance measure for passive policy will equal $\sigma^2(1 + c^2 + 2ac)/(1 - a^2)$. This is worse than for optimum policy based on a correct view of $c$, but not necessarily worse than policy based on an incorrect view.

This analysis does not, of course, tell us whether active policy is likely to make things better and nothing positive in this connection can be inferred from the diagram. It does, however, indicate the benefits and dangers of active policy, and how lack of full information is a cost but not necessarily one which will cause us to give up policy making altogether.

Later in this chapter we shall return briefly to the question of the possible harmful effects of policy. Before that we return to the problem of prediction and its relationship to policy.

In the model we are currently discussing let us determine the optimum one period ahead prediction for income. Applying the method of chapter 7 and, in particular, equation (7.16), the prediction of $Y_{t+1}$ at time $t$ is given by

$$\hat{Y}(t + 1/t) = aY_t + U_t + A + ce_{t-1} \qquad (9.28)$$

(The difference between this and the previous example of prediction is that the model now includes $U_t + A$; it is obvious that the effect of this is to add $U_t + A$ to the prediction.)

Let us compare this with the formula for optimum control for period 2 given by equation (9.11):

$$U_t = Y^* - aY_t - A - ce_t \tag{9.11}$$

If this value for $U_t$ is placed in equation (9.28) we infer

$$\hat{Y}(t+1/t) = Y^* \tag{9.29}$$

In other words, in conditions of optimal control the predicted value for $Y$ is its most desired value. In equation (9.28) the optimal predicted value of $Y$ is a function of $U$. We may, therefore, regard policy making as choosing that value for the policy instrument that makes the predicted value of $Y$ equal to its desired value. For the sort of case we have been discussing this means that the policy problem may be divided into two stages:

(a) predict the target variables as functions of the instrument;

(b) select the instrument so that the predicted value of the target equals the desired value.

This separation of the activities of prediction and control is one which economists take for granted. It seems perfectly sensible to ask for each instrument: What happens if we do this?' and, 'What happens if we do that? Having answered these questions, we can then go on to choose the best setting for each instrument. It is worth remarking, therefore, that it is possible to choose criterion functions and economic models in which it is not correct to make this separation between prediction and control. If, for example, we rejected the quadratic utility function and assumed that the policy maker's preferences were represented by something more complicated (to include, perhaps, $Y^3$ as well as $Y^2$), separation would disappear.

There is another technical point to be made relating prediction to control. If we look at equation (8.16) we find the one-step ahead prediction error is equal to $e_{t+1}$. Equation (9.12) tells us that for period $t+1$, the difference between the optimally controlled level of income and its desired value (to be called the control error) is also equal to $e_{t+1}$. We have, therefore, the conclusion that in models of the type we have considered the control error is equal to the prediction error.

Let us now go on to examine what happens if the control instrument takes longer to work. Suppose the lag between the actual and the nominal instrument is two periods and not one.

$$Y_t = aY_{t-1} + U_{t-2} + A + ce_{t-1} + e_t \tag{9.30}$$

Using equation (8.22) we may rewrite this as

$$Y_t = \frac{a(a+c)}{1+cB} Y_{t-2} + \frac{1}{1-aB} U_{t-2} + \frac{A}{1-aB} + (a+c)e_{t-1} + e_t$$

(9.31)

We then can infer

$$E(Y_t - Y^*)^2 = E\left[\frac{a(a+c)}{1+cB} Y_{t-2} + \frac{1}{1-aB}U_{t-2} + \frac{A}{1-aB} - Y^*\right]^2$$
$$+ [1 + (a+c)^2]\sigma^2$$

(9.32)

To make this as small as possible we must put the first expression in square brackets on the right-hand side equal to zero:

$$U_{t-2} = -\frac{a(a+c)(1-aB)}{1+cB} Y_{t-2} + (1-a)Y^* - A$$

(9.33)

If we substitute this into equation (9.31), we have

$$Y_t = Y^* + e_t + (a+c)e_{t-1}$$

(9.34)

Compared with the previous case the control error has now increased by $(a+c)e_{t-1}$ and the performance indicator has deteriorated by $(a+c)^2\sigma^2$. It is also worth noting how much more complicated the policy making rule has become. Comparing equation (9.33) with equation (9.14) the key difference is now the $1+cB$ in the denominator of the expression by which the income term is multiplied. This tells us essentially that optimal control now depends on all past values of income and not just on the current value.

Let us now work out the optimum two-step ahead prediction for this model. Applying equation (8.27) we discover

$$\hat{Y}(t+2/t) = \frac{a(a+c)}{1+cB} Y_t + \frac{1}{1-aB}U_t + \frac{A}{1-aB}$$

(9.35)

If this is set equal to $Y^*$ we get immediately the rule given by equation (9.33). In other words, we may control the economy by predicting income two periods ahead and setting government expenditure so that desired income equals predicted income. [Comparing equation (9.34) with equation (8.30) we see that the prediction error equals the control error again.]

The effect of increasing the lag between the nominal and actual

instrument is to lower the extent to which optimal policy improves
the performance of the economy. It is also worth mentioning that
it also increases the risk of policy leading to a deterioration in
performance. The range of values narrows within which the policy
makers can assume $c$ to lie and still improve the performance of the
economy.

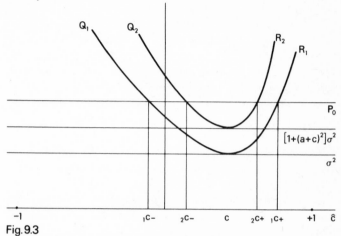

Fig. 9.3

Figure 9.3 corresponds to figure 9.2. $Q_1 R_1$ is the active policy
performance curve when the lag is one time period and $Q_2 R_2$ is the
active policy performance curve when the lag is two time periods.
The best possible level of performance in the former case is $\sigma^2$ and
in the latter case $[1 + (a + c)^2] \sigma^2$. $P_0$ is the level of performance
when policy is passive. $Q_2 R_2$ lies above $Q_1 R_1$ although they both
reach a minimum when policy makers act on the correct value of $\hat{c}$
equal to $c$. The curve $Q_1 R_1$ intersects $P_0$ at $_1 c-$ and at $_1 c+$. This is the range
within which active policy making yields net benefits. $Q_2 R_2$
intersects $P_0$ at $_2 c-$ and at $_2 c+$. The range from $_2 c -$ to $_2 c +$ is
clearly less than the range from $_1 c -$ to $_1 c +$.

While this warns us of the dangers of active policy making, it
must not be taken to imply that such policy making is harmful
always or ever. Such a view depends on the study of actual economic
systems and of the way policy is carried out within them. The
important lessons to be learned are (a) that policy must be related
to actual situations and is limited by what the policy maker knows,
(b) that the dynamic behaviour of the economy is likely to be of

considerable importance, (c) that correct policy rules may be rather complicated, and (d) that mistakes are easily made. In particular, the propensity to make mistakes will increase as the relevant time lags increase and as available information deteriorates. What the policy maker wants are quick acting instruments, the effects of which he can be pretty confident of within a system, the behaviour of which he is able to predict.

This may be regarded as a rather utopian requirement and not likely to be met in practice. The available instruments may be slow acting and unreliable, and may need to work within an imperfectly understood economic system. It is worth emphasising, however, that policy making is itself a dynamic process and is capable of improving over time. New information is collected and economic theory advances so that we become (in principle, at least) less likely to make mistakes about the effects of the instruments or the ways in which exogenous variables influence the system. We may even make 'technical advances' in economic policy and invent new instruments superior to existing ones. It is certainly my own view that all this is worth doing and that one benefit stemming from the mistakes of the past might be a capacity for better policy making in the future.

# Bibliography

Allen, R.G.D., *Macroeconomic Theory*, Macmillan, 1968.

Anderson, L.C. and Carlson, K.M., A monetarist model for economic stabilisation, *Federal Reserve Bank of St Louis*, April, 1970.

Ando, A., Cary-Brown, E., Solow, R. and Kareken, J., Lags in fiscal and monetary policy, in *Commission on Money and Credit: Stabilization Policies*, Prentice-Hall, 1964.

Argy, V., Rules, discretion in monetary management, and short-term stability, *Money, Credit and Banking*, 3, 1971.

Arndt, P.W., Policy choices in an open economy: some dynamic considerations, *Journal of Political Economy*, 81, 1973.

Artoni, R., The coordination of fiscal and monetary policies, *Public Finance*, No. 3, 1970.

Ashom, K., *Introduction to Stochastic Control Theory*, Academic Press, 1970.

Baumol, W.J. Pitfalls in contracyclical policies: some tools and results, *Review of Economics and Statistics*, February 1961.

Benishay, H., A framework for the evaluation of short term fiscal and monetary policy, *Money, Credit and Banking*, 5, 1973.

Brainard, W., Uncertainty and the effectiveness of policy, *American Economic Review*, May 1967.

Bristow, J.A., Taxation and income stabilisation, *Economic Journal*, June 1968.

Chow, G.C., Optimal stochastic control of linear economic systems, *Money, Credit and Banking*, 2, 1970.

Chow, G.C., Optimal control of linear econometric systems with finite time horizon, *International Economic Review*, February 1972.

Chow, G.C., Effect of uncertainty on optimal control policies, *International Economic Review*, October 1973.

Colwell, P.F. and Lash, N.A., Comparing fiscal indicators, *The Review of Economics and Statistics*, **55**, 1973.

Dow, J.C.R., *The Management of the British Economy*, Cambridge University Press, 1964.

Fischer, S. and Cooper, J. Phillip, Stabilisation policy and lags, *Journal of Political Economy*, **81**, 1973.

Friedman, M., The logic effect of monetary policy, *Journal of Political Economy*, **69**, 1961.

Friedman, M., *The Optimum Quantity of Money*, Macmillan, 1969.

Fromm, G. and Taubman, P., *Public Economic Theory and Policy*, Macmillan, 1973.

Haavelun, T., Multiplier effects of a balanced budget, *Econometrica*, October 1945.

Hall, R.E., The dynamic effects of fiscal policy in an economy with foresight, *Review of Economic Studies*, **38**, 1971.

Hamburger, M.J., The lag in the effect of monetary policy: a survey of recent literature, *Federal Reserve Bank of New York: Monthly Review*, December 1971.

Hansen, B., *The Economic Theory of Fiscal Policy*, Allen & Unwin, 1958.

Hansen, B., *Fiscal Policy in Seven Countries, 1955–65*, OECD, 1969.

Helliwell, J. and Gorbet, F., Assessing the dynamic efficiency of automatic stabilisers, *Journal of Political Economy*, **81**, 1973.

Henderson, D. and Turnovsky, S., Optimal macroeconomic policy adjustment under conditions of risk, *Journal of Economic Theory*, April 1972.

Holbrook, R.S., Optimal economic policy and the problem of instrument instability, *American Economic Review*, March 1972.

Holt, C., Linear decision rules for economic stabilization and control, *Quarterly Journal of Economics*, February 1952.

Howrey, E.P., Stabilisation policy in linear stochastic systems, *Review of Economics and Statistics*, August 1967.

Johansen, L., *Public Economics*, North Holland, 1965.

Kaldor, N., Conflicts in national economic objectives, *Economic Journal*, March 1971.

Livesey, D.A., Optimising short-term economic policy, *Economic Journal*, September 1971.

Meade, J.E., *The Controlled Economy*, Allen & Unwin, 1971.

Mundell, R.A., *International Economics*, Macmillan, 1968.

Musgrave, R.A. and Miller, M.H., Built-in flexibility, *American Economic Review*, March 1948.

Nerlove, M., Lags in economic behaviour, *Econometrica,* March 1972.

Ott, D.J. and Ott A.F., Monetary and fiscal policy: goals and the choice of instruments, *Quarterly Journal of Economics,* May 1968.

Peacock, A.T., A note on the balanced budget multiplier, *Economic Journal,* June 1956.

Peacock, A. and Shaw, G.K., *The Economic Theory of Fiscal Policy,* Allen and Unwin, 1971.

Peston, M.H., Generalising the balanced budget multiplier, *Review of Economics and Statistics,* **40**, 1958.

Peston, M.H., The tax mix and effective demand, *Public Finance,* No. 3, 1971.

Peston, M.H., The correlation between targets and instruments, *Economica,* November 1972.

Peston, M.H., Economics and quantitative economics: a defence, *Minerva,* April 1974.

Phillips, A., Stabilisation policy in a closed economy, *Economic: Journal,* June 1954.

Phillips, A., Stabilisation policy and the time form of lagged responses, *Economic Journal,* June 1957.

Pindyck, R.S., Optimal stabilisation policies via deterministic control, *Annals of Economic and Social Measurement,* 1972.

Pook, W., Optimal choice of monetary policy instruments in a simple stochastic model, *Quarterly Journal of Economics,* May 1970..

Shaw, G.K., Monetary-fiscal policy for growth and the balance of payments constraint, *Economica,* May 1967.

Shaw, G.K., *Macroeconomic Policy,* Martin Robertson, 1971.

Shaw, G.K., *Fiscal Policy,* Macmillan, 1972.

Smyth, D.J., Can 'automatic stabilisers' be destabilising?, *Public Finance,* No. 3–4, 1963.

Smyth, D.J., Built-in flexibility of taxation and automatic stabilisation, *Journal of Political Economy,* August 1966.

Symth, D.J., Tax changes linked to government expenditure changes and the magnitude of fluctuations in national income, *Journal of Political Economy,* **78**, 1970.

Theil, H., A note on certainty equivalence in dynamic planning, *Econometrica,* April 1957.

Tinbergen, J., *On the Theory of Economic Policy,* North Holland, 1952.

Turnovsky, S., Optimal stabilisation policies for deterministic and stochastic linear economic systems, *Review of Economic Studies,* **40**, 1973.

Willes, M.H., The scope of countercyclical monetary policy, *Money, Credit and Banking*, 5, 1973.

Worswick, G.D.N., Fiscal policy and stabilisation in Britain, in Sir Alec Cairncross (ed.): *Britain's Economic Prospects Reconsidered*, Allen & Unwin, 1971.

# Index

211